KUWAIT

KUWAIT

The Transformation
of an Oil State

Jill Crystal

Westview Press

BOULDER • SAN FRANCISCO • OXFORD

Westview Profiles/Nations of the Contemporary Middle East

Photos courtesy Kuwait Oil Company, Press and Publications Division, unless otherwise attributed

Published in 1992 in the United States of America by Westview Press, Inc., 5500 Central Avenue, Boulder, Colorado 80301-2847, and in the United Kingdom by Westview Press, 36 Lonsdale Road, Summertown, Oxford OX2 7EW

Library of Congress Cataloging-in-Publication Data
Crystal, Jill.
   Kuwait : the transformation of an oil state / Jill Crystal.
      p.   cm. — (Westview profiles. Nations of the contemporary
Middle East)
   Includes bibliographical references and index.
   ISBN 0-8133-0888-7
   1. Kuwait.   I. Title.   II. Series: Profiles. Nations of the
contemporary Middle East.
DS247.K8C79   1992
953.67—dc20   92-6019
                                                                        CIP

Printed and bound in the United States of America

The paper used in this publication meets the requirements
of the American National Standard for Permanence of Paper
for Printed Library Materials Z39.48-1984.

10   9   8   7   6   5   4   3   2   1

To my son, Malcolm

Contents

Tables and Illustrations

ix

Maps

Preface

The Iraqi invasion of Kuwait in August 1990 brought tremendous upheaval to a state that had already experienced unprecedented change in the previous three decades because of oil. This book analyzes the transformations wrought both by oil and by Iraq, placing them in their broader social context and drawing attention to the linkages among changes in the economic, social, and political realms. Although this book pays explicit attention to oil and its impact, it also goes beyond oil to analyze the previously neglected patterns of life in Kuwait and to introduce the reader to the specific contours of this Gulf state.

An overview of the state is given in Chapter 1, and the environment in which present-day Kuwait was forged is introduced. The major transformations in Kuwait's history are introduced in Chapter 2, and attention is drawn to some of the radical, if less well known, changes that preceded oil. In Chapter 3 an overview of Kuwait's oil economy is given: the economy it supplanted, the changes it induced, the policy decisions associated with oil, and the problems and advantages connected with that kind of economy. Kuwaiti society is analyzed in Chapter 4 by looking at the forces that have forged a unified community and by examining the major social structural divisions—family, class, tribe, sect, gender, and nationality. Politics in Kuwait is looked at in Chapter 5, with an examination of both the formal structures of politics (the institution of the ruling family, the consultative institution of the National Assembly, the sustaining institutions of the bureaucracy) and the informal ways in which these structures have operated through each of the most important political crises of the 1980s. Kuwait's foreign policy is analyzed in Chapter 6. The historical roots of that foreign policy and the continuity and deviations in policy that occurred during the years of the Iran-Iraq War are examined as well as the events leading up to Iraq's invasion of Kuwait. Kuwait's relations with the superpowers, with the region, and with its immediate neighbors are examined. The chapter concludes with an overview of the postinvasion foreign policy environment. The domestic impact of the Iraqi invasion is examined in Chapter 7. The effects of the invasion, occupation, and war on Kuwait's economy, society, and politics are traced, and the problems of postwar reconstruction are considered. An analysis of political liberalization and its limits in Kuwait concludes the chapter.

The book is based on several years familiarity with Kuwait and on research trips to the state. It builds on the existing research on Kuwait in English and in Arabic and on a synthesis of British, U.S., and Gulf primary and secondary sources.

A number of people made helpful comments on drafts of the book. I am thankful to Dale Eickelman, Bernard Reich, and F. Gregory Gause III for reading all or part of the manuscript. Dr. Hassan al-Ibrahim and Dr. Fawzi al-Sultan very kindly provided useful recent material. I also owe thanks to my writing companions, Majnoon and Bob, who offered no intellectual support whatsoever. My husband, Russell Balch, deserves, as ever, my thanks for reading and commenting on the entire draft and for other, less tangible support. I owe a special thanks to my son, Malcolm, whose arrival proved that it is possible to be both productive and reproductive.

Jill Crystal

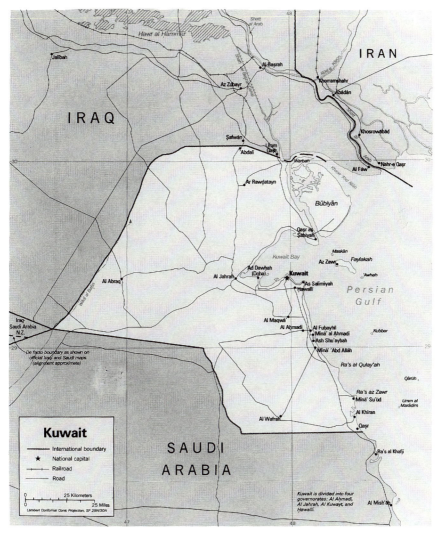

Kuwait. *Source:* Central Intelligence Agency

1

Introduction

One of the main themes that has dominated Kuwait's history is the development and protection of its small community from external threats. Although oil restructured the domestic and international environment, it did not weaken either Kuwait's sense of identity or its perceived vulnerability. Since the mid-eighteenth century Kuwait's people have had a distinct sense of themselves as Kuwaitis. Kuwaitis have also, however, always had a larger political identity as well—as Gulfians, as Arabs, as Muslims, and as members of the world community.

The second main theme in Kuwaiti history is internal rivalry: the recurring tension over the rules governing relations among members of the community. The sense of being Kuwaiti has never been equally shared by all members of the community; community has never meant equality. Although Kuwaitis close ranks against outsiders, this front has always masked internal tension over access to power, status, and wealth. These rivalries often find expression in explicitly political debates over the conventions governing the relationship between rulers and ruled, resulting in a recurrent alternation between representation and repression in Kuwaiti politics as the extent of political space is defined and redefined. Rarely, however, have these debates been allowed to threaten the basic consensus on the larger Kuwaiti national identity.

ECOLOGY AND ECONOMY

Kuwait's location and size have contributed to its particular identity. Kuwait is a small state. From north to south, it is about 200 km; from east to west, about 170 km. Its population is likewise small. The 1985 census, the most recent, put the number of inhabitants officially at 1,697,301—of whom less than half, only 681,288, were Kuwaitis. Kuwait's small size makes it internally more cohesive but also more vulnerable to outside aggression. Kuwait has big neighbors: Saudi Arabia to the south, Iraq to

1

the west and north. Only in the east does Kuwait open to the waters of the Gulf, where still other threats lie.

Kuwait has a harsh desert climate. Summers are long and hot, with temperatures ranging from 85° to 115° Fahrenheit. In July and August the daily temperature hovers around 110°. Sandstorms and humidity, especially from late July through October, add to the discomfort. Winter temperatures range from 45° to 65° Fahrenheit. Although the climate is sometimes humid, rainfall is scarce, averaging 82 mm a year. Agriculture has never thrived in this climate, and an isolated subsistence economy has never existed. Kuwaitis have had to look outward, to the desert and the sea, for food and even water (in the past, imported from Iraq). Consequently, long-distance trade and, later, pearl diving came to dominate Kuwait's economy. Until the early 1930s the pearling industry was the heart of Kuwait's economy. Since then, however, with the decline of the pearl industry owing to the development of cultured pearls in Japan and the rise of the petroleum industry following the discovery of oil in Kuwait in the 1930s and the export of oil following World War II, the economy shifted almost entirely toward this new commodity.

Oil soon came to dominate Kuwait's economy, accounting for 90 percent of its export revenues. Once simply an exporter of crude, Kuwait also developed its own oil industry. By the mid-1980s it was processing 80 percent of its crude oil in local refineries and selling 250,000 barrels a day of these refined products under the logo Q8 through its recently acquired network of about 4,400 European gas stations. Kuwait also invested in oil exploration abroad. Kuwait's efforts to manipulate its international economic environment by pushing both upstream (exploration) and downstream (refining, retailing) petroleum investments made Kuwait a leader in the oil industry, a new addition to the oil majors that historically dominated the field.

Kuwait tried to diversify away from oil in two directions. First, it invested conservatively in local industry and in banking and services. Second, it invested its oil income in overseas property and industry so effectively that by the 1980s these foreign investments brought in more revenue than did the direct sale of oil. Its overseas investments gave Kuwait a small buffer against the price fluctuations of oil and offer the best possibility for income when the oil industry eventually declines. Overseas investments alone made it possible for the Kuwaiti economy to continue to function after Iraq shut down its revenue-producing oil facilities. Nonetheless, Kuwait remains heavily dependent on oil and oil markets. It has little productive capacity outside that industry, and the damage done to the industry by the Iraqi invasion in August 1990 will be felt for some time to come.

SOCIETY

Most of the people who live in Kuwait are not Kuwaitis; they are foreign workers from Asia and the Arab world. Non-Kuwaitis formed 60 percent of the preinvasion population and over 80 percent of the work force. Slightly more than half of these foreigners were Asian. Most of the remainder were Arabs: Palestinians, Jordanians, Egyptians, and others. The national and nonnational communities are separated formally and informally. Legislation and customary practices governing economic rights (from property and business ownership to trade union activity), social rights (access to the welfare state's education, health, housing, and other services), and civil and political rights distinguish on the basis of citizenship. Housing, socializing, and marriage patterns reinforce this distinction. Ironically, the presence of so many foreigners and the Kuwaitis' vague fear of social and cultural inundation by these foreigners have been important factors in consolidating the strong sense of identity among the Kuwaitis. The Iraqi invasion has reinforced this sense.

Almost all Kuwaitis are Muslims—most are Sunni; about 15 percent are Shia. Because citizenship laws grant Kuwaiti nationality only to families long resident in Kuwait, most citizens are descendants of Kuwaitis resident since at least 1920. The most important divisions within Kuwaiti society are sectarian and class. The economic division between the rich and the not-so-rich (most of Kuwait's poor are expatriates) is reinforced by the social division between the Bani Utub, those merchant families (including the ruling family) descended from the original founders of Kuwait, and the rest of the national population. The key sectarian division is between Kuwait's majority Sunni and its minority Shia. Other social divisions—between rulers and ruled, women and men, and tribal and long-settled families—have also been important from time to time, particularly as these groups have found a political voice.

POLITY

Kuwait is unusual among its neighbors in that it has a well-established national identity and a long history as a nation, dating back to the eighteenth century. Kuwaiti law and custom draw a sharp distinction between those who belong to the Kuwaiti community, who enjoy a recognized historical right to participate in the formal life of that community, and outsiders, who do not. Oil and the recent transformations associated with it have forced Kuwait to draw this line more clearly—drawing in, for example, Kuwait's poorest citizens, historically on the margins of Kuwaiti political life, and excluding the immigrant workers.

Kuwait has established and maintained this community only with difficulty. To sustain unity, the government and social elite have had to contain internal divisions and conflicts. Hierarchy has always existed and has always been a source of contention. Groups unequal in power, status, and wealth vie to maintain or better their position within Kuwait's political structures. Although Kuwait closes ranks against outsiders, tension has always existed within Kuwait over the precise definition of its identity and over the rights and responsibilities held by those who share in that identity. This tension finds expression in social debates over norms of behavior governing public and private life. Women, inside the Kuwaiti national community but often outside the political community, have been one important focus for this debate. Public expressions of private faith have been another arena. Although Islam and politics have always been intertwined, Islamist politics, an explicitly political version of Islam, have become particularly important in the 1980s and 1990s.

Internal rivalry has often found expression in overtly political debates over the rules governing political life. State institutions such as the bureaucracy and National Assembly established the framework within which the Kuwaiti political identity emerged. Ideas of the state and the opposition played out inside and outside this institutional framework forged the Kuwaiti identity. Since 1962 that debate has expressed itself in the National Assembly. With the assembly's suspension in 1976 and again in 1986, dissent appeared in the form of demands for a return to parliamentary life. Prodemocracy advocates, active in 1989 and 1990, continued to work both inside and outside the state for parliamentary restoration in an independent Kuwait after Iraq's invasion; and following the liberation in 1991, they launched a new attack on the amir's authoritarian tendencies. The result of this ongoing discussion between the opposition and the ruler has been a pattern of alternation between representation and repression in Kuwaiti politics, as loyal and disloyal opposition are defined and redefined.

Throughout these debates a tacit understanding remains that these disagreements will not be allowed to threaten the basic consensus on the Kuwaiti national identity. The result has been a strong national identity with workable national institutions but an identity that has involved a constant process of maintenance and reconstruction.

FOREIGN POLICY

The consolidation of national identity in Kuwait has taken place in the face of external threats. Kuwait has had to reconcile necessary interdependence with a strong sense of independence and to balance the tension between its inward-looking sense of community and its need for close ties with the outside world. Kuwait's relations with its neighbors have historically been governed by two factors: a confidence borne of a strong national identity and a vulnerability borne of weakness—Kuwait is a small state in a big world. Long before oil, Kuwait was wholly dependent on the outside world for pearl markets and for subsistence goods. Oil did not change this basic structure of interdependence, but it raised the stakes by creating both greater constraints and greater opportunities. Confidence and vulnerability have always prompted Kuwait to try to manipulate outside forces to serve its own security needs—as it did on independence in 1961 when, threatened by Iraq, it called in Arab League and British forces and as it did in 1987 during the Iran-Iraq War when it secured U.S. reflagging for its threatened tankers. Kuwait could manipulate its environment, but being a small power, it could not control it. In 1990 its efforts failed. Unable to assess the true nature of the Iraqi threat and overconfident of the ability of its newly strengthened alliance with the United States to actually prevent Iraqi aggression, Kuwait was unable to anticipate or resist the Iraqi incursion of August 2.

The invasion had a thoroughgoing and devastating effect on all aspects of Kuwaiti life. The destruction of so many of Kuwait's oil-producing facilities had long-term economic and environmental consequences. Financing reconstruction cut deeply into Kuwait's foreign reserves. The social impact of the invasion was more subtle but perhaps as far-reaching. The occupation deepened one rift—that between Kuwaitis and expatriates, especially those who had supported Iraq—and created a new rift between those Kuwaitis who fled the country and those who stayed behind and endured the occupation.

Politically, the invasion restructured the relationship between the ruler and the opposition. Although the U.S.-led coalition forces restored Kuwait's independence, a return to the political status quo ante was no longer possible. Opposition groups in exile and under occupation joined to reactivate the preinvasion prodemocracy movement, calling on the amir to hold elections. The amir's ambivalent response—his reluctant agreement to hold future elections—satisfied neither the opposition nor the emerging hard-liners in his own family. The invasion also left Kuwait heavily and unequivocally dependent on the United States and Saudi Arabia—hence vulnerable to their interference in its domestic affairs, an interference that increasingly gave rise to the tendencies of repression rather than representation. In manipulating the international environment, Kuwait's rulers have always tried with only limited success to keep regional powers from interfering in Kuwaiti politics. Kuwait's leaders may again decide that to achieve harmony with their neighbors they must constrain expressions of disunity and dissent at home.

2

History

Kuwait was well on its way to becoming a nation long before it was a state. Kuwait has been an independent state only since 1961, but it has been a distinct political entity since it was founded early in the eighteenth century. Although the original families who migrated to Kuwait from central Arabia did not differ ethnically or religiously from the families they left behind, the act of migrating and establishing a new community created strong new bonds among them. From the start, Kuwait was thus set apart from its neighbors by its possession of the rudiments of a national identity. Like Kuwait, many of the Gulf states are still grappling with the issues involved in coercing or co-opting radically disparate groups into one national as well as political community, but Kuwait has had two centuries to work with these issues. Although Kuwait has not resolved its national problems, it does have a solid core with which to work.

NATIONAL FORMATION:
THE ESTABLISHMENT OF A KUWAITI COMMUNITY

The town of Kuwait was built in the early eighteenth century (the historian Ahmad Mustafa Abu-Hakima put the date at 1716) by members of the Bani Khalid tribe, at that time the dominant tribe of northeastern Arabia.[1] Originally called Grane, the town was known as Kuwait by the mid-eighteenth century. The name itself, the diminutive of the word *kut*, means small castle or fort and suggests, as Abu-Hakima noted, the town's somewhat humble origins.

The Bani Utub, the founders of the political city-state of Kuwait, did not arrive in Kuwait until the early eighteenth century. Originally, the Bani Utub were no more than loosely bound, interrelated families who came to Kuwait together from central Arabia, where they traced their origins to the Anaizah tribal confederation. These families left Arabia as migrants in the late seventeenth century, a period when famine forced many to migrate, and traveled a roundabout route that took them through eastern Arabia, where for a while they settled in Qatar, bringing them and their descendants gradually to Kuwait. The journey of migration itself was a key formative event in establishing the sense of community by creating a new social bond among the migrant families. By the time they arrived in Kuwait, these families had begun to think of themselves not merely as members of the Arabian tribes they had left, but as members of a new tribe, the Bani Utub. Indeed, the name Bani Utub itself may have its origin in the act of migration. According to Abu-Hakima, the name Utub comes from the Arabic root 'ataba, to travel from place to place (Bani, "people of"), and the ruling family mythology adopted this interpretation.[2] Shaikh Abdallah, the ruler of Kuwait from 1950 to 1965, told H.R.P. Dickson, the long-serving British political agent, that the Bani Utub assumed that name after they had traveled to the north (in Arabic, 'atabu ila al-shamal).[3] To this day, Kuwait's social elite traces its roots to this original Bani Utub clan.

After settling in Kuwait, the Bani Utub began to earn a living through pearl diving, boat building, and trade, taking advantage of Kuwait's fine harbor. Their undertakings were successful, and the colony grew. Its fleet soon rivaled that of Muscat, the other large Gulf naval power. In addition to the maritime trade with India and Africa, Kuwait also became an important stop on the land trade routes that linked India, Persia, and Arabia to Europe. The nineteenth century was a period of general prosperity for Kuwait. European travelers, who began passing through Kuwait sporadically in the late eighteenth century, noted the active commerce on land and sea.[4] When the British political resident visited Kuwait in the 1860s, the town had 20,000 inhabitants.[5]

Kuwait could enjoy prosperity and political stability in part because of the protected political space in which it developed. In the eighteenth century, when Kuwait was founded, that area of eastern Arabia enjoyed a certain peace and stability as a result of Bani Khalid rule. The Bani Khalid allowed Kuwait the space to grow and offered a measure of protection from outside threats. As Abu-Hakima notes, the late eighteenth century was also a period of rapid state formation and destruction in the region, with new forms of political rule appearing and disappearing throughout the Gulf: in Oman, Qatar, Bahrain, and central Arabia as well as in Kuwait.[6]

Kuwait's location and size, however, left it vulnerable to outside powers. From the earliest days, Kuwait's leaders could only survive by careful diplomacy and manipulation of the local balance of power. From the surrounding tribes to the Ottoman forces to the European traders, Kuwait was forced to strike a series of deals with all the regional powers. These shifting alliances allowed Kuwait to develop a surprising degree of autonomy by the mid-nineteenth century. Although most of the states in the region gradually fell under direct Ottoman or European rule, Kuwait

TABLE 2.1   Kuwait's Rulers

Ruler	Reign	Ruler	Reign
Sabah I	1752-1756	Jabir II	1915-1917
Abdallah I	1756-1814	Salim	1917-1921
Jabir I	1814-1859	Ahmad	1921-1950
Sabah II	1859-1866	Abdallah III	1950-1965
Abdallah II	1866-1892	Sabah III	1965-1977
Muhammad	1892-1896	Jabir III	1977-
Mubarak	1896-1915		

remained independent. This precarious autonomy reinforced a sense of Kuwaiti identity.

Establishing Community: Internal Threats

The Bani Utub built a new identity for themselves in Kuwait. Although they remained loyal to the Bani Khalid, the new settlers soon eclipsed the few Bani Khalid in their midst, and in Kuwait the Bani Utub ruled themselves by adding new political institutions to contain and regulate the life of the community. The most important institutions were those involving leadership. By the mid-eighteenth century, the al-Sabah had become the leading political family, from whose ranks all successive rulers have arisen (see Table 2.1). The first recognized ruler was Sabah I, who ruled for a short time in the 1750s. His rule is poorly documented, but Alan Rush, who has written the family's genealogy, put the dates of Sabah's rule tentatively at 1752–1756.[7] Tradition has it that Sabah came to Kuwait in the early eighteenth century as one of the first Bani Utub. Initially Sabah may have shared power in a semiformal division of labor with two other families: The al-Khalifah, who, tradition has it, handled the sea industries of pearling and trade, and the al-Jalahimah, who handled coastal security. The al-Sabah had responsibility for explicitly political functions such as city security and diplomatic, especially tribal, relations.

This division of labor among the three families, apocryphal or real, did not last. At first, the succession process seemed to work smoothly: When Sabah I died in about 1756, he was succeeded by his son Abdallah I. Abdallah faced one major internal challenge to his rule in this early period; its resolution entrenched the al-Sabah as Kuwait's rulers. In the 1760s the al-Khalifah had a disagreement with the al-Sabah—perhaps over the very fact of the emerging al-Sabah dynasty (the al-Khalifah, too, had some historical claim to lead) or perhaps over economics (the al-Khalifah were by now becoming wealthy merchants who wished to be still wealthier). The dispute was so sharp that it could not be resolved internally; the al-Khalifah left Kuwait for Qatar and, after a stay there, for

Bahrain, where they established political power and where their descendants continue to rule. Soon after the al-Khalifah departure most of the al-Jalahimah also left (those who stayed became known by the family name of al-Nisf [half], that is, the half that stayed).[8] There, however, the dispute seems to have ended. At the time such departures were a common and politically acceptable means of settling disputes in the Gulf. Following the move, the al-Sabah maintained good relations, political as well as commercial, with the al-Khalifah in their new home. Their departure removed the major internal challenge to al-Sabah hegemony and left the family's rulers in firmer control. During Abdallah's rule, then, the al-Sabah became the uncontested ruling family of Kuwait. The early leadership structures proved durable, guaranteeing an unbroken succession of Sabah rulers from the mid-eighteenth century on.

Originally the al-Sabah rule was based more on competence than on conquest or hereditary claims to greatness. The al-Sabah had only a conditional right to rule, dependent on continued political performance and on the support of the town notables who, through the nineteenth century, played a role in selecting the ruler from among the leading members of the ruling family. Never absolute rulers, the early al-Sabah leaders, or Shaikhs (the term *shaikh* refers to any male within the ruling family; the title *Shaikh* alone refers to the ruler), governed in consultation with the leaders of the Bani Utub families who had accompanied the al-Sabah on their Arabian migration, families that had now become the leading merchants. The rulers also maintained good relations with the many nomadic tribes, such as the Ajman, in the desert outside Kuwait town who would regularly camp near Kuwait for short periods to trade. These relations formed the basis for political alliances that emerged in the twentieth centuiry when the tribes settled. The family ruled well, and the Sabahs' continuing competence deepened their legitimacy.

Establishing Autonomy: External Threats

Abdallah's long rule helped solidify the leading political institution of the new community, the ruling family. In his early years he consolidated Sabah power. He spent his later years on external matters—in particular, the struggle between the Bani Khalid and the Wahhabis. The Wahhabis, followers of the eighteenth-century religious leader Muhammad Abd al-Wahhab, were a group of religious and political reformers who joined forces with the central Arabian house of Saud to create the alliance that would eventually establish the modern state of Saudi Arabia. From the late eighteenth to the early twentieth century, Wahhabi forces episodically posed a serious threat to Kuwait. For much of the eighteenth century Bani Khalid forces had kept the Wahhabis at bay. In the last years of the century, however, the Wahhabis succeeded in defeating the Bani Khalid, putting Kuwait at risk. Only a combination of hastily fortified internal defenses and new external alliances saved Kuwait from Wahhabi absorption.

It was during this period of insecurity that Abdallah established Kuwait's relationship with Britain through its local agent, the British East India Company. Kuwait's first formal contact with Britain came in 1775 when the Persians occupied Basra, the port near Kuwait that housed the company representatives. As a result of tension between Britain and Persia in this period, Britain rerouted some of its trade through Kuwait. In the 1790s Abdallah housed the company's Basra representatives for two years while the company sorted out disagreements with the Ottoman authorities. In return, the representatives offered Abdallah some temporary help against Wahhabi attacks but discouraged further requests for support. The Wahhabi expansion, meanwhile, prompted the Ottoman Empire to respond by encouraging the Egyptian leader, Muhammad Ali, to send forces into Arabia where they defeated the Wahhabis in 1818.

Through the nineteenth century Abdallah's successors consolidated al-Sabah supremacy within Kuwait and maintained Kuwait's autonomy from its Arabian and Ottoman neighbors. It was with the rule of Abdallah II (1866–1892) that Kuwait began to move away from a century of neutrality, as Abdallah began turning toward the Ottomans, who had long wanted a closer relationship. Abdallah, anxious to contain growing Ottoman power in Arabia, approached the Ottomans with the offer of a closer Kuwaiti alliance in exchange for guarantees of local autonomy in Kuwait, going so far as to accept the Ottoman title of *qaimmaqam* (provincial governor) of Kuwait in 1871. The title was largely a formality, however, as the Ottomans never sent administrative personnel or otherwise interfered in Kuwait's domestic affairs as they did in the areas actually under their rule. In any event, the relationship was soon severed. Although Abdallah's brother and successor, Muhammad, maintained his predecessor's Ottoman alliance, Muhammad was overthrown after four years in power by his brother Mubarak. It is with the rule of Mubarak that Kuwait's modern history commences.

Mubarak the Great

Mubarak the Great, the founder of modern Kuwait, began his political career under Shaikh Muhammad, who put Mubarak in charge of desert security and tribal relations. Mubarak, however, had his own political ambitions, which were frustrated by Muhammad and another brother, Jarrah, who shared much of Muhammad's power. In order to achieve his political aims, Mubarak coupled his own ambitions with popular, tribal, and merchant dissatisfaction with Muhammad, some of which stemmed from a fear that Muhammad's pro-Ottoman policies might eventually lead to Kuwait's incorporation into the Ottoman Empire.

In May 1896 Mubarak gathered his supporters, among them his sons Jabir and Salim (each of whom would later rule), and launched a secret night attack on Muhammad and Jarrah, killing both and proclaiming himself ruler. This exceptional accession is the only violent transfer of power in Kuwait's history. The accession met with little opposition in Kuwait; however, it did prompt concern among Kuwait's neighbors, especially the Ottomans, and the Ottoman's Arabian allies, the al-Rashid tribe, who quickly backed the surviving supporters of Muhammad and Jarrah. Their opposition prompted Mubarak to strengthen his ties with the al-Rashid opponents, the Saudi Wahhabi forces, who had been defeated by the al-Rashid forces in 1892 and were then given refuge by Mubarak. As a result, Ibn Saud, who would later unify his forces into the state of Saudi Arabia, spent time as a boy in Mubarak's court in Kuwait.

When Mubarak came to power, British influence in Kuwait was still limited, although Britain was by then the dominant regional power. As Kuwait was not actively involved in the maritime warfare that the British called piracy, Britain felt little need to regulate its relationship with Kuwait through a series of treaties as it did with other local naval powers farther down the Gulf. During most of the nineteenth century Kuwait remained essentially nonaligned, moving toward a closer alliance with the Ottomans only under Abdallah and his successor, Muhammad. In order to curtail the growing but hostile Ottoman influence, Mubarak turned to Britain.

Shortly after assuming power, Mubarak approached Britain about a more formal alliance. Britain was interested but cautious. Its primary concern with the region lay increasingly in safeguarding its routes to India. However, Ottoman plans in the area offered a potential threat to those routes, and so Britain was anxious to develop new allies. When Mubarak requested gunboats, Britain complied. Nevertheless, Britain initially resisted Mubarak's requests for a formal treaty alliance. The decisive factor in changing Britain's position was the threat posed by an Ottoman concession to Germany for construction of a Berlin-to-Baghdad railroad with a spur line to Kuwait. In response to this threat Britain agreed to the alliance that Mubarak had pushed.

On January 23, 1899, Britain and Kuwait signed a treaty that promised Kuwait British support in exchange for an exclusive relationship with Britain and British control of Kuwait's foreign policy. In the treaty Mubarak also agreed not to grant foreigners concessions in his territory without British permission. This treaty put Kuwait squarely within the British orbit and established a relationship with Britain that would last beyond independence in 1961. With this new agreement Kuwait purchased its complete independence from regional powers but only at the price of an ultimately deeper dependence on Britain. In the short term Britain was able to provide some support for Mubarak against Ottoman opposition, sending gunboats as the occasion warranted. This protection from the Ottomans also allowed Mubarak to solidify his alliance with the Wahhabis, and under the British umbrella Mubarak was able to send expeditions against the al-Rashid forces. In 1902 Ibn Saud's forces recaptured Riyadh, and from then on Wahhabi power in Arabia grew steadily.

A formal relationship with Britain followed inevitably from the treaty. In 1904 Britain sent its first representative, a political agent, to Kuwait. In the interwar period this political agent was the local British voice, offering the ruler advice both on domestic politics, which he as frequently declined as took, and on relations with foreign powers. Britain's primary concern was with its own regional interests and hence with Kuwait's foreign policy. When Britain found that support of its Gulf policy required military aid to Kuwait, as when Arabia threatened Kuwait, then Britain helped. When it was necessary to impose conditions on Kuwait to mollify more powerful neighbors in the interest of Britain's Gulf security, as with Kuwait's borders with Saudi Arabia at the Uqair Conference in 1922, Britain did so.

When World War I broke out, Kuwait was a British ally. Britain took the opportunity of the war to promise Kuwait a closer relationship as a protectorate. By the time Mubarak died in 1915, he had established a strong bond with Britain. Although this bond left Kuwait dependent on Britain, it also assured Kuwait's political independence from its neighbors and, however inadvertently, Kuwait's eventual emergence as an independent political entity in the international state system.

STATE FORMATION: THE ESTABLISHMENT OF KUWAITI INSTITUTIONS

By the early twentieth century Mubarak had established some international protection and was in a position to develop new state institutions and economic and political policies. Kuwait's economy had been growing steadily throughout the nineteenth century as part of a larger regional land and sea trading network. With the British alliance, the economy gradually became integrated into the British trading system. Jacqueline Ismael went so far as to argue that this shift radically restructured Kuwait's regional position.[9] Until the end of the nineteenth century Kuwait was on its way to developing as part of a distinct regional economy, linked increasingly with Ottoman Iraq, as the Ottoman periphery slowly escaped the decaying empire's central control. Ismael argued that Mubarak's coup and the new British alliance led to the decline of those Kuwaiti merchants tied to a regional economy, many of whom were from Basra, and to the rise of the local Bani Utub merchants, whose economic fortunes were now increasingly tied to the British imperial economy. Local merchants played the role of middlemen, helping supply the local economy and the hinterland with subsistence goods now provided by Britain. So, one important change that resulted from Mubarak's rule was the shift in economic orientation from a regional economy to a British-dominated world economy, a shift that decreased the autonomy of Kuwait's merchants as a whole but increased the power of the local Bani Utub merchants relative to the regionally oriented merchants from Basra.

Mubarak altered the economy in other ways as well. He introduced a series of new taxes—among them, taxes on pearl boats and property—that were so unpopular that they prompted a tax rebellion in 1909. That year the leading pearl buyers and merchants joined forces to oppose the taxes, moving—along with their ships and staff—to Bahrain in protest. In the end their rebellion forced Mubarak to cancel some of the taxes to ensure the merchants' return.

These taxes were also the first step toward the development of a state administration, as Mubarak instituted a small tax-gathering bureaucracy. In 1899, immediately after signing the treaty with Britain, Mubarak established sea and land customs administrations. However, the majority of activities that would become state functions still remained private. The religious institutions, for example, had substantial independence and were dominated by one family, the al-Adasani. Education also remained in private hands. When the merchants decided they needed a school system to take students beyond the local Quranic schools to teach them accounting and other skills, they turned not to the government but to their own community, raising money privately for the Mubarakiyyah school, established in 1912. Likewise, social services were a private responsibility. Kuwait's first health care system was established privately during Mubarak's rule, although at his invitation, by doctors from the Arabian Mission of the Dutch Reformed Church in America.

Politically, Mubarak's most important innovation was to centralize power in the hands of the ruler. Throughout the nineteenth century the Shaikh had been primarily a first-among-equals tribal leader, responsive to and in part selected by the local notables. Beginning with his decision to name himself ruler, through a coup and without consulting the notables, Mubarak continued to make state decisions alone, slowly alienating many of the leading families. This centralization of power in the hands of the ruling family marked an important change, one that would continue into the oil era.

Mubarak's Successors

Mubarak was succeeded on his death in 1915 by his son Jabir, who ruled from 1915 to 1917. Jabir did not rule long enough to introduce major

The desert road to Jahrah (author's photo)

changes, but he repealed Mubarak's unpopular house and land taxes. Jabir was succeeded by his brother Salim, and it was during Salim's rule that Kuwait effectively asserted its independence from the now territorially ambitious Arabia in the Battle of Jahrah. Salim began his rule on a bad footing with Ibn Saud. Before coming to power Salim had, in the last days of Mubarak and in his capacity as head of the Kuwaiti forces, granted sanctuary in Kuwait to the Ajman tribe, at that time opponents of Ibn Saud, in order to balance growing Saudi power. When Salim came to power, Ibn Saud expressed his dissatisfaction. The spring of 1920 saw clashes between Kuwaiti and Saudi Ikhwan forces in the desert outside Kuwait. In order to guard against these attacks, Shaikh Salim had a great wall (the gates of which are preserved) built around Kuwait in the summer of 1920, a four-month project that absorbed the labor of Kuwait's entire adult male population. Guards manned the wall continuously against Wahhabi attacks. In October the Ikhwan attacked Kuwaiti forces at Jahrah, a desert village not far from Kuwait town, and dispersed Shaikh Salim's army, forcing it to take refuge in Jahrah's fort, where it spent a night under siege until a relief force from Kuwait arrived the next morning. These Kuwaiti reinforcements, along with some tribal supporters, were able to force the Ikhwan to withdraw, holding them off long enough to prevent a final assault on Kuwait. According to western doctors in the area, Kuwait's forces suffered 63 dead and 120 wounded, large casualties for the small state, leaving the mission hospital overflowing.[10] British forces, coming to Kuwait's rescue with air and sea support, finally settled the matter in Kuwait's favor. In the end, the Battle of Jahrah was declared a Kuwaiti victory.

The battle was an important milestone. In effect, it established Kuwait's independence from Saudi Arabia and reinforced the city-state's growing national identity. The easy rallying of support evidenced by the rapid construction of the town wall suggests that Salim enjoyed popular backing in his efforts to maintain Kuwait's autonomy. The success of his strategies in turn reinforced this sense of patriotism. Although the Kuwaiti forces fought well, the battle also indicated the recurring need for Kuwait's leaders to rely on careful diplomacy and balanced alliances in order to undermine militarily superior forces. The limits and costs of this essentially diplomatic strategy were felt soon after Salim's rule ended. Because Kuwait won its independence from Saudi Arabia with British help, Britain set the terms of that victory in 1922 at the Uqair Conference, which delimited Kuwait's borders with Saudi Arabia. At that conference the British representative granted Saudi Arabia a large chunk of Kuwaiti territory to compensate the Saudis for territorial losses to Iraq, reducing Kuwait's area to about one-third its previous size.[11] This border settlement effectively ended any expansionist ambitions Kuwait's leaders may have had and ensured that Kuwait would always remain a small state with big neighbors.

Shaikh Salim's short reign also saw a few important domestic changes. Mubarak had introduced a small fiscal administration; Salim now introduced a security apparatus—a new local security force under a director who divided the town into sections, each with a local overseer, in order to more closely watch for religious improprieties (such as drinking and prostitution), to which Salim gave renewed attention.[12]

When Shaikh Salim died in 1921, he was succeeded by his nephew Ahmad. Shaikh Ahmad's rule was dominated by two important events—one economic, the other political. The first was the discovery of oil. The second was the Majlis Movement, an uprising by the merchants that succeeded in establishing a brief legislative assembly and that signaled the restructuring of political relationships within the Bani Utub elite.

The Economic Base: The Discovery of Oil

Although Shaikh Ahmad's reign was dominated by the discovery of oil and the enjoyment of the new revenues accompanying this discovery, none of this was apparent when he came to power. Indeed, Ahmad first faced an economic recession, brought on in part by the lingering dispute with Saudi Arabia that finally prompted a Saudi embargo against Kuwaiti goods from 1923 until 1937. The embargo began because Ahmad refused to agree either to new tariffs on goods transiting Kuwait to Arabia or to the placement of a Saudi tax collector in Kuwait. The blockade caused economic hardships and upset existing trading patterns, turning many merchants away from Saudi Arabia and toward Iraq. The territorial loss to Saudi Arabia at the Uqair Conference was also a considerable economic setback. A more severe economic blow was the invention by Japan of cultured pearls, which suddenly lowered the price of Gulf pearls. It was in the midst of this recession that oil appeared.

The discovery of oil in Kuwait was not a sudden or single event. Kuwaitis had long known of its existence from observing seepages in the desert. The British, however, took a commercial interest in this oil. In 1911 the Anglo-Persian Oil Company (APOC), the company that would eventually become British Petroleum (BP) and was already active in Persia, approached the British government in an effort to obtain an exploratory concession in Kuwait (the 1899 treaty bound Mubarak to grant such concessions only to British-approved groups). Britain refused APOC's request but soon after, in 1913, sent in a geological survey team to look for oil. Distracted by World War I, Britain did little for the next few years. After the war, APOC approached the Shaikh for a concession, this time with British approval. While these negotiations were under way, another company—Eastern and General Syndicate (EGS), represented by Major Frank Holmes—also approached the Shaikh. In 1924 Shaikh Ahmad and Ibn Saud together gave Eastern and General permission to look for oil in the Neutral Zone, jointly administered territory between Kuwait and Saudi Arabia set up by the Uqair Conference. As discussions over concessions in Kuwait proper continued, Holmes entered into an association with an American company, Gulf Oil, to handle a concession for Bahrain. In 1927 Gulf joined forces with Holmes to press for the Kuwaiti concession, backed by the U.S. government, which was pressuring Britain to allow U.S. oil firms into the region. For a time Shaikh Ahmad listened to both Gulf and BP. In the end a compromise was reached in the form of a joint company set up by Gulf and BP in 1932, the Kuwait Oil Company (KOC). In December 1934 this new entity signed a concession agreement with the Shaikh, granting it seventy-five years of exploration rights. This agreement, with many amendments, lasted until 1976, when the company finally became fully Kuwaiti owned. Following the 1934 agreement, KOC began exploration. In 1938 it found oil in commercial quantities at the Burgan field—a field that would prove to be one of the world's largest oil reserves. By now, however, oil had begun to ooze into Kuwait's political life.

The Political Base:
The Majlis Movement of 1938

From the earliest days of Kuwait's history, political power had rested in the hands of an oligarchy dominated by the founding Bani Utub elite. Kuwait's leaders, the al-Sabah rulers, dominated this oligarchy, but never with absolute power. Their need for revenue, which they collected through taxes on pearl and trading boats, forced them to rely on the captains and boat owners who oversaw the trade, sold the pearls, controlled the crews who harvested them, and remitted the taxes. The merchants used the occasion of paying taxes to express their views on political life in the community; in a sense, they used their taxes to buy political power. When a ruler tried to govern without the merchants' consent, their organized opposition could pressure him to relent. One struggle occurred in 1909 when the leading pearl merchants left Kuwait for Bahrain to protest new taxes imposed by Shaikh Mubarak. They returned to Kuwait only after Mubarak's retraction of the taxes and virtual apology.

A deeper struggle occurred in 1921, on the death of Shaikh Salim. At that point, the notables had recent experience in organizing. In 1920, after the Battle of Jahrah, a council of leading men had persuaded the ruler to request British help. Following Salim's death, the leading merchants established a twelve-man council that petitioned the ruling family to include the merchants in the succession decision. The council succeeded in eliciting from Shaikh Ahmad a promise of ongoing consultation. Little is known of this council, which lasted only two months before collapsing from internal disagreements and perhaps al-Sabah pressure. In part, the council was a delayed response by the merchants to the increasingly authoritarian government established by Mubarak. As an effort to restrict this authoritarian government, it failed. However, it did provide an important precedent for later efforts.

With the very first trickle of oil revenues, the political relationships at the top began to change. Unlike taxes, oil revenues did not go through the pearl merchants on their way to the Shaikh but went directly from the oil companies to the ruler, thus outflanking the old Bani Utub elite and depriving them of the economic basis of their earlier political influence. In the 1930s the ruler's new oil revenues began to increase the distance between the ruler and the ruled. In 1935 Shaikh Ahmad received his first payment from KOC, and by 1938 he had a small but regular income from oil. These revenues were threatening to displace the customs and other taxes paid by the merchants as the leading state revenues.

When oil arrived, Kuwait was in the midst of an economic crisis, prompted by the decline of the pearling industry, by the Great Depression, and by the conflicts with Saudi Arabia whose trade embargo had cut severely into the traders' overland profits. The merchants, already strapped, feared correctly that they would not enjoy the same control over oil revenue that they had from the revenues generated by pearling and trade. At the first hint that their relationship with the ruler was in jeopardy, the merchants organized and fought back. Following the granting of the initial concession in 1934, they tried to climb back into the loop, arguing that the oil revenues should be considered state funds, that consequently they should go not to the Shaikh but to some state body, on which the merchants would be represented, and that these revenues should be earmarked for development—health, education, infrastructure—rather than being treated, as they were from the start, as personal funds of the Shaikh. In some deep sense the Majlis Movement was an effort by the merchants to salvage something of their imminently fading power. It did not succeed in turning back the tide, but it did allow them to retain more political power than they might otherwise have had.

The movement itself arose in 1938.[13] The merchants began to organize politically, first within the institutions they dominated: the new Education Council, which the merchants had set up to oversee the new school system they were trying to establish, and the Kuwait Municipality, an elected merchant institution, both of which were created in the 1930s. Early in 1938 merchants began circulating petitions and leaflets and putting up antigovernment posters demanding reforms: a greater say in succession and public policy, an expansion of social services such as health and education, and an end to corruption in the ruling family.

When the ruler responded with force, arresting and beating one dissident, the merchants doubled their efforts. In June 1938 the merchants held an election and chose from among their ranks a Legislative Assembly to formally protest the ruler's policies and to implement new reforms. They also organized Kuwait's first political party, the National Bloc.

Outside their new institutions the merchants sought allies in the ruling family. They found one in the person of Abdallah Salim, a prominent yet dissident shaikh who had been passed over for succession (although he would eventually rule Kuwait from 1950 to 1965).[14] Abdallah Salim agreed to lead the Legislative Assembly, and reluctantly Shaikh Ahmad also agreed to accept the assembly. In July the assembly prepared a basic law that asserted the assembly's intention and its right to pass legislation in the areas of security, finance, social policy (health, education, development), and foreign policy. Again, Ahmad reluctantly agreed. In the following six months the assembly energetically set about enacting legislation. It restructured the tax system, introduced public health regulations, opened schools, introduced reforms in the judicial system, and began new construction projects. If the ruler was displeased with some of these reforms, he was still less happy with new laws the assembly introduced restricting the expanding power of the al-Sabah family, which included restrictions on market monopolies the family and its entourage enjoyed and the family use of unpaid labor.

By December 1938 Shaikh Ahmad decided the assembly had gone too far. When the assembly demanded that it, rather than the Shaikh, should henceforth receive checks from the oil company, the ruler recognized this as an attempt by the merchants to reassert their historical economic power over him. Since he no longer needed the merchants' taxes, he no longer needed to listen to their ideas on policy. He had no intention of formally relinquishing the new independence oil had given him, and in December he dissolved the assembly.

When the assembly members and their supporters fought back, Shaikh Ahmad rallied beduin forces, who surrounded the assembly supporters and forced their surrender. The ruler then held elections to a new assembly; but when this body refused to ratify the constitution he submitted, one that would have significantly enhanced the ruler's power, he dissolved this assembly, too. The opposition fought back one last time. In March 1939 when a dissident was arrested for giving an antigovernment speech, his supporters' efforts to obtain his release erupted in a small melee in which the police opened fire, killing one merchant and wounding two others. Having subdued the crowd, the ruler now introduced harsher measures, executing the speaker who had set off the disturbance and arresting the assembly members. So new was this kind of political opposition that the ruler had to build a jail for the detainees: Kuwait's security force was growing. Those opponents who could escape left for Iraq, which had given moral support to the opposition. Ahmad had demanded a showdown and won.

The assembly failed for two reasons. First, the opposition was unable to expand its merchant base into a unifying national movement. Second, in its effort to develop new allies, the opposition looked to forces outside Kuwait—to Iraq and Britain—and in this effort threatened Kuwait's security, losing still more popular support. At home the merchants were unable to consolidate their support among dissidents in the ruling family. Although Abdallah Salim backed them for some time, he was never able to produce many other supporters from the family, nor was he willing to support the merchants to the hilt. When the ruling family as a whole felt threatened, Abdallah Salim did not stand against them.

But the problem ran deeper than that. The merchants who joined the assembly and took part in the Majlis Movement were overwhelmingly Sunni. However, a significant number of Kuwaitis were then (as now) Shia, members of a sectarian minority. Although many Shia families had long lived in Kuwait, others were newly arrived in Kuwait, the consequence of migrations from Iran during the early part of the century.

Kuwait's Shia never joined the Majlis Movement, which they saw, correctly, as an exclusively Sunni movement. Indeed, the movement leaders were very concerned about the growing Shia presence and tried to introduce a census, in part to count and ultimately to restrict the Shia. As the movement progressed, its actions and those of the assembly only confirmed Shia fears. When the assembly tried to oust the Shaikh's personal secretary, a Shia supporter, the Shia grew apprehensive. Shia efforts to obtain assembly representation through formal complaints and even street demonstrations failed. In the end many Shia felt so threatened that they made active efforts to leave—in 1938 over 4,000 Kuwaiti Shia approached Britain with requests for citizenship.[15]

The merchants were ultimately no more successful in obtaining support from abroad. They first approached the British political agent in Kuwait, who offered them some tentative support, in part out of vague sympathy for a movement that would put some checks on autocratic power, in part from an underestimation of the movement's strength and, in part, to wean the opposition from its ties to anti-British Iraqi forces. For a time the agent made a public show of meeting the assembly members. But this support was short-lived. As opposition grew, the British became more concerned that the assembly could eventually mutate into a genuinely national institution, one that might take a harder look at Britain's role in the area and that might take a more difficult stand on oil-related issues. By December 1938 Britain had come around to the ruler's view that the assembly had assumed too much power. Ironically, it was partly this reversal on Britain's part that began to turn the merchants into precisely the nationalist force that would eventually offer opposition to the British presence; the merchants who organized against the ruler in 1938 were the leaders of the opposition to Britain's Palestine policy.[16]

When British support failed to materialize, the merchants looked to Iraq for support. Iraq had its own interest in Kuwait: an interest in its new oil potential that Iraq now expressed in territorial claims for, alternately, all or some of Kuwait, arguing that it had inherited the Ottoman claim to the region. Because the Ottomans had never actually ruled Kuwait, this assertion was based on the never-ratified Anglo-Ottoman Convention of 1913, which declared Kuwait an autonomous district of the Ottoman Empire, a claim rejected by Britain and Kuwait.[17] In the 1930s, as in the 1980s, Iraq's disagreements with Iran over the Shatt al-Arab, Iraq's opening to the Gulf, also caused Iraq to look to Kuwait. Iraq was interested in extending its access to the Gulf by building another port on Kuwait's longer coastline, freeing Iraq from its dependence on Basra. In 1938, as the Majlis Movement was growing in Kuwait, the Iraqi foreign minister went before his parliament to claim Kuwait—Iraq's natural outlet to the sea, as he saw it—as an inseparable part of Iraq for the first time.[18] In the

1930s the growing sense of Arab nationalism in the region and in Iraq in particular furthered this interest, as did the related Iraqi goal of generally discrediting Britain and encouraging anti-British opposition.

Consequently, Iraq offered significant verbal and some material support to the movement. It began working with some three dozen large Kuwaiti families who also owned land in Iraq. As the movement deepened, many of these families took Iraqi nationality. Iraqi leaders began meeting with the dissidents, offering them promises of state contracts and possibly government posts if the movement succeeded. The Iraqi government also encouraged a newspaper and radio disinformation campaign to encourage Kuwaiti opposition. In the final moments of the movement, however, the Iraqis held back from offering military assistance.

Although Iraqi support gave the merchants some short-term leverage, it did so at the cost of casting suspicion on the national loyalty of the pro-Iraqi dissidents. Some merchants actually favored the most radical Iraqi claim—annexation. Others accepted Iraqi support in the hope that they could manipulate it to their own ends. But this distinction was lost on those Kuwaitis who did not want to be absorbed by Iraq. For them, the connections with Iraq were a threat to the Kuwaiti national community. The fleeing dissidents' departure for Iraq when the movement failed only reinforced these fears.

Once the movement had been defeated, the Shaikh was free to spend his revenues with little constraint. But then, just as the Majlis Movement ended, just as oil operations were about to take off, World War II came along. In production terms, the war was a near disaster for Kuwait. Although the British maintained some repair operations in Kuwait, providing some local jobs, they did not maintain oil production. The British capped the wells, suspended operations, and left Kuwait, on the verge of prosperity, all but penniless. It was only with the end of the war that operations resumed. In 1946 the first barrel of oil was exported and from there on the industry developed rapidly.

INDEPENDENCE: THE ESTABLISHMENT
OF KUWAIT AS A STATE

In January 1950 Shaikh Ahmad died and was succeeded by his cousin Abdallah Salim. By 1950 Abdallah had long been an important force in Kuwait. Under his father, Shaikh Salim, Abdallah had held the post of tribal liaison, an important position in a period when tribal ties were the key to defining Kuwait's relations with its Saudi neighbor. When Shaikh Salim died, Abdallah temporarily assumed his duties, and for a time some family members supported Abdallah as a permanent successor. The majority, however, backed Abdallah's cousin, Ahmad Jabir. Abdallah was never happy with this decision and for some time continued to issue orders in his own name; he tried, for example, to introduce fixed salaries, giving himself a stipend equal only to the Shaikh's. When the leading family members joined forces against him, he was forced to retreat. During the 1930s Abdallah again distanced himself from the family by backing the merchants and the supporters of parliamentary politics. This experience apparently left Abdallah with an abiding commitment to representative politics; when he finally came to power, he was instrumental in opening the National Assembly. With the renegotiation of power following the defeat of the Majlis Movement, Abdallah gained control of the Finance Department, which he headed from 1937 until Ahmad's death in 1950. Abdallah succeeded him with no serious family opposition.

Abdallah's rule witnessed Kuwait's transformation from a poor and dependent British protectorate to a wealthy independent state. Indeed, Abdallah's accession day, February 25, is celebrated as Kuwait's national day because of the pivotal role Abdallah played in bringing Kuwait from poverty and dependence to independence and wealth. By Abdallah's accession, Kuwait was already on its way to prosperity: In 1950 Kuwait earned about $16,000,000 from oil.[19] Abdallah now set about spending that money, immediately inaugurating a broad development program. This development plan was an important departure from the ad hoc development funding of Ahmad's last years. The plan built, however, on Abdallah's personal experience in development as finance director under Ahmad where he had overseen development expenditures on health and education. It could not yet, however, draw heavily on the examples, successful or otherwise, of neighboring oil-producing states, as Kuwait was already well ahead of them as an emerging oil economy. In fact, in key ways Kuwait soon became the example these other states would follow. The early 1950s in Kuwait saw the rapid expansion of new development projects and state spending on infrastructure: communications, transportation, and state administration. In the late 1950s Abdallah shifted the emphasis toward a broadly based and highly popular program of social services, providing Kuwaitis with free health care and education, a variety of welfare benefits, and guaranteed state employment. New hospitals and clinics were built by the hundreds, schools by the thousands. Where such services were still inadequate, the government paid Kuwaitis to go abroad for treatment or further education. Teachers and health care personnel were trained or imported to provide the new services.

The new oil revenues proved, however, to be a mixed blessing. The Majlis Movement was the first suggestion of trouble, the first hint that oil could have volatile, dislocating political effects. Under Abdallah, new problems rapidly appeared. First, the new services soon exhausted Kuwait's indigenous labor supply, especially its supply of skilled labor. As a result, the government turned to foreigners. So many foreign workers arrived in Kuwait that by Abdallah's death in 1965 the nonnationals outnumbered the Kuwaitis. Second, in the first few years the development plans proved highly inefficient. Large sums of money went to inappropriately selected, poorly designed, and improperly executed projects. By the early 1950s the new spending had brought Kuwait to the verge of bankruptcy.

The crisis had its roots in a number of factors, among them the simple optimism prompted by revenues so sudden and so large. The more immediate cause, however, lay in some measure with the spending advice Kuwait was receiving. Abdallah initially attributed much of the blame to Britain: to the five large British firms that oversaw a good deal of the initial construction and, to a lesser extent, to the British political representatives who tried to force their advisers on the Kuwaiti government. Oil thus prompted an important change in Kuwait's relationship with Britain.

Restructuring the Relationship with Britain

Kuwait's new revenues and its expanding market transformed its relationship with and raised its importance to Britain. With the end of the war and the resumption of oil operations, Britain now made a concerted effort to increase its influence in Kuwait. What had previously been primarily a political relationship took on a new economic dimension as the British Agency tried to encourage the Kuwaiti government to invest its revenues in and through British firms. Initially Britain succeeded: Virtually all the early state contracts went to just five large British firms, firms that charged the highest price, frequently for the least work. These contractors all but fleeced Kuwait in the first years of operation, bringing the country to virtual bankruptcy by the early 1950s. Unlike his successors in other oil-producing states who would later resort to debt to extricate themselves from similar crises, Abdallah simply called a halt to all nonessential state spending, sending contractors home and turning away ships in the harbor. When this response met with political protests, Abdallah called the opposition's bluff, threatening to resign if his policies were not accepted; they were. Kuwait was thus able to emerge from its first real oil crisis with leaner and more careful spending policies.

Britain also tried to deepen its political as well as its economic relationship with Kuwait. From the beginning of Abdallah's rule, the British tried to force him to take on new British advisers. Although Britain never succeeded in convincing him of the value of the advisory system in general, it did convince him to take a handful of junior advisers in finance, development, customs, and airport management. These advisers, in turn, directed development spending toward the British firms, aggravating Abdallah's economic problems.

As Britain's local presence and its pressure on the ruler grew, tensions began to develop beneath the surface. That the British were never greeted with unbridled affection is suggested by the street taunt reported by one of the first Western physicians to serve in Kuwait: "Englishman, Englishman, with a swelled head. We're hoping tonight will find him dead!"[20] Some of these tensions first appeared in 1938 when Britain backpedaled on its support for the Majlis Movement. The postwar problems with Britain over the advisers and the five British firms deepened Abdallah's resentment of Britain.

Abdallah might have been more resistant to Britain initially were it not for the problems he faced from his own family. The trouble with the family came from two powerful shaikhs: Abdallah Mubarak, the last living son of Mubarak the Great, the security chief, and for many years the leading contender for ruler; and Fahad Salim, Shaikh Abdallah's brother, who ran the departments of public works and health as well as the Kuwait Municipality, sources of much development work. Fahad, who hoped to use his state positions to benefit from the growing revenues, in part by using contracts as patronage, was especially opposed to Kuwait's growing dependence on these British firms.

These relatives and other family members took every opportunity to siphon development funds away from state projects and into their own tanks. Their actions prompted Abdallah to look for other allies. Thus, at about the same time that Britain began looking for ways to involve itself more deeply in Kuwaiti politics, Kuwait's new ruler began looking for new ways to consolidate his own power within the state, particularly against Abdallah Mubarak and Fahad. These separate quests brought Britain and the Shaikh together briefly. It was partly the desire to contain those shaikhs most anxious and able to siphon off the new revenues that convinced Abdallah to allow in the British advisers in the hope that they would control his relatives. The advisers, however, were no more successful than Abdallah in containing Fahad and Abdallah Mubarak. When the advisers failed, Abdallah had no further use for them, particularly as their commercial ventures had nearly bankrupted him. As the advisers, one by one, quit in frustration, Britain was forced to relent and by the mid-1950s it decided to stop pushing for more direct internal control and reverted to dealing directly with the ruler. As Britain had been defeated in its efforts to deal with the Shaikh as any but a de facto ruler, it had little to gain from maintaining Kuwait's formal dependent status. The stage was set for independence.

Kuwait's Postindependence Rulers

On June 19, 1961, Britain granted Kuwait independence. Shaikh Abdallah and the resident replaced the 1899 agreement with new letters of friendship. Kuwait's early independence from Britain, a decade before the other Gulf shaikhdoms, is in some measure due to Abdallah's successful resistance to British administrative pressures. In external affairs the relationship remained little changed at first, as an Iraqi claim on Kuwait following independence forced Abdallah to turn to Britain and the Arab League for military support. As for the shaikhs, in the end Abdallah had to confront them himself. It was a difficult struggle, but he succeeded. With family support Abdallah engineered the exile of Fahad Salim in 1959 and of Abdallah Mubarak in 1961. Fahad Salim died soon after his exile; Abdallah Mubarak spent decades abroad before retiring to Kuwait. Throughout the 1950s Abdallah had held off naming a successor. In 1962, he named his brother Sabah, who was deputy prime minister and foreign minister, heir apparent. This appointment marked the end of the long struggle with Fahad and Abdallah Mubarak.

Ironically, it was this centralization of Abdallah's own power over his own family that allowed Abdallah to embark on a policy that ultimately involved substantial decentralization. Abdallah's last accomplishment, following independence, was to introduce more representative institutions to Kuwait. Abdallah had the political imagination to smooth Kuwait's transition to independence by adding a measure of formal participation, building on a now popularly valued Kuwaiti tradition. The ouster of Fahad and Abdallah Mubarak, who had opposed expanding participation, helped Abdallah make the change, as did the Iraqi threat and the need for a united front at home. Immediately on signing the treaty with Britain, Abdallah set up a Constituent Assembly to draft a constitution. Following the approval of the draft document in November 1962, elections were held in January 1963 for Kuwait's first National Assembly.

Abdallah Salim died in 1965 and was succeeded by Sabah Salim, whose rule saw the consolidation of the leadership and other institutions introduced by Abdallah Salim. Sabah came to the post with a long history of service: He headed the police force until 1959, served briefly as head of the Health Department, then as head of the new Foreign Affairs Department, and on independence, as Kuwait's first foreign minister. Abdallah's nomination of Sabah as heir apparent in 1962 had been at that time a surprise choice—first, because Sabah, like Abdallah Salim, came from the Salim rather than the Jabir line of the ruling family, breaking an alternation in the two sides that had prevailed since the reigns of Shaikhs Jabir and Salim early in the century; second, because politically Sabah was a very low-profile shaikh. Overshadowed in the 1950s by Fahad Salim and Abdallah Mubarak, Sabah came to prominence only in the vacuum their departure created. Nonetheless, he proved a competent ruler, consolidating the policies introduced by Abdallah Salim. In his development plans Sabah benefited from the rising revenues that accompanied the oil

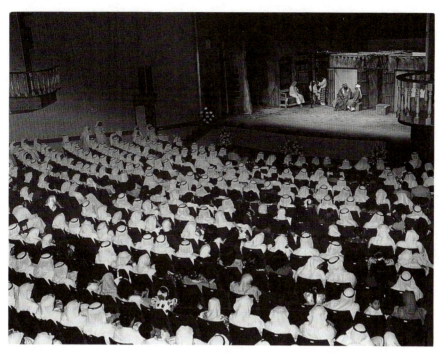

Kuwaiti theatre production (courtesy Ali al-Shati)

price increases of 1973, allowing him to expand the services introduced by Abdallah. Sabah used the new revenues not only to pursue development spending but also to introduce new diversification efforts and to create a Reserve Fund for Future Generations, into which a portion of all oil revenues automatically went. Under Sabah's leadership, Kuwait also assumed full ownership of the Kuwait Oil Company, increasing Kuwait's direct control over the source of revenues.

Sabah had more trouble in his narrowly political goals. From Abdallah he inherited a newly elected assembly with an articulate opposition. With the encouragement of shaikhs Jabir (since 1977, amir) and Sa'ad (since 1978, heir apparent), Sabah responded with a somewhat more authoritarian touch than his predecessor, instituting press controls, limiting public assembly, deporting suspicious foreigners, and interfering in the electoral process. In 1976, shortly before his death, he finally suspended the assembly. Through delegation of authority, Sabah did arrange a smooth transition to the rule of his successor, his cousin Jabir Ahmad, whom he appointed heir apparent in 1966 and on whom he relied heavily as prime minister during most of his rule. When Sabah died on December

31, 1977, Shaikh Jabir succeeded him, returning Kuwait to the pattern of alternation between the Jabir and Salim lines.

Shaikh Jabir came to power after long service in the government.[21] He had been head of security and liaison with the oil company at the oil town of Ahmadi in the 1950s. He then served as head of the Finance Department and as founding director of the Kuwait Fund for Arab Economic Development. After independence he was finance minister in 1962–1963 and then both deputy prime minister and finance minister from 1963 to 1965. Following Sabah's accession in 1965, Jabir served as prime minister until Sabah's death in 1977. Jabir's rule saw a series of crises: economic problems associated with the decline in oil prices in the 1980s, political problems associated with the second dissolution of the assembly in 1986, growing violent opposition in the 1980s and nonviolent opposition in the prodemocracy movement of 1990, and finally, the Iraqi invasion of 1990 and its aftermath. The successes and failures of the policies that Jabir adopted are detailed in Chapters 5 and 6.

NOTES

1. Ahmad Mustafa Abu-Hakima, *The Modern History of Kuwait* (London: Luzac, 1983), p. 1.

2. Abu-Hakima, p. 3.

3. H.R.P. Dickson, *Kuwait and Her Neighbours* (London: George Allen and Unwin, 1956), p. 26.

4. Jill Crystal, *Oil and Politics in the Gulf: Rulers and Merchants in Kuwait and Qatar* (Cambridge: Cambridge University Press, 1990), p. 19.

5. Lewis Pelly, "Remarks on the Tribes, Trade, and Resources Around the Shore Line of the Persian Gulf," *Bombay Geographical Society Transactions* 17 (1863), p. 73.

6. Abu-Hakima, p. 17.

7. Alan Rush, *Al-Sabah: History and Genealogy of Kuwait's Ruling Family, 1752–1987* (London: Ithaca Press, 1987), p. 193.

8. Rush, p. 196.

9. Jacqueline Ismael, *Kuwait: Social Change in Historical Perspective* (Syracuse: Syracuse University Press, 1982).

10. Eleanor Calverly, *My Arabian Days and Nights* (New York: Thomas Y. Crowell, 1958), pp. 118–121.

11. M. W. Khouja and P. G. Sadler, *The Economy of Kuwait: Development and Role in International Finance* (London: Macmillan, 1979), p. 263.

12. Rush, p. 80.

13. See Crystal, *Oil and Politics in the Gulf,* Chapter 3.

14. Jill Crystal, "Abdallah al-Salim al-Sabah," in *Political Leaders of the Contemporary Middle East and North Africa,* edited by Bernard Reich (New York: Greenwood Press, 1990), pp. 8–14.

15. Crystal, *Oil and Politics in the Gulf,* p. 54.

16. Rosemarie Said Zahlan, "The Gulf States and the Palestine Problem, 1936–48," *Arab Studies Quarterly* 3 (1981), pp. 1–21.

17. Daniel Silverfarb, *Britain's Informal Empire in the Middle East: A Case Study of Iraq, 1929–1941* (Oxford: Oxford University Press, 1986), p. 67.

18. Crystal, *Oil and Politics in the Gulf*, p. 52.

19. Khouja and Sadler, p. 26.

20. Calverly, p. 19.

21. See Jill Crystal, "Jabir al-Ahmad," in *Political Leaders of the Contemporary Middle East and North Africa*, edited by Bernard Reich (New York: Greenwood Press: 1990), pp. 277–283.

3

The Oil Economy

Kuwait at first glance would seem to have few resources besides oil. The territory is dry and to the untrained eye nearly barren. The early settlers, however, must have recognized Kuwait's most important economic resource: its trade links to the outside world. The interdependence of the oil era is hardly new; from the earliest days, Kuwait's economy has been linked to distant lands across the desert and the sea.

THE DESERT AND THE SEA: THE PRE-OIL ECONOMY

The desert itself provided Kuwait with little before oil was discovered. The arid, stormy climate and the sandy soil allowed little agriculture. Only a few exceptional villages, such as Jahrah, provided real crops—enough to supply Kuwait with vegetables but not with grains.[1] The desert economy was strong enough to sustain only the beduin, and even they required strong trade links with Kuwait and other settlements. From the desert economy came the products of sheep and camels: skins, wools, dairy products, occasionally meat, and especially trade—caravan trade with distant cities. Indeed, the harshness of the desert and its productive limits virtually forced Kuwait to trade. The desert trade was dominated by caravans to Baghdad and Aleppo.

The sea provided still more resources. One of Kuwait's first attractions to early settlers was its sheltered harbor. From the beginning the Bani Utub took advantage of the harbor to send boats out to trade. Pearl diving was the first Kuwaiti industry to flourish. The pearl banks of the Gulf are among the richest natural banks in the world, providing the basis for what was in the nineteenth century an entire Gulf economy. Just before World War I, when the industry was near its peak, Kuwait had 700 boats and employed 15,000 men.[2] Pearl diving was a seasonal occupation, with the diving season running from mid-May to mid-September. Boats would leave port in the spring and remain at sea the entire season. The industry was labor intensive, highly structured, and hierarchical. The division of labor began with the boat owner at the top, followed by the captain (sometimes the same person), and a crew, which included the divers who collected the oysters, the haulers and their helpers who pulled up the divers, and various ancillary members down to the child apprentices. The pearl trade also had a well-marked division of labor, with distinctions drawn between the middlemen, who bought the pearls directly from the boats, and the pearl merchants, who sold them to the foreign markets of Iraq, India, and Europe.

Crew members were tied to the merchants through a system of debt bondage. The captains would lend the crews what money their families needed to survive their absence at sea, and the crews were obliged to work to repay the loans. Wages were rarely high enough to allow a sailor to escape from the system. Most were in debt their entire lives and beyond, as the debt became part of the pearl diver's estate, an obligation on his children and relatives. For most Kuwaitis this was a hard life—a life of poverty, work, debt, and early death. Drowning, shark attacks, or malnutrition (from the paucity of fresh food on board) were all common causes of death at sea.[3] From time to time the sailors would protest this system either individually (by feigning illness, disobeying orders, jumping ship) or collectively (by striking or appealing to the Shaikh for intercession).[4] Through these means they could occasionally win concessions, but they could not change the system as a whole.

Trade flourished as a natural counterpart to the pearling industry. Although some ships worked the pearl fisheries near Sri Lanka during the winter months when the Gulf pearls could not be harvested, most pearl boats and crews turned to local trade (Kuwait being a natural link for cross-Gulf trade) and long-distance trade.[5] Kuwait became a conduit for transit trade between the Gulf and the Far East, Europe, and Africa. By the early nineteenth century Kuwaiti ships were prominent in this long-distance trade. From the Gulf the ships took dates and pearls. From India, Kuwait's leading trading partner by the early twentieth century, the boats brought rice, coffee and tea, spices, wood, cotton, and other goods and sold (among the more profitable items) smuggled gold.[6] In the years just after World War II, the gold trade, although illegal, was so lucrative that it could turn a profit even if one boat in four was confiscated; to spread risks, merchants could even buy confiscation insurance.[7] From Africa the boats brought wood for construction of more boats and houses, so much wood that Kuwait's rooms came to be measured in mangrove poles.[8] From Europe the Kuwaitis bought manufactured goods, including guns.

Other economic activities based on the sea emerged alongside pearling and trading. Boat building, for example, became an important local industry. Beginning with its own boat market, Kuwait was soon exporting its ships to other Gulf ports. Fishing also became a small but significant

A Kuwaiti pearl merchant, circa early 1940s

industry, not only feeding the local population but also providing a small surplus for export. At the turn of the twentieth century the fishing industry provided jobs for over 1,000 Kuwaitis.[9] Even after the discovery of oil, shrimp remained one of Kuwait's few nonpetroleum exports.

During the nineteenth century these industries allowed Kuwait to prosper. The population grew steadily and rapidly in the last few decades of the century through both natural increase and migrations from eastern and central Arabia, Qatar, and Persia. By 1905 the population was about 35,000. After the turn of the century growth continued but at a slower rate. By 1919 the population had reached 85,000, with 60,000 people in Kuwait town, and by 1947 the population was 120,000.[10] By that time a number of sea changes had occurred in the larger economic network to which Kuwait was increasingly tied. In particular, Kuwait's ties to Europe had grown.

Kuwait had always had trade links to Europe. Archaeological evidence of ancient trade routes tying Greece to Kuwait's Failakah Island date from 400 to 100 B.C. In the nineteenth century Kuwait's modern trade links to Europe developed in an at first imperceptible but ultimately radical way. The reason for this change lay outside Kuwait, in Europe, where from the sixteenth century on the newly developing European capitalist states were spreading their trade links and their economic system

Workers building pearl-diving boats (*dhows*)

to the entire globe. This new European expansion first brought Portugal and then Holland, France, and most notably Britain to the Gulf. The long-term impact was to tie Kuwait to these European economies, primarily through Britain, in the process shifting Kuwait's own economy from its local and regional orientation to an international orientation. The tie that connected Kuwait's oil to European gas stations was merely the last knot in a rope that stretched back at least to the nineteenth century. From a historical perspective the transformation Kuwait experienced was part of a much larger process that came to tie most of the Third World to the First World and indeed, in some sense, to create the distinction between the two.

For Kuwait, however, what was important was the particular local effect this transformation had. In the nineteenth century the British presence began to change the nature of the regional Gulf economy. The British economic presence was felt first and most clearly in trade, where British ships propelled by steam edged Gulf vessels out of many trade routes. Competition from British products complemented this process. Britain did not edge the local traders out completely; Gulf sailors continued to find trading niches, routes where they could turn profits, but British ships increasingly limited those routes. The economic effect of the growing British presence was not as great on Kuwait as it was on other states: first, because the Kuwaitis were particularly successful in locating economic niches of their own; second, because Britain's primary interest in Kuwait was still strategic—its concern lay with protecting its access to India. Nonetheless, the economic impact of Britain's presence was felt in Kuwait, most clearly during the reign of Mubarak. As Ismael argued, Mubarak's British alliance accelerated economic changes already under way, turning Kuwait's economic orientation from a regional to an international one, in a process that ultimately subordinated Kuwaiti traders to Britain. As Kuwaiti merchants were increasingly forced to limit their trade to local subsistence products and desert trade, they were marginalized. In time this process led to a drain of local capital to Europe and to the removal of any impulse toward indigenous, autonomous economic development, a process that occurred throughout the Third World.[11] In Kuwait, however, the impact was tempered both by the belated British economic interest in the settlement and by the constraints on Kuwait's potential for independent economic development created by its limited resources and strong trade ties.

This economic integration into a British and ultimately a world economy deepened after the Mubarak period. World War I caused serious dislocation to Kuwait's economy. In order to limit supplies reaching Ottoman forces, the British banned caravan trade at Kuwait; although many merchants were able to evade the restrictions by smuggling (turning

The old market in Kuwait, 1940s

handsome individual profits), the economy as a whole suffered. The recession deepened after the war when Ibn Saud demanded a 7 percent transit tax on goods crossing Kuwait destined for central Arabia. When Kuwait refused, he countered with an embargo. This action, along with the desert Ikhwan raids, was costly to Kuwait. Finally, the Japanese invention of cultured pearls lowered the price of natural pearls dramatically, mortally wounding the Gulf pearling industry. The invention of the culturing process, a seemingly random event, was itself part of the broader expansion of a world economy that linked European pearl buyers with Japanese producers. The final link tying Kuwait to Britain was oil. But even when oil arrived in the 1930s, it brought little immediate benefit; it was a European timetable that determined the exploitation of oil. Hardly had it been discovered than the wells were capped as Britain prepared for World War II. During the war, the Kuwaiti economy again suffered. Food was rationed, and goods were scarce. It was only after the end of the war that oil could assume its leading economic role in Kuwait.

MULTINATIONALS AND THE STATE: THE HISTORY OF OIL

The oil industry in Kuwait has, since its development in the interwar period, been dominated by one company—the Kuwait Oil Company—originally a fifty-fifty joint holding of the Anglo-Persian Oil Company (the predecessor of British Petroleum) and Gulf Oil, a U.S. company. KOC's domination of the Kuwaiti market was the result of a long and competitive negotiating process.

The history of the oil industry in Kuwait began in 1911 when APOC, which had already found oil in Iran, asked the British political resident in the Gulf to approach Shaikh Mubarak with a request for a concession. Britain postponed the request because of the political uncertainty in the area but kept the matter in mind. In March 1913 Britain carried out the first geological survey for oil in Kuwait and in November approached Mubarak. In an exchange of letters with Britain in October 1913 Mubarak agreed that if oil were found, he would grant no concessions except to groups approved by the British government. During World War I the question of oil was put aside, but by the end of the war Britain was prepared to try again in Kuwait. Britain had made the decision to convert its navy to oil, and to that end Britain had purchased a majority ownership in APOC. The company began negotiating with Shaikh Ahmad for a concession in his territory, putting forward an offer in 1922.

However, by then competition had appeared. Following the war a New Zealand businessman, Frank Holmes, began canvassing the area for concessions that his group, Eastern and General Syndicate, would then resell. Interested in the Kuwaiti concession, Holmes approached Shaikh Ahmad in 1923, letting him know the terms EGS had offered Ibn Saud— terms that were far better than what APOC was offering Ahmad. On this basis, Ahmad rejected the offer from APOC and requested and received British permission to entertain Holmes's proposals. Shaikh Ahmad now began talking to both companies, playing each against the other. Each offer had its weakness. EGS offered potentially higher revenues, but it was a small, financially strapped company that might not be able to exploit the oil concession properly. The APOC offer was one that could be delivered, but the revenues would be lower, and the offer came with an implicit promise of closer ties with Britain, a mixed prospect. While Holmes and APOC pursued separate negotiations with the Shaikh, Holmes also obtained a concession for Bahrain and for the Saudi-Kuwaiti Neutral Zone, the 2,000-square-mile border territory jointly administered by Saudi Arabia and Kuwait. It was this latter concession that brought Gulf Oil into the negotiations. In 1926 EGS was stretched to the limit and, for a price, was willing to offer its interest to APOC. APOC, however, found the price (£50,000) too high, especially as its geologists were not optimistic about finding oil (thus far, no one had actually discovered exportable quantities of oil on the Arabian coast). So EGS turned to Gulf Oil, which was anxious to find new sources of oil and was optimistic about Bahrain and Kuwait. Gulf had been unable to get concessions in the area because the British had already tied up the region with their exclusive treaties with the Gulf leaders. In 1927 Gulf agreed to purchase EGS interests in the area.

The Gulf purchase changed the dynamics of the negotiations. Unlike EGS, Gulf was a major player, a respectable competitor to APOC. Shaikh Ahmad saw opportunity in this new situation. It meant he could play off the two companies for the best deal and be sure either winner could deliver; it also meant he could balance his British alliance with that of another powerful state, the United States, and perhaps even get a measure of protection from other states by attaching both countries' interests to Kuwait.

At first Britain tried to keep Gulf out, holding up negotiations by insisting on a British nationality clause. Gulf, however, was willing to wait. Behind the scenes, Gulf benefited from a new U.S. initiative to pressure Britain into letting more U.S. oil firms into the area, pushed in part by Andrew Mellon, the U.S. ambassador in London and previously head of Gulf Oil. In April 1932 Britain agreed to remove the nationality clause. In May 1932 oil was found in Bahrain in commercial quantities.

While these discussions were taking place abroad, APOC and Gulf Oil faced off in the Gulf, each trying to better the other's offer to Shaikh Ahmad. Ahmad enjoyed this competition; the oil companies did not. Considering that the discovery of oil in Kuwait was becoming increasingly likely, both companies were growing more impatient. And once it was clear to APOC that it could not keep Gulf Oil out of the Gulf altogether, both companies hit on a new strategy: They decided to cut a deal with each other and in 1933 formed a joint company, the Kuwait Oil Company. KOC then approached Ahmad with an offer that fell well below either Gulf's or APOC's previous offers. Fortunately for the Shaikh, he still had room to negotiate because in the interim a new company, Traders Limited, had appeared with a better offer. With this competition the Shaikh went back to KOC, demanding more money (which he got) and also the right to nominate a KOC board member (which he did not get). KOC backed off its lower offer, and a deal was struck.

On December 23, 1934, Shaikh Ahmad signed the first Kuwaiti concession with KOC, giving the company a seventy-five year exclusive grant to explore for oil in Kuwait (in 1951 the concession was extended an additional seventeen years). In return Ahmad received $178,000 down and an annual exploration fee of $35,000 or $1.13 per ton of oil until oil could be exported and thereafter $94,000 a year or $1.13 a ton, whichever was greater.[12] In time the terms of the original concession were altered to reflect the growing bargaining power of the oil-producing states and the competition from smaller oil companies. But this was the basic agreement that governed oil production until nationalization of oil companies occurred in 1976.

The search for oil began immediately, and in 1938 oil was discovered in the Burgan field, ultimately one of the most productive oil fields in the

TABLE 3.1 Annual Oil Production in Kuwait (in millions of barrels)

1946	1950	1955	1960	1965	1970	1975	1980	1985
5.9	125.7	402.7	619.1	861.5	1,090.6	760.7	607.268	387.363

Sources: M. W. Khouja and P. G. Sadler, The Economy of Kuwait (London: Macmillan, 1979), p. 26; Kuwait, Annual Statistical Abstract, 1989, Table 200.

world. Operations were halted during World War II, and for the next few years Kuwait slipped back into the recession it had hoped oil would prevent. However, when the war ended, operations quickly resumed. In June 1946 the first barrel of oil sailed out of Kuwait's harbor.

Although KOC has dominated the oil industry in Kuwait, other companies have obtained smaller concessions. In 1948 Aminoil signed a sixty-year concession for Neutral Zone (later, Divided Zone) oil. In 1958 a Japanese consortium, the Arabian Oil Company, received the concession for the Neutral Zone offshore area. In 1961 Royal Dutch Shell got the concession for the area offshore Kuwait proper. In 1962 a national firm, the Kuwait National Petroleum Company (KNPC), took the concession for an area in western Kuwait relinquished by KOC and in 1967 formed the Kuwait-Spanish Petroleum Company with Spanish Hispanoil to develop this concession. KOC has always remained dominant, however; in 1976 when KOC was nationalized (retroactively to 1975), the company was still producing almost 90 percent of Kuwait's oil.

From 1946 on, oil production and revenues grew steadily and rapidly (see Table 3.1). Oil production rose from 5.9 million barrels in 1946 to 16.2 million in 1947. From there it soared, peaking at 1.202 billion barrels in 1972 (over 3.8 million barrels per day); thereafter political considerations, in addition to physical capacity, governed production levels. As production levels increased, so too did Kuwait's revenues, from $76,000 in 1946 to over $1 billion in 1972. And as oil income rose, government expenditures grew dramatically, and the entire economy witnessed an unprecedented expansion. Within a decade or two of the first export of oil, Kuwait enjoyed a level of economic development that made it one of the richest states in the world on a per-capita basis.

DEVELOPMENT STRATEGIES:
THE ECONOMIC ROLE OF THE STATE

Oil Agreements and Oil Pricing

Because Kuwait's economy rested in the first instance on oil, Kuwait's first economic strategy was to ensure a high price for that commodity. In the early years, as was fairly typical at that time, Kuwait had virtually no control over oil prices or other oil policies: BP and Gulf set Kuwait's production levels and prices. The price Kuwait received for its oil on the basis of the 1934 concession worked out to 13 cents a barrel, considerably below the 22 cents per barrel that Saudi Arabia, Iran, and Iraq received at the time.

Shaikh Ahmad, well aware of the need to influence pricing policies, tried in the initial oil negotiations to use the competition between APOC and Gulf to his advantage. He even tried to include Kuwait in management decisions, unsuccessfully requesting a Kuwaiti seat on the KOC board of directors. Once the 1934 concession agreement was signed, Ahmad had less room to maneuver, and his subsequent efforts to renegotiate the terms of the agreement failed. The government did do somewhat better with later concessions: Both the 1948 Aminoil concession and the 1959 Arabian Oil Company concession involved some state participation, but these concessions were for a small percentage of Kuwait's oil. The KOC concession covered almost all of Kuwait's territory, it was exclusive, and it was long—good for seventy-five years (with amendments, ninety-two years) as initially agreed upon.

In order to gain control over pricing, it was necessary for Kuwait to join forces with other oil-producing states. In the first years of oil production this kind of political organization was not possible, but by the postwar period the international economic and political environment had begun to change. More countries were becoming independent, and political and economic organization among them was now possible. In the 1940s the Venezuelan government negotiated a new payments agreement with the oil companies whereby profit-sharing arrangements replaced fixed per barrel prices. By the time Abdallah came to power in 1950 he was able to build on the success of other states and to trade on Kuwait's own importance, which grew rapidly after the rise of the Iranian nationalist leader Mussadeq, whose policies prompted a British oil boycott and a decline in Iranian exports—a decline largely met by an increase in Kuwaiti production. In 1951 a fifty-fifty oil agreement was applied to Kuwait, giving the state revenues equal to half of KOC's export profits, and KOC's concession was extended seventeen years. The new agreement increased Kuwait's revenues and gave Kuwait the incentive for further pressuring the companies. In 1955 Abdallah reached another agreement with KOC, in which the company relinquished 50 percent of its initial concession area.

It took changes in the international environment and in the structure of the international oil market, however, to give Kuwait real negotiating power. At first Kuwait worked through the Arab League, which in the 1950s began trying to coordinate oil policy among its producing members. In the late 1950s two factors prompted greater organization on the part of the oil-exporting states. One was the arrival on the scene of smaller independent oil companies, which would change the structure of the negotiating environment by breaking the large companies' united front. The immediate factor, however, was a unilateral reduction in posted prices by the oil companies in response to a world surplus of oil. In 1959 and then again in 1960 the oil companies, without consulting the producing countries, introduced two rounds of price reductions—decreases that totaled about 27 cents a barrel. This reduction provided the incentive to act, and five producers—Iraq, Iran, Venezuela, Saudi Arabia, and Kuwait, who together produced 85 percent of the oil sold internationally—met in Baghdad in September 1960 and created OPEC, the Organization of Petroleum Exporting Countries.

OPEC had three goals to start with: first, to raise oil prices to their pre-reduction level; second, to abolish quantity discounts granted by concessionaires to their affiliates; and third, to change the method of calculating company payments by expensing royalties—that is, by subtracting royalties as expenses before, rather than after, calculating profits—an adjustment designed to increase the share of profits the producing states received.

In 1962 OPEC presented its demands to the oil companies but at first made little progress. OPEC's most important success was in affecting the agenda by broadening the debate over division of profits to a debate over price and production levels. In addition, it did succeed in stopping, although not reversing, the decline in oil prices. In 1964 the oil companies also agreed to the principle of expensing royalties but insisted they be allowed to discount the posted price, a technique that lowered taxable profits and partially offset the agreement on expensing.

From the start Kuwait was an active member of OPEC. It was a founding member, joining in 1960 even before obtaining independence, and it supplied OPEC's second secretary general in 1965. For the first critical years Kuwait was the Middle East's largest oil producer (it was surpassed by Saudi Arabia in 1966 and by Iran and Libya in the late 1960s). When OPEC negotiated the 1964 agreement on expensing royalties, the Kuwaiti government, as an OPEC member, agreed to accept the new arrangement. However, when the amir brought the agreement home, the new National Assembly balked, refusing to ratify it, and called instead for the expensing of royalties without discount off posted prices. The assembly also devoted considerable attention to other oil-related issues: the marketing of oil in Kuwait, payments schedules, production levels, gas flaring, and employment and training of Kuwaitis. Oil soon became the assembly's key concern and a major source of conflict between it and the government. In December 1965 twelve assembly members resigned in protest over the government's oil policy. The Kuwaiti press, especially the progressive weekly *al-Ta'liah,* now picked up the issue, giving extensive coverage to oil negotiations. The government soon reached its limit and in May 1966 suspended *al-Ta'liah.* As for the assembly, the government simply waited for its term to end. When elections for the second National Assembly were held in 1967, the government, through various forms of electoral interference, assured itself a more docile body, one that lacked the dissenting members. This assembly ratified the oil agreement. In the interim, however, KOC had made some concessions: it agreed to refer tax disputes to the Kuwaiti courts, it agreed to a government investigation of production costs, and it gave the government the option of taking its royalties in either oil or cash.[13] The company also gave more attention to hiring Kuwaitis; by the early 1980s about half of KOC's staff, including high-level management and skilled labor, was Kuwaiti.

The 1967 Arab-Israeli War was the next turning point in the oil negotiations. During the war some of the Arab states, notably Iraq and Algeria, proposed an oil boycott. Kuwait, however, along with Libya (then still ruled by King Idris) and Saudi Arabia, opposed this measure. The dissenting members joined in 1968 to form OAPEC, the Organization of Arab Petroleum Exporting Countries, a group with a more specifically political agenda. As with OPEC, Kuwait was an early and active member of OAPEC, providing it with headquarters in Kuwait. Following the war, the companies agreed to eliminate the discounts on posted prices. But major developments were still to come.

By 1970 the oil environment had begun to change. Oil consumption had increased so rapidly after World War II that by 1970 it was a seller's market. The producing states took advantage of this turn. Libya, now under the leadership of Mu'ammar Qaddafi, led the way, building on the fact that its concessionaire, Occidental, was a small company highly dependent on Libyan oil. Libya refused to negotiate with the companies as a group, focusing instead on Occidental. When it obtained a price increase from Occidental, other small companies followed, and eventually the large companies fell into line. In November 1970 Kuwait and Saudi Arabia obtained increases in oil prices of 10 cents a barrel. The successes of 1970 were followed by the Tehran agreement of February 1971, which raised posted prices by 40.5 cents a barrel and set a schedule for further increases. This agreement was an important turning point because it introduced the principle that prices would be set through negotiation between the producing states and the oil companies, not through unilateral oil company action. By the eve of the 1973 Arab-Israeli War the producing states had made significant progress toward participating in pricing, production, and marketing decisions.

The turning point came in 1973. On October 17 the OAPEC members met and announced an oil boycott of countries helping Israel, and they also raised prices by 70 percent (prices rose 300 percent above the prewar level by January 1974). Kuwait benefited directly from the price increases and used them to expand its control over more of the local oil industry. After gaining control over pricing, Kuwait moved to increase control over production. Production levels had long been a concern in Kuwait, certainly since the early years when overproduction damaged the Burgan field.[14] Production levels had fluctuated radically in the 1950s and 1960s as the oil companies used Kuwait to compensate for production changes elsewhere, most notably in 1951 when the companies increased Kuwaiti production to offset Iranian losses and again in 1961 when the companies increased Kuwaiti production following a dispute with Iraq. By the 1970s, however, Saudi Arabia had begun to play the role of swing producer, and Kuwait was able to introduce production limits. During the assembly discussions of the oil issue in the 1970s, technical concerns about production expanded into a larger discussion about a national policy relating production to national needs. Kuwait introduced serious production limits after hitting its peak production level of 3.86 million barrels per day in March 1972. In April the government set its first limit at 3 million barrels per day. The 1973 price increases allowed it to limit production still further, and in 1975 the level was lowered to 2 million barrels per day. From 1972 to 1975 oil production fell by nearly half. In 1979, following Iranian production disruptions, the government briefly went above its ceiling but in the early 1980s lowered its production ceiling to 1.5 million barrels per day, with actual production falling below 1 million barrels per day in 1982. Only in the mid-1980s, as oil prices fell, did Kuwait slowly lift its ceiling, rising toward 2 million barrels per day by 1990.

Kuwait also moved to expand control of the oil industry itself. The precipitating issue was the use of associated natural gas. Gas is often found with oil, and in the early years this associated gas was simply burned off, or flared. In 1971 the assembly called for national control of this wasted gas. When the oil companies proved unresponsive, the assembly voted to nationalize the gas industry in late 1971. As a result the utilization of gas rose from 33 percent in 1970 to 70 percent in 1977.[15] Lowering production levels on oil was another way of handling the flaring problem, one that was only too successful: Oil production cuts eventually so limited the production of associated gas that by the early 1980s Kuwaiti industry was actually short of gas supplies. Efforts to find new sources of gas only produced new oil fields.

From control of gas, Kuwait moved to control of oil. In 1973 the assembly refused to approve an agreement granting the government a minority share in KOC, demanding instead a larger share. In January 1974 the government took a 60 percent share in KOC, and at the end of 1976 it took full control of KOC, retroactively effective from March 1975. The concessionary agreement was now replaced with a commercial contract through which Gulf and BP bought Kuwaiti oil. The government also extended more control over the smaller companies operating in its territory. In 1977 Kuwait terminated Aminoil's concession, replacing it with national control.

Since the successes of the 1970s OPEC has seen many setbacks in its efforts to control oil prices, and in the 1980s Kuwait had to deal with all the problems associated with falling oil prices. Nonetheless, from 1973 on generally higher revenues allowed Kuwait to embark on an ambitious program of both oil-based development and diversification away from oil.

Oil-based Development

Almost from the first days of the oil era Kuwaitis expressed concern over the need to ensure that steady economic growth would continue after oil. Much of the concern grew out of the weakness of Kuwait's non-oil industries. Kuwait's pre-oil industries, notably pearling, were in decline even before oil arrived; oil ensured that they would never revive. Very quickly the pearling boats stopped sailing altogether, and the industries of boat building and long-distance trade withered. As old industries were destroyed, however, new ones emerged.

The most important, of course, was oil. Kuwait continues to rely heavily on the export of crude, although it has tried to diversify its trade partners (see Tables 3.2, 3.3, and 3.4). It has also made a concerted effort to move away from its reliance on the simple export of crude (see Tables 3.5 and 3.6). Kuwait's oil sector is controlled by the Kuwait Petroleum Corporation (KPC), established in 1980. KPC, an integrated oil company, includes the Kuwait Oil Company, which handles domestic production and exploration, and the Kuwait National Petroleum Company (KNPC), which handles refining, as well as other oil-related companies such as the Kuwait Foreign Petroleum Exploration Company and the Petrochemical Industries Company. KPC is a large international corporation, a rival eighth sister among the leading oil companies.

Kuwait has long been interested in downstream expansion in refining and marketing. The advantage of oil-based diversification lies not only in the guaranteed outlets for Kuwaiti oil that it provides but also in the higher profits and pricing flexibility that refined products command, giving Kuwait money and time to diversify. Perhaps the most important downstream area for Kuwait has been refining. At first Kuwait tried to enlist the cooperation of KOC in its downstream expansion goals, but in the 1960s the company was uninterested in setting up a local refining capability, and the government lacked the leverage to force it to do so. So Kuwait moved independently, creating the Kuwait National Petroleum

TABLE 3.2 Kuwait Government Revenues (in 000 Kuwaiti dinars, 1KD = $3.40)

Revenues	1985-86	1989-90
Oil revenues	2,094,675	1,941,969
Taxes on net income and profits, non-oil Companies	11,634	13,000
Taxes on real estate (Property transfer)	1,348	2,250
Entry and registration fees	477	538
Customs duties and fees	59,481	65,877
Security and justice	9,091	7,733
Education	4,538	5,606
Health	581	720
Housing and public utilities	10,645	10,038
Electricity and water	50,311	60,078
Transport and communication	67,014	89,425
Financial stamps revenue	6,410	14,800
Other services	974	670
Miscellaneous revenues and fees	20,718	17,546
Sales of land and real estate	7,196	250
TOTAL	2,345,093	2,230,500

Source: Kuwait, *Annual Statistical Abstract, 1989*, Table 257.

Company in 1960, originally as a 60 percent state-owned venture (the state bought out the private shares in 1975). KNPC's immediate goal was to market refined products within Kuwait; its long-term goal was to become an integrated oil company. KNPC first bought KOC's local distribution network, becoming the sole local distributor. In 1968 it began operating a refinery at Shu'aibah to exploit flared gas and to refine crude oil. Kuwait's earliest attempts at refining were not promising, however, as technical operation problems, high production costs, high input costs, and high labor costs left KNPC near bankruptcy by 1970. Although the early years did provide invaluable training in the oil industry for skilled Kuwaiti labor and management, it was only after the 1973 price increases that Kuwait could begin running its refineries at a profit. By the late 1980s Kuwait had the third largest refining capacity in OPEC, following Saudi Arabia and Venezuela, and was exporting almost 90 percent of its oil as refined products.

Having refined its products, Kuwait then had to market them. Although the initial focus was on domestic refining, KNPC also took Kuwait's first steps into overseas marketing, refining, and exploration. Until the

TABLE 3.3 Kuwaiti Exports of Crude Oil by Importing
Countries, 1984 (in 000 Barrels)

Importing Country	Barrels
Arab countries	**2,803**
European Countries	
United Kingdom	---
France	1,165
Holland	34,238
Italy	1,144
Greece	---
W. Germany	1,509
Spain	505
Belgium	967
Romania	575
Others	2,783
Total	**42,886**
American countries	
United States	6,068
Canada	---
Brazil	5,484
Total	**11,552**
Asian Countries	
Japan	64,824
Singapore	32,754
South Korea	15,855
Taiwan	28,297
Philippines	11,946
Thailand	---
Malaysia	1,901
Others	3,187
Turkey	---
Total	**158,764**
African countries	**400**
Oceanic countries	
Australia	4,983
New Zealand	---
Total	**4,983**
Other countries	**21,196**
TOTAL	**242,584**

Source: Kuwait, *Annual Statistical Abstract, 1989*,
Table 201.

TABLE 3.4 Kuwaiti Exports and Imports, by Destinations and Origins, 1987 (in 000 Kuwaiti dinars, 1KD = $3.40)

Groups of countries	Exports Value	Percentage Distribution
Arab countries	138,385	66.62
African countries	755	0.36
American countries	7,753	3.73
Caribbean countries	1	0.00
Asian countries	42,471	20.45
European Economic Community	11,012	5.30
Free market countries	5,316	2.56
Other European countries	946	0.46
European centrally planned economies	948	0.46
Oceanic countries	123	0.06
Others	2	0.00
TOTAL	**207,712**	**100.00**

Groups of countries	Imports Value	Percentage Distribution
Arab countries	168,764	11.03
African countries	3,166	0.21
American countries	181,540	11.86
Caribbean countries	11	0.00
Asian countries	590,885	38.60
European Economic Community	432,483	28.25
Free market countries	73,036	4.77
Other European countries	29,797	1.95
European centrally planned economies	18,658	1.22
Oceanic countries	31,959	2.08
Others	412	0.03
TOTAL	**1,530,711**	**100.00**

Source: Kuwait, *Annual Statistical Abstract, 1989*, Table 221.

early 1980s Japan and Pakistan together accounted for about 40 percent of Kuwait's exports of refined products. By 1990 Kuwait's refined products fed into a large, primarily Western European downstream retail network, selling under the logo Q8. In 1983 KNPC bought Gulf's marketing operations in Scandinavia and the Benelux countries. In the following years it bought 1,300 gas stations in the United Kingdom, giving Kuwait some 4,800 gas stations in seven European states (Sweden, Denmark, the

TABLE 3.5 Kuwaiti Exports of Refined Products by Destination, 1985

Importing Countries	Barrels (in thousands)	Importing Countries	Barrels (in thousands)
Arab		**American**	
Egypt	4,371	United States	5,984
South Yeman	403	Brazil	---
United Arab Emirates	1,133	**Subtotal**	**5,984**
Sudan	----		
Syria	445		
Lebanon	1,166	**Oceanic**	
Others	429	Australia	6,459
Subtotal	**7,947**	Haiti Islands	---
		New Zealand	---
		Subtotal	**6,459**
European			
England	5,973	**African**	
Holland	17,034	Zimbabwe	3,453
Italy	39,593	Tanzania	463
West Germany	1,630	Others	1,016
France	9,902	**Subtotal**	**4,932**
Others	1,880		
Subtotal	76,012	**Other**	15,660
Asian			
Japan	13,183		
Indonesia	526		
Singapore	7,759		
South Korea	225		
Taiwan	1,437		
Phillipines	----		
Malaysia	945		
Hong Kong	200		
India	4,796		
Pakistan	18,746		
Other	----		
Subtotal	47,817		

Subtotal all countries	**164,811**
Bunkers	5,130
Total	**169,941**

Source: Kuwait, *Annual Statistical Abstract, 1989*, Table 203.

TABLE 3.6 Value of Kuwaiti Exports and Imports, 1976-87 (in million Kuwaiti dinars, 1KD = $3.40)

Year	Imports	Total^a Exports	% Oil Exports
1976	972	2,874	92.5
1977	1,387	2,793	91.5
1978	1,264	2,864	91.7
1979	1,437	5,089	93.9
1980	1,765	5,527	92.6
1981	1,945	4,531	87.6
1982	2,385	3,128	83.3
1983	2,149	3,364	87.2
1984	2,041	3,631	89.6
1985	923	1,653	89.3
1986	1,661	252	----
1987	1,531	208	----

^{a} Includes re-exports

Source: Kuwait, Annual Statistical Abstract, 1989, Table 218.

Netherlands, Belgium, Luxembourg, the United Kingdom, and Italy).[16] In 1983 Kuwait also bought two European refineries with a capacity of 135,000 barrels per day, giving it an overseas refining capacity of about 250,000 barrels per day. When prices collapsed in 1986, Kuwait was refining over 80 percent of its oil and selling much of this amount directly overseas. Kuwait also expanded downstream by moving into the transportation of both crude and refined oil through the Kuwait Oil Tanker Company. And it expanded into petrochemicals, primarily fertilizers, investing in fertilizer production both at home and abroad, especially in fertilizer plants in Tunisia and Turkey.

The downstream projects have not been without their problems. World oil refining is already at overcapacity, a problem that will only grow as more states follow Kuwait into refining. Kuwait also entered the transportation field during a period of excess world tanker capacity. Weak international demand for fertilizer coupled with competition has also limited Kuwait's success in this area, forcing it, for example, to suspend production of ammonium sulfate in 1976. However, Kuwait considered its downstream projects long-term investments and was patient about the payoff.

Kuwait also engaged in upstream expansion. Long before the oil era Kuwaiti merchants posted sons in ports up and down the Gulf and on to

India to oversee the satellite trade operations. When Kuwait moved into oil it followed this historical pattern, attempting first to control and then to expand its own sources of oil. By 1988 Kuwait was producing 20,000 barrels per day of oil abroad, half in the United States and half in the North Sea.[17] Although North Sea oil is more expensive to produce, its transportation costs to European outlets are lower, and its location outside the Gulf gives Kuwait some insurance against threats to Gulf shipping. Kuwait also owns shares in Egyptian and Indonesian oil fields. In 1981 Kuwait acquired a U.S. drilling and exploration company, Santa Fe International, at a cost of $2.5 billion. Kuwait immediately began expanding the company and integrating it into its oil operations, with the company taking on downstream and upstream operations in the Americas and the North Sea. Kuwait's investments in the United States also included small percentages of ARCO, Conoco, Phillips, AMOCO, and other oil-related firms. Through the Kuwait Foreign Petroleum Exploration Company (KUFPEC), a KPC subsidiary established in 1981, Kuwait began exploring for oil in Morocco and the United States. KUFPEC has not, to date, been a financial success, steadily losing money, but again the government viewed it as a longer-term investment. KUFPEC's future interests include the former Soviet states, Yemen, Asia, Australia, Egypt, Tunisia (where it discovered oil in 1989), Algeria, the Congo, and Gabon.

Kuwait's most public oil-related investment has been in British Petroleum. In 1986 the Kuwait Investment Office set out to acquire almost 21.6 percent of the shares of BP, a plan that would have absorbed more than 7 percent of Kuwait's overseas investments.[18] BP gave Kuwait access to North American and Asian markets, a nice addition to its European retailing operations. Kuwait had failed in a 1984 attempt to buy Getty Oil's 50 percent share of Mitsubishi Oil with its access to Japan's market of 4.4 million barrels per day. The purchase of the stake in BP, however, prompted British fears that Kuwait would exert undue influence over BP, perhaps risking harm to its overseas operations.

The British Monopolies and Mergers Commission ruled that Kuwait would have to sell over half its BP holdings. In January 1989 BP announced it would buy 11.7 percent of its shares back from Kuwait, leaving it with 9.9 percent. Although Kuwait still made a sizable profit, it was unable to achieve its initial investment goals. After the problems with BP the Kuwaiti government undertook a restructuring of the investment administration, recalling most of the top bureaucracy of the London-based Kuwait Investment Office (KIO), a setback for KIO in its long battle with the Kuwait Investment Authority, based in Kuwait, which had been set up in 1980 under the Finance Ministry to control KIO but which had thus far succeeded only in becoming a parallel organization handling the General Reserve and some other investments.

Diversification

From the start Kuwait has also had an interest in developing its non-oil economic potential, assuring it some control over the inevitable transition to a postoil economy. Until the 1960s, however, the government's top priority was the expansion of social services. What development occurred was as an adjunct to that goal. A tentative shift toward development came in the 1950s with the replacement of the Development Board with the Planning Board. Among the early projects were Kuwait's first refinery and a desalination plant.

The first big push for industrialization came in the 1960s. In 1961 the government established the Shu'aibah Industrial Zone to provide subsidized industrial facilities at one location. In the early 1960s the government established the Kuwait Flour Mills and the National Industries Company, of which one operation, the Kuwait Metal Pipes Company, did manage to export successfully. A World Bank study led to a $3 billion development plan for 1967–1971, emphasizing industry. In addition to oil-related investments (refining, fertilizers) the plan also called for the Shu'aibah Industrial Development Board to oversee a variety of projects in the new Shu'aibah industrial area, including electricity and water distillation plants, port expansion, roads, dry dock, and expansion of metalworks and plants manufacturing chlorine, asphalt, cement, pipes, and prefabricated houses.

Following the first plan an Industrial Development Committee established in 1965 set up the next phase, for 1971–1976, which emphasized export-oriented industries. In the domestic sector, the government set up incentives for private sector participation—tax exemptions, technical aid, and preferential government purchases. The Industrial Bank of Kuwait, established in 1974, was another part of the push for industrial investment. In the mid-1970s the government began building electric plants and desalination plants. One of the few areas in which the government did not invest heavily was agriculture, although it did invest as early as 1953 in the Kuwait Experimental Farm, designed to focus on locally appropriate crops and animal breeds.

After the 1973 price increases the government had the funds to expand its projects. The new five-year plan, for 1976–1981, was funded at over $16 billion. When this spending spurt produced inflation as well as shortages and bottlenecks, the government slowed expenditures in 1978–1979, ultimately abandoning the second plan. Since then the government has continued to pursue some industrialization but far more cautiously.

Despite government statements supporting industry, this sector has never been the funding priority in Kuwait that it has been in other states; and although there has been some rhetoric to the contrary, the Kuwaiti government has essentially acknowledged that the prospects for non-oil based industrialization are limited. Among the problems Kuwait faces are a relatively small market, a small labor force coupled with the problems inherent in importing a larger force, and limited natural resources other than oil.

Perhaps the most important area of diversification has been investment abroad. Kuwait began investing overseas in modest amounts in the early 1950s, primarily in Britain. In the 1960s, following independence, Finance Minister (since 1977, amir) Shaikh Jabir expanded the investment program. In the 1970s foreign investment emerged as a leading strategy, in part because of the surge of new revenues following the price increases, in part because of the real limits on Kuwait's industrial potential, and in part because of some opposition to industrialization at home from Kuwaitis who felt that the revenues would earn more if invested abroad. It was partly in response to these criticisms that the government in 1976 established the Reserve Fund for Future Generations and decreed that in addition to the $7 billion initial investment it would put 10 percent of the oil revenues into the fund annually. These funds were not to be touched until the turn of the century.

Besides its oil-related overseas investment, Kuwait invested in other areas—for example, property in the United States and Britain, bonds, and blue chip stocks. Until the 1980s almost all of Kuwait's foreign investments were in the United States and Western Europe. Kuwait spent about $2 billion in Spanish industry and invested in such German firms as Hoechst (25 percent) and Daimler Benz (17 percent). The U.S. seizure of Iranian assets in 1979 was one factor prompting the government to broaden its investments. In the 1980s Kuwait began to diversify its overseas holdings, beginning with the 1980 purchase of $26 million worth of shares in leading Japanese corporations.

Kuwait's foreign investments were so successful that by the early 1980s they were generating more income than was the direct sale of oil. In 1987 Kuwait's foreign investments produced $6.3 billion, compared to $5.4 billion from oil.[19] The *Financial Times* estimated Kuwait's overseas investments at more than $100 billion, two-thirds of which was in the Reserve Fund for Future Generations.[20] It was these overseas investments that enabled Kuwait's government in exile to continue to function in the months following the 1990 Iraqi invasion and that provided the funds to finance reconstruction and the repair of the damaged oil industry.

RETRENCHMENT STRATEGIES:
THE ECONOMY IN A PERIOD OF FALLING PRICES

In the early 1980s the international oil market again changed, this time from a sellers' to a buyers' market. Increasingly the producers found themselves unable to set the price of oil. Several factors contributed to this situation, among them heavy stocking by the importing states following the price increase of 1979, the Iranian revolution that year, and the Iran-Iraq War the following year. Conservation in the West and energy substitution also contributed, as did a shift toward non-OPEC oil, particularly oil from the North Sea and Mexico.

In 1985 the oil market began contracting. By 1986 prices had fallen to their lowest point, below $10 a barrel, and in early 1986 the OPEC price structure collapsed. The decline came shortly after the Iranian capture of the nearby Iraqi Faw peninsula, which destroyed much of Kuwait's export to Iraq, with the Iran-Iraq War already absorbing much of Kuwait's revenues in aid to Iraq. The still unresolved Kuwaiti stock market crash of 1982 (see Chapter 5) further depressed the economy. In 1981 the government announced Kuwait's first nominally deficit budget, and the next year the deficit doubled. In 1986 Kuwait's GDP fell by 16 percent, the trade surplus dropped by 70 percent, and the state budget (as the Kuwaitis calculate it, omitting investment income) continued to run a deficit.[21]

The October 1986 OPEC meeting instituted strict production controls, and Kuwait initially agreed to a production limit of 1.25 million barrels per day (it did not, however, count its Divided Zone production of 150,000–200,000 barrels per day in its quota, as most of the revenues from this production went to Iraq until 1988). However, the growing world demand for oil coupled with increasing cheating by other OPEC members prompted Kuwait to take an increasingly hard line. In the June 1989 Vienna OPEC meeting Kuwait simply refused to be held by OPEC's decision to raise total production to 19.5 million barrels per day, to be distributed proportionally among its thirteen members on the basis of their current market shares, thus giving Kuwait a quota of 1.093 million barrels per day, up from its old quota of 1.037 million barrels per day, but far short of either its then current production level of 1.7 million barrels per day, its quota request of 1.35 million barrels per day (a 30 percent increase from its old quota), or its production capacity that Kuwaitis officially put at 2.5 million barrels per day (although many feel 1.7 million barrels per day is closer).[22] In this meeting Kuwait opposed Saudi Arabia, with which it had historically been allied, placing Kuwait (instead of Saudi Arabia) as the advocate of lower prices. The Kuwaitis (along with Saudi Arabia) also rejected a compromise put forward that would have granted quotas for the first million barrels production over 20 million barrels per day on the regular formula, with another 474,000 barrels to be allocated among states, like Kuwait, demanding special treatment. Of the 474,000 barrels Kuwait would get 200,000, or roughly two-thirds of its demanded increase.[23] In the end, Kuwait's oil minister, Ali Khalifah, signed the agreement with a stipulation that virtually made a fiction of his signature, saying that Kuwait "neither accepts nor is bound by its assigned quota"—in effect, that Kuwait itself would decide how much to produce.[24] Following the conference, the minister said Kuwait would reduce production to 1.35 million barrels per day, promising further limits should prices fall sharply.[25] But by early 1990 Kuwait was producing at 1.9 to 2 million barrels per day. These production levels and the flouting of quotas were key factors later cited by Iraq in its decision to invade.

Kuwait took this position for a number of reasons. It argued that quotas should be based on size of reserves and production capacity, both large in Kuwait's case. (Other states—Venezuela and Algeria faced with riots, Iran and Iraq with reconstruction costs—naturally put forward other principles, such as economic or political need.) The Kuwaitis also argued that their position was really the first step toward a more rational restructuring of production quotas, one that would allow more fluctuation in production with changes in demand. In the long run a more stable market might lead to better planning by oil-producing countries. In part, the position was simply intended to gain more revenues. In part, it was intended to meet the demands of Kuwait's new refining capacity, which the oil minister put at 1.35 million barrels per day.[26] In part, perhaps, it was an effort to give Kuwait more visibility regionally, as its visibility had diminished since the gradual decline in the level of U.S. forces following the Iran-Iraq War. In part, it reflected the government's inability to raise revenues from other sources, either internally, through taxation, or externally.

Kuwait's position on production indicates it was feeling the pinch of falling prices. Nonetheless, falling prices did not have as harsh an effect on Kuwait as they had elsewhere. Unlike many of its neighbors, the Kuwaiti government not only failed to cancel any major projects but instead embarked on new ones. Several factors account for this reaction. First, Kuwait is a very small and very wealthy state with large reserves and production costs among the lowest in the world. It could lose some fat without losing muscle. Second, unlike some of its small Gulf neighbors, Kuwait had already largely completed the development of basic infrastructure: new roads, communications systems, state administration. The oil price decreases came at a time when Kuwait was prepared to begin retrenching anyway. Third, the optimism of the early price increases was paralleled by a pessimism connected with the price decreases in the mid-1980s. In the late 1980s, oil revenues actually proved higher than expected. Finally, Kuwait's previous policies, especially its investments abroad, gave it a buffer.

Nonetheless, Kuwait also developed strategies to deal with the decrease in revenue. First, Kuwait simply increased production to partially offset falling prices. Unlike many producers, Kuwait, with its vast oil resources, could afford to do this. In 1988 Kuwait had an estimated reserve of nearly 100 billion barrels of oil, the third largest in the world and the equivalent of 240 years of production at then current rates.[27] Both Kuwait's development of retail outlets that could disguise production levels and its outright refusal to abide by OPEC quotas, evident at the 1989 Vienna OPEC meeting, indicate the extent to which Kuwait was determined to compensate for lower prices with higher production. Second, it tried to cut costs. Government expenditures were reduced, most successfully in new construction. Where cuts were necessary, the government was careful to select the constituencies for those cuts, choosing nonnationals over Kuwaitis and expatriate contractors over local merchants.

Third, Kuwait tried to increase non-oil income. Like its neighbors, however, the Kuwaiti government was less successful in finding new sources of state revenues. The government tried public borrowing, acquiring nearly $5 billion of public debt in 1987 through a treasury bond issue, the first time a Gulf state had sold such bonds in order to offset budget deficits without touching capital reserves.[28] In 1988 it aimed to raise $3.6 billion this way.[29] However, trial balloons by government officials announcing the introduction of new taxes or curtailments of state subsidies provoked such resistance that they were abandoned. In 1986, following approval of a budget with a planned revenue drop of almost 40 percent, several cabinet members began testing the idea of introducing new, or what they called "symbolic," charges for previously free services. The planning minister even called publicly for the introduction of taxes and a formal taxing system. Heated assembly opposition prompted the government to backpedal on this policy. This inability to tax the population is a problem shared by other oil-producing states and stems from the fact that the administrative structures that have grown up as a result of oil, although large in terms of personnel, are nonetheless relatively inflexible and ineffective because they have been set up to carry out the easiest state functions—distribution of revenues—functions that, unlike extraction of revenues, are least likely to provoke opposition from the population. One result is a relative inability to tax when taxes are needed.

Finally, some Kuwaitis welcomed the falling oil prices as an opportunity to break oil's hold on the local economy and to allow more diverse and, they argued, more authentic development that would in the long run prove more advantageous to Kuwait. To understand that position, it is necessary to examine the two-edged sword that is oil.

THE BENEFITS AND THE COSTS OF OIL

The Benefits

Oil revenues allowed the state to provide a wide range of new services to the population (Tables 3.7 and 3.8 give an overview of state

TABLE 3.7 Kuwait Government Expenditures, by Ministry, 1987/1988
(in 000 Kuwaiti Dinars, 1KD = $3.40)

Ministries and Departments	Expenditures (in 000 Kuwaiti dinars)
Head of state allotments	8,000
Amiri Diwan	7,155
Audit Department	1,971
Council of Ministers	
Diwan	8,667
National Council of Culture, Arts and Literature	2,791
Fatwa and Tashri Department	1,552
Planning	18,793
Civil Service Commission	20,991
Foreign Affairs	28,933
Finance	
General Administration	134,611
General Accounts	757,296
Administration of Customs	14,976
Commercial Affairs and Industry	19,599
Oil	41,494
Defense	286,760
National Guard	28,336
Interior	153,210
Justice	11,400
Awqaf and Islamic Affairs	13,344
Education	288,979
Information	44,681
Public Health	203,051
Social Affairs and Labor	64,688
Housing	---
Electricity and Water	426,451
Communication	
Telegram and telephone	57,550
Post	8,284
Civil Aviation	9,378
Public Works	143,047
Complimentary Credit	---
TOTAL	**2,805,988**

Source: Kuwait, Annual Statistical Abstract, 1989, Table 260.

Physical education class at a Kuwaiti elementary school (courtesy Ali al-Shati)

spending). In a sense, the first social service the state provided was the development of infrastructure. The first town plan was drawn up in 1954 and in the following years largely implemented. New roads were built along with a new harbor, a new communications system, and a new water system, critically important to arid Kuwait.

The government also used the new revenues to develop a variety of social services. Education was one of the earliest priorities in the oil era. In the early 1950s the government embarked on a large-scale education project involving school construction and the hiring of new teachers. In 1965 school was made compulsory for Kuwaitis to age fourteen. In the 1960s the government introduced a major adult literacy program. Consequently, the school population and level of education rose quickly (see Tables 3.9 and 3.10). The government also developed higher education, primarily through the establishment of Kuwait University in 1966. Today Kuwait has one of the best school systems in the region and one of the highest literacy and educational rates as well. Free education for school-children includes books, uniforms, meals, transportation, and even a parental allowance. The system is well-funded, modern, and comprehensive. At the university, free education includes not only tuition but also dormitories, meals, and such perks as free sportswear, transportation, and field trips. The government also sends students abroad on state fellowships.

TABLE 3.8 Kuwait Government Expenditures, by Type of Expenditure, 1984/1985-1988/89 (in million Kuwaiti dinars; 1KD = $3.40)

Type of Expenditure	1984/85		1985/86		1986/87[a]		1987/88[a]		1988/89[a]	
	%	A/C	%	A/C	%	A/C	%	Budget	%	Budget
Salaries	24.6	675.1	31.2	730.5	43.7	756.5	42.4	838.5	43.1	886.3
Purchase of goods and services	13.9	381.9	12.7	297.8	12.1	208.9	13.4	266.0	12.9	264.0
Transport and equipment means	0.7	20.9	0.8	19.9	1.2	20.8	1.2	24.5	1.3	26.5
Construction projects	22.9	628.8	24.0	536.6	29.0	501.9	32.8	650.0	31.0	657.0
Public Properties	4.8	150.0	6.8	160.6	6.9	120.0	5.1	100.0	5.8	100.0
Unclassified expenditures and exchangeable payments	49.1	1,348.2	56.9	1,333.3	72.3	1,252.0	64.6	1,279.0	61.4	1,261.0
Funds added to the capital of K.F.A.E.D.[b]	1.0	30.0	1.3	30.0	----	----	----	----	----	----
Fund added to capital reserve	(27.8)[c]	(764.7)	(43.7)	(1025.1)	(75.2)	(1,302.3)	(69.5)	(1,376)	(65.5)	(1,346.2)
Reserve for future generations	10.0	274.5	10.0	234.5	10.0	173	10.0	197.9	10.0	205.4
Total Revenues	100.0	2,744.7	100.0	2,345.1	100.0	1,730	100.0	1,979.4	100.0	2,054

[a] General Budget Estimates
[b] K.F.A.E.D.: Kuwait Fund for Arab Economic Development
[c] Figures in parentheses are negative

Sources: Kuwait, Annual Statistical Abstract, 1989, Table 258.

TABLE 3.9 Education in Kuwait by Numbers of Teachers, Students, Schools,
1962-1963 to 1988-1989

Years	Teachers			Students			Classrooms	Schools
	Total	Female	Male	Total	Female	Male		
1962/63	2,941	1,390	1,551	59,551	23,877	35,674	1,844	140
1965/66	5,036	2,356	2,680	91,788	38,238	53,550	2,878	176
1970/71	9,085	4,446	4,639	138,747	60,384	78,363	4,644	230
1975/76	15,472	7,988	7,484	201,907	92,034	109,873	6,932	326
1980/81	22,885	12,335	10,550	302,610	141,623	160,987	9,681	481
1985/86	26,490	15,231	11,259	360,227	173,291	186,936	11,119	591
1988/89	28,431	16,145	12,286	372,687	182,063	190,624	11,780	642

Sources: Kuwait, Annual Statistical Abstract, 1989, Table 305.

Health care was also provided (as shown in Table 3.11). After World War II the state began taking over what was then a rudimentary health care system, based on a small hospital and clinic program introduced by the American Mission of the Dutch Reformed Church. The first postoil development in the health sector was the construction of the Amiri Hospital, which was completed in 1949 and opened with a staff of four doctors. In the 1950s a comprehensive health care system was developed, making Kuwait the first Gulf state to introduce a health system that offered free comprehensive service to the entire population and since then has continued to provide free health services to all its nationals and most expatriates. Improvements in public health as well as health care have dramatically extended the Kuwaiti life expectancy.

Affordable housing has been a state priority. Significant state funds have been dedicated to providing low-cost and no-cost housing to the population. The government introduced its first low-income housing program in 1953. In the next two decades, 75,000 Kuwaitis (15 percent of the national population) received directly subsidized housing.[30] Others received subsidized housing through low-interest housing loans provided by the state.

Other social services also grew. Direct transfers through the Ministry of Social Affairs helped low-income families in several categories including the old and the handicapped. Marriage allowances helped the young. A generous social security program gave pensions to retirees. From 1972 to 1981 the share of government spending on social services more than quadrupled.[31] Government subsidies on water, electricity, telephone service, some basic food items, and gasoline benefited rich and poor alike.

TABLE 3.10 Educational Status of the Kuwaiti Population, 1985 (10 years and older)

Educational Status and Sex		Non-Kuwaiti		Kuwaiti	
		Percent	Number	Percent	Number
Illiterate	Male	21.2	109,800	15.5	33,466
	Female	19.1	54,717	36.9	82,407
	Subtotal	20.4	164,517	26.4	115,873
Read and write	Male	23.5	122,067	13.3	28,670
	Female	20.3	58,057	10.6	23,666
	Subtotal	22.5	180,124	11.9	52,336
Primary	Male	13.4	69,453	26.9	58,150
	Female	16.7	47,660	20.5	45,699
	Subtotal	14.5	117,113	23.6	103,849
Intermediate	Male	15.1	78,514	25.4	54,694
	Female	17.6	50,487	17.5	39,027
	Subtotal	16.0	129,001	21.3	93,721
Secondary and below university level	Male	16.6	86,285	14.0	30,299
	Female	18.6	53,298	11.2	25,065
	Subtotal	17.3	139,583	12.7	55,364
Graduate and post-graduate degrees	Male	10.2	52,926	4.9	10,625
	Female	7.7	22,150	3.3	7,532
	Subtotal	9.3	75,076	4.1	18,157
Total	Male	100.0	519,045	100.0	215,904
	Female	100.0	286,369	100.0	223,396
	Total	100.0	805,414	100.0	439,300

Source: Kuwait, Annual Statistical Abstract, 1989, Table 35.

TABLE 3.11 Government Hospitals, Clinics, and Medical Staff, 1979–1988

	1979	1980	1981	1982	1983	1984	1985	1986	1987	1988
Hospitals and sanitoriums	9	11	14	15	15	17	16	16	16	16
Clinics	49	53	55	54	56	62	62	62	63	65
Dental clinics	78	94	105	114	137	140	157	169	192	193
Mother care centers	15	18	17	18	19	21	22	22	22	23
Child care centers	24	28	28	28	30	32	36	38	40	42
Preventive Health centers	16	23	23	23	23	25	25	28	29	29
School clinics	420	457	480	494	517	540	575	626	682	688
Physicians	1,555	1,921	2,133	2,254	2,354	2,442	2,528	2,548	2,535	2,641
Dentists	167	181	203	223	238	259	277	294	306	320
Pharmacists	228	252	322	345	363	388	392	416	422	437
Assistant pharmacists	350	338	336	342	240	331	342	353	351	368
Therapists	144	185	202	202	217	201	201	201	213	213
Health officers	223	–	210	230	237	240	231	265	257	–
Laboratory assistants	567	661	806	860	884	927	982	1,000	1,148	1,020
Dental technicians	51	56	55	70	62	59	72	76	77	84
Qualified nurses and assistants	3,882	5,407	6,128	6,251	7,023	7,565	6,851	6,794	6,878	7,977
Assistant nurses	501	385	323	596	562	429	330	264	–	–
Radiographers and assistants	263	329	423	438	437	444	453	439	438	450
Male nurses	939	918	1,101	1,019	NA[a]	NA[a]	1,006	1,011	1,093	162
Other									2,587	2,982

[a] Not available

Source: Kuwait, *Annual Statistical Abstract, 1989,* Table 339.

One estimate put these subsidies at $1800 per Kuwaiti in the early 1980s.[32] Finally, state employment was often a form of social security. The government's policy was to hire any Kuwaiti needing a job. As a result, wages and salaries as a share of public expenditures rose from just over one-quarter of the total expenditures after independence to 40 percent a decade later.[33]

State aid went to the rich as well as the poor, most notably through the land purchase program begun in 1952. Through this program the government purchased large tracts of land at high prices, kept some in the city center for roads and other public uses, and resold the rest to the private sector at very low prices. As many of the landowners were members of the ruling family (often, members who had literally staked out a claim to desert land in the 1940s as the value of private property began to rise) or merchants (many of whom had built stately homes on prime downtown land or acquired other property through indebted crews), the program was largely a transfer of wealth from the state to the rich. In the early 1960s one-quarter of the state budget went to this program, and in 1964 land purchase was the largest category of government expenditure, surpassing development.[34]

The Costs

Oil has been such a benefit to Kuwait that it is hard to imagine that it might also have serious costs. But it does, and those costs are very real. Economic development has led to overspending, corruption, inefficiencies, inflation, shortages, and bottlenecks.

Each of the major social welfare programs produced unintended side effects. In education, the expansion of schools led the government to rely on foreign teachers. In the late 1950s almost 90 percent of Kuwait's teachers were non-Kuwaiti.[35] Most of these teachers were Arab—many were Egyptian—and often brought with them political ideas that troubled the regime. Nor was the system as successful as hoped in matching trained Kuwaitis to the necessary jobs. In higher education, the system continued to turn out more graduates than jobs in liberal arts. The government was particularly unsuccessful in encouraging Kuwaitis to enroll in vocational programs. The result was a bad match between the graduates and the needs of the economy.

In health care, very expensive medical equipment was rapidly purchased with less attention given to priority needs or to the ability of the system to maintain and use the equipment.[36] Treatment received more emphasis than prevention. And, as in education, the state remained dependent on foreign health care workers.

The housing program expanded with little overall planning, resulting in long waiting lists combined with a high level of remodeling using government loans, a less efficient process than building appropriate housing in the first place.[37] The program also drove up the price of land and produced other, less-tangible social problems, as large sectors of the population were abruptly relocated and as historical family living arrangements were dislodged. To an even greater extent than the health and education programs, the housing program led to the emergence of an industry based almost entirely on foreign labor.

In general, the most dramatic problems were those associated with the rapid increase in foreign labor necessitated by all the new development programs and social services. For Kuwait, a nation of immigrants, foreign labor was not wholly new. In the period between World War I and World War II the pearl industry employed many foreigners, in particular, Omanis and Adenis. But the influx after oil was on an unprecedented scale. Kuwait's population grew from 120,000 in 1946 to over 200,000 in 1957.[38] Although the population growth was in part a result of increasing birthrates and decreasing death rates due to better living conditions, foreigners made up the bulk of the increase. By 1957 non-Kuwaitis constituted 45 percent, almost half, of the total population. The problems associated with the emergence of this new segment of society are discussed in Chapter 4.

A final social issue of some concern was that these social programs were creating a kind of dependency among Kuwaitis: expectations of wealth without any reciprocal sense of responsibility on the part of the recipient. Some Kuwaitis were concerned that this attitude would prove demoralizing or even ethically debilitating. Others were simply concerned with the state's continuing economic ability to meet this sense of social entitlement. Virtually all these programs were expensive. Each new program created new expectations, but few created new revenues. These concerns found a stronger voice as oil prices fell in the 1980s. It took the Iraqi invasion in 1990, however, to convey the importance of these concerns to the public at large.

NOTES

1. Y.S.F. Sabah, *The Oil Economy of Kuwait* (London: Kegan Paul, 1980), p. 24.

2. Sabah, p. 17.

3. Sabah, p. 16.

4. See "The Law of the Divers," translated by Jacqueline Ismael, *Kuwait: Social Change in Historical Perspective* (Syracuse: Syracuse University Press, 1982), pp. 161–171.

5. Sabah, p. 17.

6. Sabah, p. 20.

7. M. W. Khouja and P. G. Sadler, *The Economy of Kuwait: Development and Role in International Finance* (London: Macmillan, 1979), p. 16.

8. Khouja and Sadler, p. 262.

9. Sabah, p. 13.

10. Sabah, p. 25.

11. Ismael, pp. 54–78.

12. Khouja and Sadler, p. 22.

13. Sabah, pp. 29–33.

14. Sabah, p. 28.

15. Ragaei El Mallakh and Jacob Atta, *The Absorptive Capacity of Kuwait* (Lexington, Mass.: Lexington Books, 1981), p. 22.

16. *Economist*, March 26, 1988.

17. *Economist*, March 26, 1988.

18. *Middle East Economic Digest* (*MEED*), January 16, 1989.

19. *Economist*, March 26, 1988.

20. *Financial Times*, March 13, 1990.

21. *MEED*, January 16, 1988.

22. *Wall Street Journal*, June 8, 1989.

23. *Wall Street Journal*, June 12, 1989.

24. *Wall Street Journal*, June 12, 1989.

25. *Wall Street Journal*, June 9, 1989.

26. *Wall Street Journal*, June 12, 1989.

27. *Economist*, March 16, 1988.

28. *Wall Street Journal*, September 22, 1987.

29. *MEED*, February 13, 1988.

30. Khouja and Sadler, p. 33.

31. Hassan Hammoud, "The Impact of Technology on Social Welfare in Kuwait," *Social Service Review* 60 (1986), p. 56.

32. Carl Bazarian, "Kuwait: Economic Developments," *American Enterprise Institute Foreign Policy and Defense Review* 2 (1980), p. 52.

33. Hammoud, p. 56.

34. Sabah, p. 55.

35. Hammoud, p. 59.

36. Hammoud, p. 61.

37. Hammoud, p. 63.

38. Sabah, p. 51.

4

Kuwaiti Society

Unlike many Middle Eastern states, where the political borders bear no relation to the borders of the communities within, Kuwait's borders come close to surrounding a people who feel they share a distinct identity. This Kuwaiti sense of unity is built on a base of concentric circles: Islamic, Gulf Arab, and Kuwaiti. In the postwar period several factors have contributed to the consolidation of these identities, particularly the Kuwaiti identity; key among them are the family and the state. However, important divisions also cut across Kuwaiti society, including divisions along family, class, tribal, sectarian, gender, and national lines.

UNITY

Kuwait is an Islamic society. Kuwait has long had a small Arab Christian community, the product of missionary activity early in this century, and a small resident foreign Christian community. According to the 1980 census, 87,080 Christians (6.4 percent of the population) lived in Kuwait. Most are foreign workers, mainly from southern India (many nannies are Indian Christians). The constitution guarantees freedom of belief (with certain restrictions, for example, proselytizing of Muslims), and Christians hold public worship without hindrance. The non-Muslim, non-Christian population comprised 28,161 inhabitants (2.1 percent of the population).[1] A small Jewish community also existed in the period between World War I and World War II. However, the overwhelming majority of Kuwait's citizens and noncitizens today are Muslim. Kuwait's state religion is Islam, and constitutionally Islamic law is a main source of legislation. Surveys in the late 1970s indicated that Kuwaiti university students, when asked to choose abstractly, consistently chose Islam as their most important group affiliation, outranking family or citizenship.[2] Because the Islamic identity is so important, the government has consciously attempted to link the Kuwaiti state identity to Islam through pronouncements and displays of public piety, through state funding of mosques and Islamic institutes, through state support of religion in the school curriculum, and through playing a prominent role in Islamic conferences.

Kuwait is a Gulf Arab society. Kuwaitis are heir to the larger Arab tradition and identify themselves nationally as Arabs from Kuwait. But Kuwait also has a specifically Gulfian identity, a common cultural identity it shares with Bahrain, Oman, Qatar, the United Arab Emirates (UAE), Saudi Arabia, and Iraq. This identity is a unique local mix of the Islamic and Arab identities with liberal borrowing from African, Indian, and Persian cultures. These connections are evident, as Muhammad Rumaihi and others pointed out, in artifactual similarities from architecture to furniture.[3] This Gulf identity was carried and shaped by traders, posted during their careers up and down the trade routes in Gulf, Indian, and African ports; by pearl divers and sailors who moved with the economy; by slaves brought to Kuwait from Africa; by non-Kuwaiti wives from India, Africa, and other Gulf ports; and by the families and individuals who, for political and economic reasons, chose to move from one Gulf port to another. The Gulf identity was unified in its high cultural expression by the peripatetic poets of the Gulf. As Rumaihi (himself a Bahraini emigre to Kuwait) illustrated, this Gulf identity was clearly visible by the interwar period and grew in the 1950s through cultural clubs and literary magazines. In the 1980s poetry played a key role in the Gulf cultural revival. At the political level, this Gulf identity found expression in the Gulf Cooperation Council.

Finally, Kuwait has a specifically Kuwaiti identity, a sense of citizen loyalty narrower than any of these other loyalties. This particularly Kuwaiti identity emerged initially as a result of the shared experience of migration and the common effort to build a new settlement and society in Kuwait. The pre-oil economy knit society together, as all were involved in some way in the shared enterprise of wresting a living from the desert and the sea. This identity grew in the period following World War II. Surveys of Kuwaiti youths in the late 1970s found that middle school students ranked Kuwaiti citizenship second in importance in group affiliation only to religion.[4] The Iraqi invasion in 1990 did much to consolidate this sense of specifically Kuwaiti identity.

These identities have been nurtured by social institutions. As elsewhere, the family forms the basis of society in Kuwait. The importance of the family is enhanced in Kuwait by the country's small size, which allows leaders accessibility through family networks. One family network in particular has grown up as an institution designed to pass concerns upward, to link family clusters to the state. This is the *diwaniyyah*, a regular weekly meeting—generally of men who are relatives and friends—over coffee to discuss business and politics, arrange introductions, and

Kuwait towers (author's photo)

obtain or grant favors through the development and maintenance of *wastah* (connections). As an institution of socialization it maintains and consolidates the identities of the extended family, social class, and Kuwaiti society. The diwaniyyah is one of the most important social institutions linking the individual and the state. For the individual the diwaniyyah is the place not only for articulating grievances but also for establishing the personal connections with state officials that will allow those grievances to be addressed. For the state the diwaniyyahs are listening posts. Following the National Assembly's closure in 1986, the diwaniyyah became an even more important institution linking the citizen and the state, as it was one of the few through which political concerns could still be openly voiced. Indeed, following the closure the amir publicly encouraged the diwaniyyah, calling it a more genuinely representative institution than the old assembly. The diwaniyyah network was the organizational structure through which Kuwait's prodemocracy movement put forth its concerns. The diwaniyyahs also helped organize the underground resistance to Iraq following the invasion.

After the family, the state is the second major instrument of socialization. Kuwait's leaders have tried to use the state both to build a Kuwaiti identity and to inculcate values conducive to their continued rule primarily through the state education system, state media, state employment, and state services.

As elsewhere, the state school system has played a key role in political socialization. Until the 1930s Kuwait's educational system was entirely private, consisting of a network of Quranic schools. In 1938 the British political agent wrote that every boy and nearly every girl attended such a school.[5] Islamic authorities thus controlled this primary instrument of socialization. Early in the twentieth century one of the doctors of the American Mission of the Dutch Reformed Church also set up a boys school, and for a short time the American wife of one of the mission doctors also ran a girls school. Their efforts were limited, however, precisely by the public's recognition of the schools' socializing potential: Mission members were, after all, missionaries. The same Kuwaitis who showed little reluctance at visiting mission doctors were more cautious about mission teachers.

In the interwar period the merchants began to encroach on the educational prerogatives of the religious elite. Sunni merchants, unhappy with sending their sons abroad for higher education, established the Mubarakiyyah school in 1911, a more specialized school for training in writing and bookkeeping as well as history and geography. This school was followed by the Ahmadiyyah school in 1921. A merchant Education Council in 1936 established the rudiments of a more extensive school system, beginning with four new primary schools, including one for girls.

The 1930s, however, was a time of social and political dislocation, the period in which the merchants launched a concerted political attack on the rulers in the Majlis Movement of 1938. This movement began in the merchant Education Council, although it soon spread to the municipality and finally to the new Legislative Assembly. When the movement ended in defeat, the Shaikh vowed he would not allow the education of Kuwait's children to be dominated again by potential opposition leaders. No sooner had the government crushed the movement than it began establishing a new state education system. By 1945 the government had seventeen schools, enrolling 3,635 students.[6] Since 1965 education has been compulsory, a law that is largely honored and enforced, and this school system offers free education to every Kuwaiti child. The state has never let its control of education weaken. From the first oil revenues education has been a high priority, commanding substantial state funding. Almost one-third of all state employees are connected with education. The government has also tried to preempt any other potential opposition from gaining control over education. For example, the Education Ministry, in conjunction with the Ministry of Islamic Affairs, supervises Kuwait's religious training institutes. Private schools are primarily for expatriates and remain under state regulation. The state uses its educational system to actively inculcate a sense of Kuwaiti identity and loyalty to the ruler and the state.

Education as an instrument of state socialization has always, however, been inhibited by the shortage of Kuwaiti teachers and the consequent reliance on foreign teachers. This problem first appeared in the 1920s when the Ahmadiyyah School hired non-Kuwaiti teachers and continued in the 1930s when the Education Council turned to Palestinians. The state has tried to address this issue: One of its first tasks on taking over the business of education in 1939 was to send a mission of Kuwaiti students to Iraq for teacher training. Nonetheless, despite these state efforts, Kuwait came to independence with an almost totally foreign teaching staff. Many teachers were Egyptian, and in the Arab nationalist 1960s many officials feared Kuwaiti efforts at inculcating a state patriotic identity were being subverted by countersocialization at the hands of these Egyptian Arab nationalist teachers. Yet, despite an active teacher training policy aimed at Kuwaitis who, it was felt, would be less likely to teach subversive doctrines, by the early 1980s over 70 percent of the teachers were still non-Kuwaiti. The state succeeded in introducing a curriculum that inculcates a Kuwaiti identity and that reinforces the role of the leaders; it was less successful in hiring a teaching staff that has internalized those values.

The media is the second important state instrument of political socialization. As in much of the Third World, the broadcast media are state-owned, with some of the print media in private hands. The government has made affirmative use of the state media to encourage the development of a Kuwaiti identity. Other state institutions, such as the Ministry of Information and the Kuwait News Agency, also publish a regular range of historical and cultural works designed in part to educate the population to the importance of its specifically Kuwaiti identity. The print media, more apt to draw on Kuwait's Islamic, Arab, and even Third World identities, were historically quite free and consequently an agent, however unintentionally, of countersocialization. Since the closure of the assembly in 1986, new press restrictions and the dismissal of large numbers of journalists (many foreign) have made the Kuwaiti press more restrictive, leaving the government's image of Kuwaiti identity less challenged.

Finally, the state has been an instrument of socialization through its role as employer and provider of social services. The state is a massive employer, hiring the majority of working Kuwaitis. Not only does state employment directly instill a sense of state nationalism, but it encourages Kuwaitis to think of themselves as set apart in a more subtle way. State employment is, for Kuwaitis, a guaranteed right—a right non-Kuwaitis do not enjoy. The notion that being a Kuwaiti is a special status, one to which rights are attached, goes far not only to make Kuwaitis feel distinct from other less privileged, non-Kuwaiti Arabs but also to feel positive about being Kuwaiti.

The state's generous allocation of social services drives home the same point. By offering these services preferentially (in some cases exclusively) to Kuwaitis over foreigners, the government helped reinforce a sense of shared identity and social integration. The range of privileges available to Kuwaitis is, by U.S. standards, awesome. Kuwaitis are entitled to free education, from kindergarten through graduate school. The state health care system provides modern, free, efficient care. The state welfare system provides direct transfers to a variety of Kuwaitis, from widows to students and prisoners' families, with the largest disbursements of government aid going to support families in need owing to divorce, old age, widowhood, disability, parental death, illness, miscellaneous financial disability, incarceration of a family member, and educational and marital status.[7] Kuwaitis are acutely aware—and when necessary the state reminds them—that they enjoy these rights because of their special identity as Kuwaitis. The state reinforced this message by enacting laws that make it very hard to become a Kuwaiti.

Out of these state interests have grown attachments, loyalties, and eventually, affection. A study of university students in the mid-1970s found that compared to non-Kuwaitis, Kuwaiti men had a stronger patriotic identity and were notably less alienated from their state institutions.

Almost 80 percent felt they could influence the government and their feelings of trust and efficacy were quite high.[8] Their general confidence in the government was strong, and they felt their leaders were responsive to their needs. At the time, the authors attributed this feeling to three factors: the more democratic political system in Kuwait, including the relative freedom of expression; economic prosperity; and the small size of the system. Yet in studies conducted after the assembly was closed, the authors did not find a decline in the students' sense of efficacy. In a 1977 survey of Kuwaiti men Tawfic Farah found that his respondents felt politically efficacious and that this was generally so across the board, regardless of socioeconomic status.[9] These survey results indicate the state's success both in inculcating a sense of Kuwaiti identity and in linking a positive sense of patriotic identity to the state. State institutions of socialization such as the media, the school system, and the state's social services apparatus have played a key role in the development of this identity.

DIVISION

Kuwaitis have a strong and positive identity, a sense of themselves as distinct from and more privileged than non-Kuwaitis. There is a basic unity to Kuwaiti society. However, although Kuwait's historical experiences created one unified society, these experiences brought Kuwaiti society together in a particularly hierarchical way. These hierarchies created important divisions within Kuwait.

Family Divisions: Rulers and Ruled

Perhaps the most important political division is between the ruling family and the ruled families. The al-Sabah preeminence seems to have its origins in the family's historically political rather than its military, economic, or religious functions—that is, in al-Sabah competence as city administrators and as diplomatic liaisons with the neighboring tribes and with the Ottomans. In the colony's early years even this political power was shared with, or at least contested by, two other Bani Utub merchant families. Social power, likewise, was shared with the Bani Utub merchant elite and with the religious authorities. In terms of wealth and social status, the al-Sabahs did not tower above their Bani Utub peers. Through the eighteenth and nineteenth centuries al-Sabah rulers were (as foreign observers noted) not particularly wealthy compared with the other elite families. In general, the social and economic distance between these families was not great.[10] Intermarriage was the norm, and the al-Sabahs' diwaniyyahs were frequented by other Bani Utub families.

The distance between the ruling family and the merchant elite from which they come has increased in this century, especially in the years since oil. Shaikh Mubarak was the first ruler to introduce new economic restraints on, and hence distance from, the merchants, prompting a tax revolt followed by other rebellions in 1921 and 1938. By then, oil had been discovered, and it was with oil that the ruling family, with its direct access to this new state revenue, began to seriously distance itself from the merchants and other Kuwaitis. Not only did the ruler distribute revenues preferentially to his own family, but he also granted state positions and state salaries to family members in order to assure loyalty at the highest levels.

The ruling family is economically distinct from the rest of the population. The government maintains a civil list from which every al-Sabah receives a monthly check.[11] Many al-Sabahs also benefited less formally but no less effectively from the government's land purchase program of the 1960s and from inside access to various government spending and development programs. The al-Sabahs are also socially distinct, with a preference for family endogamy replacing the historically equal intermarriage with the Bani Utub merchant elite. Finally, al-Sabahs are distinct politically from the rest of the population. The family, of course, has always been the pool from which Kuwait's rulers have been drawn. Al-Sabahs are also clearly overrepresented in high government posts. Key ministries have almost always been held by al-Sabahs, among them defense, interior, information, and foreign affairs. Politically the al-Sabahs are literally above the law, their transgressions handled by family councils rather than ordinary courts. These economic, social, and political distinctions created a distance between the ruling family and the other families of Kuwait long before the Iraqi invasion of 1991 but one that became particularly apparent during the months of exile.

Class Divisions

Among the non-Sabahs, the most important social distinction is between the rich and the not-so-rich, that is, a class distinction based on wealth. Kuwait has several important class divisions that are historically grounded in the very hierarchical social stratification that emerged in the pearling and trading industry. At the top of this industry were those whose primary task was maintaining the conditions for trade, that is, the leaders, the al-Sabahs. Equal to or just below them were the traders who financed the trading expeditions. Together these traders and the al-Sabah rulers comprised the Bani Utub elite families who had migrated together to Kuwait. Historically their notion of themselves as the peak of Kuwait's social hierarchy owed something to the tribal traditions these Kuwaitis inherited, traditions that ranked these asil (original or pure) noble tribes that once engaged in camel breeding above other tribes once engaged in sheep breeding or crafts.[12] These social distinctions, originally tribal in origin, retained their importance long after the families had settled. Over time the Bani Utub used their position as the social and economic elite to acquire still more access to wealth and control over others. As the old tribal elite became shipowners and pearl merchants, they turned from a wealthy status group into a class. In turn the Bani Utub were able to use their newfound wealth to buy more status. As their trade success grew, the merchants were able to buy more and more boats without substantially increasing the wages of the crew. Indeed, as the crews fell into debt, the merchants were able to expand their wealth by confiscating the homes and property of crew members. Later, after oil was discovered and land became a much more valuable commercial commodity, the merchants' possession of this land, originally through confiscations, made them still wealthier. During the eighteenth and nineteenth centuries, Kuwaiti society seems to have become more hierarchical as this elite became wealthier and wealthier, moving away from the more egalitarian structures, norms, and values of the desert economy to the less egalitarian structures, norms, and values of a market economy.

After oil, Kuwait's class structure changed radically. Oil creates a *rentier* economy that weakens class structure by making access to the state rather than access to private property the prime determinant of wealth. Kuwait's revenues, like those of other predominantly oil-producing rentier states, have had this debilitating effect on social structure because these revenues are so large, because they come from outside the economy (that is, payments from oil multinationals), and because they go directly to the state. Once oil arrived, pearl divers and sailors who had once worked for traders left the private sector to work for the state. They lost their class identities and assumed new identities as bureaucrats and technocrats.

The one class that might have disappeared with the coming of the oil economy, but did not, was the merchant class. As I have argued elsewhere, this result was unexpected.[13] Before the oil boom, the merchants were a class, unified by shared trading interests. Their shared economic interests gave them a special relationship to the rulers, who relied on them to collect the taxes needed to run the state. After the discovery of oil, this new industry quickly came to dominate the economy. The pearling industry was already in decline; now the remaining trade sector withered, as sailors took government jobs and as the traders looked for ways to profit from the new industry.

The merchants did not disappear as a class at this point for two reasons. The first was cultural: They had developed not only merchant interests but a merchant culture and a set of social institutions (their diwaniyyahs and intermarriage patterns) that would, for a time, sustain that culture. The merchants were quite conscious of their class interests and worked actively to maintain those interests under changed circumstances. The second reason was economic: They were able to find or, rather, negotiate a new economic niche for themselves with the government. They were able to do this because of the nuisance value they provided. Simply, it was cheaper for the government to buy them out than to drive them out. In order to pacify the merchants, the government guaranteed their economic survival and used some of the mechanisms at the disposal of the state to help the merchants, including a promise that a small non-oil private sector where the merchants could reap profits would be maintained. In addition, the government promised either to pass state contracts for development work on to local merchant firms or, if contracts were given to foreign firms, to require that they take Kuwaiti (that is, merchant) partners, thus ensuring the merchants a cut. Finally, the state guarantee of economic survival included virtually direct transfers through the land purchase program, a program in the 1960s through which the government bought land at high prices from leading merchants (and some ruling family members), ostensibly for development purposes, then sold back most of the land to the merchants at low prices. The merchants did pay a price for these guarantees: They promised to keep a low profile in politics. In other words, they agreed to a trade of wealth for political power. Thus, although most classes were substantially weakened, the merchants as a class survived. In general, though, most classes and the class structure as a whole were severely weakened by the oil economy.

Following the discovery of oil, the state replaced the private sector as the most important source of social stratification. Most employed workers work for the state, and state wages determine the ranks of the salaried workers: the bureaucrats and technocrats. State services and direct transfers determine the wealth of their recipients. Some of these state employees have, from time to time, engaged in class-based behavior, organizing, for example, and even striking over economic interests, as in the oil sector. This action, however, is not the norm. The workers' relationship to the state is fundamentally different from their relationship to private industry. One key difference is ownership. The most successful ministry official might conceivably become minister, but he could never own the ministry or, consequently, pass that ownership on to his children: Economic positions are not heritable. The fact that the same organization, the state, is at once employer, law enforcer, and social services provider, as well as a host of other roles, also means it is much easier for this organization to monitor, prevent, and control class-based behavior, that is, to keep workers in line, than it would be were these roles more scattered. Finally, organization along class lines is inhibited by the fact that workers are divided along other lines as well, for example, tribal and national lines.

Tribal Divisions

Although the original founding families of Kuwait, the Bani Utub, were nomadic tribal families and although tribal norms continue to play an important role in Kuwait today, the tribal social distinctions that are important today are those between the long-settled (although once tribal) families and still-tribal families that settled only in the last several decades. Historically, these desert tribes lived on the outskirts of Kuwait town and in the desert beyond, protected by and clients to the al-Sabah. These families served as liaison to other tribes and often as armed retainers to Kuwait's rulers.

Following independence these tribes began to play a new role in Kuwait. The military threat from Iraq coupled with the tribes' historical military role prompted Kuwait's ruler to offer many previously nominally stateless beduin tribes citizenship along with all the attendant rights in exchange for military service. After the assembly opened, the rulers again encouraged large numbers of tribal families to settle in Kuwait, enticing them with new housing, social services, and jobs—including jobs with the state as soldiers, police officers, guards, and bodyguards.[14] Their children received special fellowships and guarantees of special state jobs. Other tribes of less exalted lineage have also settled in Kuwait, filling particular niches in Kuwait's economy. In exchange the government requested and received tribal support in the assembly, which it used as a counterweight to nationalist and other opposition groups, encouraging tribes to run tribally identified candidates for office. As a result tribal representation in that body grew steadily over the next twenty years. The result was a strengthening of tribal identities and a process of political retribalization. Several tribal families (for example, the Ajman) became quite powerful in Kuwait.[15] Many beduin, because of their nomadic history and political usefulness, were even able to take advantage of citizenship offers from more than one state, collecting passports from Bahrain or Saudi Arabia as well as Kuwait. Others, however, were not so lucky. Because the process of granting nationality was selective and uneven, some beduin long resident in Kuwait fell through the cracks, becoming stateless *bidun jinsiyyah* (without nationality). This group, on the edge of legality, includes a range of residents. Some are *bidun*, beduins whose families historically lived in the desert territory in or—and this is a complicating factor—near Kuwait, but who, under the government's new enforcement policy, were unable to produce papers proving historical residency in Kuwait and hence entitlement to nationality. The group of bidun, however, also includes, at one end, people who would legally have received Kuwaiti citizenship but whose fathers or grandfathers never registered them with the government and, at the other, expatriate workers who opportunely lost their passports and hoped to better their economic lot by blending into and hoping for eventual mass naturalization of the bidun. The status of the bidun became an issue again following the Iraqi invasion in 1990. Most bidun had naturally stayed in Kuwait, fearing that without papers they would be unable to return if they left. Although many proved to be loyal Kuwaitis, suffering the occupation and serving in the resistance, others—some with historical family ties to Iraq—joined the other side.

In general, then, tribal identity has survived and thrived because of its economic uses to the beduin and its political uses to the government. Both tribal identification in general and identification with specific tribes remain important lines of stratification today. The tribe, in addition to being a real line of division in Kuwaiti society, is also the source of the socially dominant symbols and institutions. Tribalism, as Nicolas Gavrielides argued, provides the symbolic framework for interpreting and incorporating new groups.[16] Historically tribal institutions also provide some of the most important social links between the individual and the state. The diwaniyyah is probably the most important such institution, as Farah noted:

> The *diwaniya* is a men's social institution, the importance of which cannot be overlooked in the Middle Eastern society. Although it is ostensibly an informal gathering of men on a regular basis—a man's private club, if you will—behavior patterns are quite formalized. In tribal societies, where maintaining consensus was crucial to the survival of the tribe, the *diwaniya* provided an arena for social intercourse that concomitantly served the very vital function of settling disputes and arriving at decisions. As urbanization set in, the *diwaniya* lost something of its catholic character and began to reflect the stratifications within the society itself. A *diwaniya* today will tend to embrace members of similar social standing, religion, and even age. Thus, a man cannot really choose to "join" a *diwaniya*; he is born into one.[17]

Thus, an historically important tribal institution has been reworked to serve new social, economic, and political functions.

Sectarian Divisions

One of the most important divisions in Kuwait is the sectarian division between Sunni and Shia. The Shia community is diverse, comprising Arab Shia Gulfians who emigrated from Bahrain and Saudi Arabia's eastern Hasa province; Arab Shia who had emigrated to Persia, settled, and later returned; and Persian Shia who emigrated to Kuwait but continued to speak Persian as well as Arabic and maintained family, social, and business ties to coreligionists in Iran.

At the turn of the century the Shia, mainly of Persian origin, already comprised a substantial segment of the settled population in Kuwait. Most were poor, although a few Persian Shia retailers and a dozen or so well-to-do Persian Shia merchant families, such as Bahbahani and Qabazard, did well, particularly those with historical business connections to the al-Sabahs. In the interwar period the Shia community expanded greatly owing to immigration from Persia. Whereas the British had estimated the resident Persian population at about 1,000 early in the century, they put it at about 10,000 by the early 1930s. By the early 1950s the entire Shia population had reached about 30,000. Figures today are far harder to come by as they are not publicly released: Estimates range anywhere from 10 to 25 percent of the national population.[18]

The Shia population developed its own Kuwaiti subcultural identity through two opposite processes. On the one hand, an organic sense of shared identity has grown up naturally within a community with shared beliefs and practices. A certain sectarian economic and social segregation, especially a strong tendency toward endogamy within sectarian groups, has given the community a sense of itself. Discrimination by and conflict with the politically, economically, and socially dominant Sunni community has also sharpened the Shia sense of identity. This sharpening goes back at least to the interwar period when Sunni and Shia faced off in the Majlis Movement of 1938 after the Sunni organizers excluded Shia from the new political institutions. Tension reappeared in the 1950s when the Shia felt excluded from the new Sunni-dominated government bureaucracy. In the 1960s and 1970s Shia candidates formed a distinct bloc in the assembly.

In the 1980s the Shia social identity became much more pronounced, at least in its public expressions. The Iranian revolution prompted both a new sense of community on the part of Kuwait's Shia and a new fear of that community on the part of Kuwait's Sunni. Early efforts by the Shia Iranian clergy to export that revolution inevitably politicized the Shia community. Although the bulk of Kuwait's Shia seemed as happy with their Shia-Kuwaiti identity as Sunni are with their Sunni-Kuwaiti identity, some Kuwaiti Shia were drawn to their revolutionary coreligionists in Iran, prompting Sunni leaders in Kuwait, acting on a combination of preexisting fears and genuine Shia opposition, to introduce discriminatory measures that in turn inadvertently alienated many more Shia, previously loyal to the regime. Thus sectarianism remains an important element of social stratification in Kuwait. Although the concern with Iran on the part of Kuwait's Sunni waned with the Iraqi invasion, the sectarian split reappeared under occupation as relatively more Shia than Sunni remained in Kuwait, the Shia feeling less welcome in Sunni-dominated Saudi Arabia, home to Kuwait's new exile community.

Gender Divisions

As elsewhere, gender is an important social division in Kuwait. To say this, however, is not to say that Kuwaiti women are trapped in harems, enslaved to their husbands, oppressed by Islam, or governed by any of the usual popular misconceptions. Rather, it is to say that gender is a meaningful line of social stratification and that different identities and interests have developed along this line.

Both custom and law enforce a division of labor between the sexes. The family remains the center of Kuwaiti social life, and a woman's place in the family is intimately tied up with her role as wife and mother. Kuwaiti women (and men) marry and stay married, remarrying if they have to. In 1985 only 7 percent of women over twenty-four had never married. By the age of forty the percentage of Kuwaitis, male and female, who have never married drops to 0.6 percent.[19] Even unmarried women continue to live in families: According to the 1985 census only 225 Kuwaiti women lived in households of one.[20] The importance of family life and the customary divisions of labor within the family combine to create different roles for women and men.

The law, in treating women differently, reinforces many customary distinctions. Personal status laws, dealing with family issues, are based largely on Islamic law and draw many distinctions based on sex. In a legal sense a woman never comes fully of age: Even if she is over twenty-one, she needs her father's permission to marry. Her choice of marriage partners is also restricted by law. She cannot marry a non-Muslim, although a man may, and she can marry only one spouse at a time, but a man may marry up to four. In law, men's rights to divorce are largely unrestricted; women's are highly regulated, with divorce permitted only in proven cases of nonsupport, impotence, long imprisonment, or serious physical or emotional incapacity.[21] Women have full property rights; however, in accordance with Islamic law, their inheritance is half that of men.

Laws, including Islamic laws, may help institutionalize social practice, but they are also interpreted through and shaped by social practice. So, for example, although polygamy in Kuwait is legal, it is rare. The legal ease of divorce is moderated by the family opposition such divorce is likely to provoke. Social restrictions and family pressure effectively restrict the legal right of divorce for men, and a woman's power in a marriage will vary radically depending on family origin, social class, and the peculiarities of her circumstances.

However, for those women who fall through these social cracks—for those whose families will not, for whatever reason, support their position—formal recourse and external sources of support are few. One such group is the Kuwait Women's Cultural Society, established in 1985 by

Su'ad al-Tarawah, a Kuwaiti attorney, which provides, among other services, free legal advice to women who cannot afford it. Divorce, alimony, and child custody (the issues being closely related, as without custody women are entitled to only limited support) are the subjects of the most sought-after legal help.[22] The demands on al-Tarawah's group indicate the size of the crack through which women can fall.

Despite these legal distinctions, the government has always supported a degree of equality between the sexes. Women's access to state services such as housing, health care, and education is excellent, with education serving as a good example. Until early in this century girls' formal education, like boys', consisted essentially of Quranic schools. The first non-Quranic girls primary school opened in 1937 as part of the merchants' educational initiative, and the first secondary school opened in 1951. Education has since become compulsory for both sexes to age fourteen. As of 1991 girls comprise just barely under 50 percent of the students from kindergarten through high school. The picture is not perfect, as literacy rates for women remain lower than for men. In 1985 24.1 percent of Kuwaiti females, but only 9.9 percent of Kuwaiti males, over the age of six were illiterate. Nonetheless, the situation is improving: In 1961 60.9 percent of Kuwaiti women were illiterate, compared to 37.7 percent of the men.[23]

Access to higher education for women has also improved, although more slowly. In 1960 the first group of Kuwaiti women sent to Cairo University on state scholarships graduated. When Kuwait University opened in 1966, women soon came to constitute a majority: By the late 1980s 60 percent of the incoming class and 66 percent of the Kuwaitis were female.[24] Women do well at the university, graduating in higher numbers than men and often pursuing historically male-dominated majors. Among the Kuwaiti students, 70 percent of the science majors are women. However, Kuwaiti women are underrepresented in law and Islamic law (34 percent of the Kuwaiti majors are women) and engineering and petroleum (38 percent are women).[25]

If women have easy access to education, their participation in the labor force is more problematic. Women, of course, have always worked, carrying out the bulk of the activities associated with child care, food processing, and the household economy. In the pre-oil days when most adult men spent considerable time away at sea during the pearling season, women's household autonomy was quite pronounced.

Women's lives have been radically affected by the economic, social, and political changes of the last few decades. Oil has affected the household economy by raising incomes, giving many Kuwaiti households the economic ability to hire nannies and servants to perform many of the tasks historically carried out by Kuwaiti women. Oil wealth and the concomitant social changes it has introduced, such as increasing women's educational levels, have also introduced some demographic changes, inducing women to marry somewhat later and bear somewhat fewer children. Somewhat unexpectedly, oil—and the geographical mobility it has given men—has also produced a new, small, but important pool of unmarried women. A tradition of Kuwaiti men marrying foreigners that comes from Kuwait's trading history continues in a new form today as men studying abroad (where they do so in greater numbers than women) frequently marry foreign women, leaving an equal number of Kuwaiti women, on whom endogamy is more binding, without partners. In a 1970 survey female college graduates expressed concern with the shrinking pool of marriageable Kuwaiti men that was leaving many older women unmarried.[26]

Outside the household economy, women's salaried participation rate in the public work force is low. In 1985 only 13.8 percent of Kuwaiti women age fifteen and over were employed, a figure that, though low, indicated substantial growth since 1975 when only 6 percent were in the work force.[27] Overwhelmingly, those women in the work force are in social services, clerical positions, and education; over one-third of working Kuwaiti women are teachers. Several women, however, are active in the business world, some in the larger trading firms, others as owners and managers of small, fashionable shops.

Although women's participation in the labor force has risen slowly in the last few decades, it remains low. There are a few explanations. First, women, like men, usually work because they need money, and in Kuwait fewer people than in other countries need to work for the salary alone. In 1985, of the 69,154 adult Kuwaitis not working, 25 percent were not working because they had other income.[28] Although the labor-force participation rate for men is far higher than for women, it is still very low compared with most states: According to the 1985 census only 59 percent of Kuwaiti men (and 13.8 percent of Kuwaiti women) were economically active.[29]

Second, social norms and restrictions direct and limit women's employment. Because Kuwait is so wealthy, those opposed to women working cannot make the argument that women are taking jobs from men. Instead they emphasize norms of female modesty, generally couched in Islamic terms. One of the most important norms governing appropriate work for women is the value placed on limiting contact between the sexes. Sometimes women internalize these norms. In a 1984 survey of 553 working and nonworking women, less than 20 percent expressed a preference for work in historically male positions.[30] Female opposition to women working was significantly higher among older, less educated, and highly religious respondents. Sometimes women are obliged to respect the norms of the men in their household, as husbands or fathers can effectively prevent women from working. Although most of those represented in the 1984 survey who did not work gave as their reasons the greater importance of housework (44 percent), substantial numbers cited opposition from husbands (19 percent), parents (7 percent), or family (17 percent).

Third, women who work face problems. In 1961 the first women in government employment were initially refused entry to their jobs because they refused to veil (at that time, discarding the veil was a symbol of emancipation for these women). It was only after the foreign minister, Shaikh Sabah, allowed unveiled women to work in his ministry that other ministries followed.[31] A 1970 survey of women university graduates indicated that many felt little entry-level discrimination in employment but felt discrimination acutely in promotions and subsequent pay.[32]

Practical and political considerations having to do with child care can also restrict women's public work. Kuwaiti women have many children, and even though the birthrate is lower for working women, it is still high. Most working women have children, and most intend to have more.[33] This is not as great a problem as it might seem. Women who work for the government (the majority) work (as do men) a short week with a workday that ends by one o'clock, bringing mothers home by nap time. There also seems to be a little more slack allowed to mothers with child-care problems (for example, sick children). For working women, one practical advantage of the high value placed on children is that their child-care responsibilities are acknowledged as socially important—that is, there is no equivalent to the U.S. norm of forcing women to choose between work and family, with its concomitant work-place silence about the children of women who do work. However, not all is so rosy. Kuwait has almost no day-care centers or nursery schools, except for a few for the children of foreigners (the first of which was founded in 1963 by Salwah Abu-Khadrah for Palestinian families cut off from support networks).[34] For those who can afford them (and many Kuwaiti households can, regardless of whether parents work), nannies are common, but with these nannies political problems arise.[35] Recent years have seen growing opposition to the use of foreign nannies (the only sort available), on the grounds that they inculcate non-Kuwaiti ideas and values.

If there are so many obstacles, why, then, do women work at all? In Jamal A. Sanad and Mark A. Tessler's 1984 survey, self-fulfillment (35 percent) and income (34 percent) were the most common reasons given.[36] Al-Sabah's 1980 survey of women had similar findings: Married women generally worked for the income; unmarried women worked to fill time.[37] Women who do work enjoy generous benefits—in some cases benefits more generous than those men earn. Married female state employees can retire after fifteen years (unmarried women after twenty) on a pension only slightly below their salary.

Concerns about foreign workers have also led some prominent Kuwaitis to advocate an increased role for women in the work force because the potential male Kuwaiti workforce remains small and the alternative to Kuwaiti women is non-Kuwaiti employees. The conflation of these two issues emerged in a public way in 1986 when the National Assembly passed a law granting women generous (by U.S. standards) maternity leave—two years off at half pay.[38] One of the arguments put forward in the law's defense was that it would restrict the importation of foreign nannies. When the law was passed, public comment shifted to the observation that working women, many of them teachers, who took advantage of the law would themselves need to be replaced, undoubtedly by foreigners, thus providing no net advantage. Women were not unified in their position on the law. Some saw it as a progressive maternity leave policy; others as an attack on women's economic independence and right to work.

Finally, most of the working women in Kuwait are foreign. The labor picture for these women is rather different and considerably bleaker. In general, these women are younger than male foreign workers, they are somewhat more highly educated, far less adequately compensated (their salaries are about half of men's salaries), they work longer hours (in 1983 women worked on average 49-hour weeks compared with 45-hour weeks for men), and they stay a shorter time in Kuwait.[39] The position of these women, however, must be understood in the context of foreign workers generally.

National Divisions: Expatriates and Citizens

Foreign workers have long played a large role in Kuwait's economy. Although foreign workers have always been important, the composition and number of the foreign work force have changed dramatically in the last few decades (see Table 4.1). The percentage of foreigners grew from 45 percent in 1957 to nearly 60 percent in 1985.[40] Their role increased dramatically after the oil price increases of the 1970s prompted the government to undertake large, labor-intensive development projects.

Some generalizations can be made about the composition of the expatriate population. According to a survey conducted in the 1970s, most foreigners are in Kuwait by choice, that is, because they can earn more money there than they could elsewhere, and are generally happy in Kuwait.[41] The majority of foreigners (62 percent in the 1985 census) are men. Most foreigners stay in Kuwait for short periods, 40 percent for under five years. About three-quarters work for the state.[42] As Table 4.2

TABLE 4.1 Kuwaiti Population by Nationality, 1957-1990

Census	Kuwaiti		Non-Kuwaiti		
Years	Percentage	Number	Percentage	Number	Total
1957	55.0	113,622	45.0	92,851	206,473
1961	50.3	161,909	49.7	159,712	321,421
1965	47.1	220,059	52.9	247,280	467,339
1970	47.0	347,396	53.0	391,266	738,662
1975	47.5	472,088	52.5	522,749	994,837
1980	41.7	565,613	58.3	792,339	1,357,952
1985	40.1	681,288	59.9	1,016,013	1,697,301
1990[a]	38.6	826,586	61.4	1,316,014	2,142,600

[a] Estimated mid-year population
Source: Kuwait, *Annual Statistical Abstract, 1989*, Table 11 and 12.

indicates, they dominate certain industries such as construction. Gavrielides described an ethnic division of labor in Kuwait: Maids and nannies are Christian Indians; doorkeepers at Kuwaiti buildings are Baluchi and at non-Kuwaiti buildings they are Egyptian; cooks are Nubians; social sciences and humanities teachers are Egyptian; English and science teachers are Palestinian; car repair is done by Armenians from Aleppo (body), by Syrians from Hawran (tires), and by Sikhs (parts).[43]

There are important divisions within the foreign community (see Table 4.3). The first is between Arabs and non-Arabs. Most foreigners are Arab. According to the 1985 census 37.9 percent of the population was non-Kuwaiti Arab, and 21 percent was Asian. Africans, Europeans, and Americans each constituted less than 1 percent.[44] Arab workers pose a dilemma for the government. On social grounds they are more attractive, and Arabization of the labor force has been the stated government policy. Yet over the last two decades the number and percentage of non-Arab workers has grown. In 1970 Arabs comprised 68 percent of the foreign workforce and Asians only 29 percent. By 1975 the percentage of Arabs had fallen to 65 percent, and the percentage of Asians had risen to 33 percent; by 1980 Arabs made up 60 percent, Asians 38 percent.[45] In 1985 slightly more than half the non-Kuwaiti work force was Asian (52 percent), and slightly less than half (46 percent) was Arab. The rise in Asian workers has been even more dramatic among foreign women: In 1970 80 percent of the foreign working women were Arab and only 18 percent Asian; in 1985 31 percent were Arab, 68 percent Asian.[46]

The reason for this discrepancy lies, first, in the lower wages Asian labor commands and, second, in the political problems Arab workers pose. Both their linguistic and cultural compatibility and their political sense of entitlement, as members of the larger Arab nation, make them in practice

TABLE 4.2 Estimated Distribution of Labor Force, by Economic Activity, Sex, and Nationality, 1983

Economic activity	Total			Non-Kuwaiti			Kuwaiti		
	Total	Female	Male	Total	Female	Male	Total	Female	Male
Agriculture, hunting, and fishing	3,182	37	3,145	2,553	37	2,516	629	---	629
Mining and quarrying	6,475	518	5,957	2,701	333	2,368	3,774	185	35,89
Manufacturing industries	39,664	740	38,924	36,482	703	35,779	3,182	37	31,45
Electricity, gas, and water	5,365	---	5,365	4,551	---	4,551	814	---	814
Construction	81,363	555	80,808	80,290	555	79,735	1,073	---	1,073
Wholesale, retail trade, restaurants and hotels	54,797	2,146	52,651	50,283	2,072	48,211	4,514	74	4,440
Transport, storage and communications	31,561	2,146	29,415	22,903	1,406	21,497	8,658	740	7,918
Finance and business services	17,575	2,997	14,578	13,690	2,516	11,174	3,885	481	3,404
Social services	251,896	83,435	168,461	164,280	65,046	99,234	87,616	18,389	69,227
Total	**491,878**	**92,574**	**399,304**	**377,733**	**72,668**	**305,065**	**114,145**	**19,606**	**94,239**

Source: Kuwait, *Annual Statistical Abstract, 1989*, Table 161.

TABLE 4.3 Kuwaiti Population by Region of Origin, 1975-1985

Groups of Countries	1975		1980		1985	
	Percent	Number	Percent	Number	Percent	Number
Kuwait	47.5	472,088	41.7	565,613	40.1	681,288
Arab	42.2	419,187	42.3	574,495	37.9	642,814
Asian	9.8	97,813	15.0	204,104	21.0	355,947
African	---	440	0.1	1,601	0.1	2,039
European	0.4	4,280	0.8	9,984	0.7	11,908
American	0.1	814	0.1	1,997	0.2	3,142
Others	0.0	47	0.0	158	0.0	163
Not stated	0.0	168	0.0	---	0.0	---
Total	100.0	994,837	100.0	1,357,952	100.0	1,697,301

Source: Kuwait, *Annual Statistical Abstract, 1989*, Table 17.

more of a threat to the state. This larger shared loyalty to one Arab nation (not state) has its roots not only in a shared cultural history but also in a shared opposition to colonial rule and in the history of the shared political movement for Arab independence that was defeated by Britain and France. It found political expression not only in recurrent movements for political integration but in the lip service paid to Arab nationalism by leaders of virtually every Arab state. As oil wealth divided Arab rich and poor, each group appealed to a different logic of entitlement to serve its interests. The oil-producing states, Kuwait and Saudi Arabia, came increasingly to link entitlement to state sovereignty, whereas members of the poorer states increasingly stressed this larger Arab identity as justification for sharing the revenues. This division, which began to emerge in the 1970s, explains in part the support of so many Arab nonnationals for Iraq, defending the invasion, in part, in terms of this larger Arab entitlement.

Arab workers have been a source of concern since at least the 1960s when Kuwaiti leaders worried about Egyptian teachers preaching Arab nationalism. This is a special concern since Arabs, especially Palestinians and Iraqis, tended to stay in Kuwait longer than others—over fifteen years on average. In 1985 106,604 non-Kuwaitis, the majority Arab, had been in Kuwait for twenty years or more.[47] Arab workers are also somewhat more likely to bring dependents along, the group with the highest dependency ratio being the Palestinians.[48] Non-Kuwaiti Arabs pose political problems. Their interests often touch on topics of concern to Kuwait but their loyalties, it is feared, lie outside the state.

Kuwaitis have long been alarmed by the size of the foreign population, Asian or Arab. Although most foreign workers leave after short periods, enough stay. According to the 1985 census, nearly 30 percent of the foreigners in Kuwait were born there.[49] According to one survey of foreign labor carried out in the 1970s, most foreigners acknowledged Kuwait's right to exclusivity, but still most did not want to leave Kuwait and did not intend to leave voluntarily.[50] Most reported weak emotional ties to their homelands, findings of understandable concern to Kuwait. By the late 1970s the authors were reporting increased alienation among the expatriates due to their unequal legal status and job insecurity.

Kuwait responded to the presence of so many foreigners with numerous restrictions. It placed economic limitations on non-Kuwaitis: They could not hold certain jobs and generally did not earn wages as high as Kuwaitis or enjoy the same fringe benefits. Although they could join existing unions, they could do so only after five years residence, and they could not vote in union elections or hold union office. They could not own land or businesses, they could not participate in the stock market, and in general, they were excluded from the most lucrative areas of the economy. Kuwait also placed social limitations on non-Kuwaitis. Zoning separated Kuwaitis and non-Kuwaitis residentially. Marriage to Kuwaitis, especially to Kuwaiti women, was rare. Hence foreigners did not participate in Kuwaiti family networks or in the usually nationally segregated Kuwaiti sports and cultural clubs.[51] Foreigners did, of course, form their own social networks and organizations, but these generally functioned apart from their Kuwaiti counterparts.

Kuwait placed political limitations on non-Kuwaitis. First, the state had strict naturalization laws. In the past it had required thirty years residence for non-Arabs, fifteen for Arabs (acknowledging the greater sense of Arab entitlement, noted above), and fulfillment of a series of conditions, among them being a Muslim, knowing Arabic, and contributing to the state. Until 1980 the state limited naturalizations to fifty a year.[52] Even then, naturalization did not entitle these Kuwaitis to vote for twenty years or to hold elective or ministerial posts. In 1980 the government amended the Nationality Law, allowing the naturalization of some residents after fifteen years if Arab, otherwise twenty, and ending the fifty-person-a-year rule. However, the rate of naturalization did not increase dramatically.

The government also carefully controlled the entry of nonnationals. The first Nationality Law was issued in 1948; the first Aliens Residence Law in 1959 (both were later amended). Undocumented workers (and even documented workers) were regularly expelled when political tensions developed. Restrictions on and efforts to reduce foreigners increased dramatically after the rise in political violence in the early 1980s. Both political and economic need gave the issue new meaning after the Iraqi invasion of 1990.

Finally, concerns with foreign labor prompted the government to try to reduce its dependence on foreign workers and to Kuwaitize the workforce. In an effort both to control foreign labor and to create more jobs for Kuwaitis, a new labor law in 1989 limited the ability of foreign workers to switch employers. These policies met with only limited success. State policies aimed at increasing the level of Kuwaitis in vocational and technical training programs repeatedly met with low enrollments and high costs. Efforts to increase the number of Kuwaiti women in the labor force prompted Islamist opposition. The government thus faced a dilemma: It could not replace foreign workers, nor was it wholly comfortable with their large presence in the Kuwaitis' midst. This dilemma has only intensified following the Iraqi invasion.

NOTES

1. Kuwait Ministry of Planning, Central Statistical Office, *Annual Statistical Abstract 1988 (ASA 1988)*, p. 28.

2. Tawfic Farah, *Political Behavior in the Arab States* (Boulder: Westview Press, 1983), p. 29.

3. Muhammad Rumaihi, *Beyond Oil: Unity and Development in the Gulf*, translated by James Dickins (London: Al Saqi Books, 1986), p. 97.

4. Farah, p. 27.

5. Jill Crystal, *Oil and Politics in the Gulf: Rulers and Merchants in Kuwait and Qatar* (Cambridge: Cambridge University Press, 1990), p. 45.

6. Kuwait Ministry of Information and Al-Arabi, *Kuwait on the March* (Kuwait: 1989), pp. 53–54.

7. *ASA 1988*, p. 436.

8. Tawfic Farah and Faisal Al-Salem, "Political Efficacy, Political Trust, and the Action Orientations of University Students in Kuwait," *International Journal of Middle East Studies* 8 (1977), p. 318.

9. Tawfiq Farah, "Inculcating Supportive Attitudes in an Emerging State: The Case of Kuwait," *Journal of South Asian and Middle Eastern Studies* 2 (1979), p. 67.

10. Alan Rush, *Al-Sabah History and Genealogy of Kuwait's Ruling Family: 1752–1987* (London: Ithaca Press, 1987), p. 10.

11. Nicolas Gavrielides, "Tribal Democracy: The Anatomy of Parliamentary Elections in Kuwait," in *Elections in the Middle East: Implications of Recent Trends*, edited by Linda Layne (Boulder: Westview Press, 1987), p. 158.

12. Gavrielides, p. 156.

13. See Crystal, *Oil and Politics in the Gulf.*

14. Gavrielides, p. 160.

15. Mohammad al-Haddad, "The Effect of Detribalization and Sedentarization on the Socio-Economic Structure of the Tribes of the Arabian Peninsula: Ajman Tribe as a Case Study," Ph.D. diss., University of Kansas, 1981.

16. Gavrielides, p. 154.

17. Farah, "Inculcating Supportive Attitudes," p. 61.

18. For historical estimates, see Crystal, p. 40.

19. *ASA 1988*, pp. 65–66.

20. *ASA 1988*, p. 41.

21. Nesta Ramazani, "Islamic Fundamentalism and the Women of Kuwait," *Middle East Insight*, January-February 1988, p. 24.

22. Ramazani, p. 24.

23. *ASA 1988*, p. 53.

24. *ASA 1988*, pp. 340, 401.

25. *ASA 1988*, p. 404.

26. Kamla Nath, "Education and Employment Among Kuwaiti Women," in *Women in the Muslim World*, edited by Lois Beck and Nikki Keddie (Cambridge: Harvard University Press, 1978), p. 185.

27. Jamal A. Sanad and Mark A. Tessler, "The Economic Orientations of Kuwaiti Women: Their Nature, Determinants, and Consequences," *International Journal of Middle East Studies* 20 (1984), p. 445.

28. *ASA 1988*, p. 131.

29. *Financial Times*, March 13, 1990.

30. Sanad and Tessler, p. 445.

31. Nath, p. 185.

32. Nath, p. 185.

33. Suad al-Sabah, *Development Planning in an Oil Economy and the Role of the Woman: The Case of Kuwait* (London: Eastlords, 1983), p. 142.

34. Shafeeq Ghabra, *Palestinians in Kuwait: The Family and the Politics of Survival* (Boulder: Westview Press, 1987), p. 44.

35. Noura Al-Falah, "Kuwait: God's Will and the Process of Socialization," in *Sisterhood Is Global*, edited by Robin Morgan (New York: Doubleday, 1981), pp. 410–413.

36. Sanad and Tessler, p. 445.

37. Al-Sabah, p. 149.

38. Ramazani, p. 25.

39. Nasra Shah and Sulayman Al-Qudsi, "The Changing Characteristics of Migrant Workers in Kuwait," *International Journal of Middle East Studies* 21 (1989), p. 45.

40. *ASA 1988*, p. 31.

41. Tawfic Farah, Faisal Al-Salem, and Maria Kolman Al-Salem, "Alienation and Expatriate Labor in Kuwait," *Journal of South Asian and Middle Eastern Studies* 4 (1980), p. 3.

42. *Middle East Economic Digest (MEED)*, May 16, 1987.

43. Gavrielides, p. 161.

44. *ASA 1988*, p. 29.

45. *ASA 1988*, p. 128.

46. *ASA 1988*, p. 128; Shah and Al-Qudsi, p. 32.

47. Shah and Al-Qudsi, p. 58.

48. Shah and Al-Qudsi, pp. 37–38.

49. *MEED*, May 16, 1987.

50. Farah, Al-Salem, and Al-Salem, p. 3.

51. Sharon Stanton Russell, "Migration and Political Integration in the Arab World," in *The Politics of Arab Integration,* edited by Giacomo Luciani and Ghassan Salame (London: Croom Helm, 1988), p. 202.

52. Russell, p. 192.

5

Political Institutions and Processes

When Kuwait became independent in June 1961, the new state faced two crises. The first was a foreign policy crisis stemming from an Iraqi claim to part of the newly independent territory, a claim that Iraq asserted within days of Kuwait's independence. The second crisis was a national crisis of identity and loyalty stemming from the ideological and practical demands of independence. The first crisis was quickly addressed. A new treaty arrangement between Kuwait and Britain provided for British military support against threats. Britain sent forces to Kuwait, which, along with Arab League forces, forestalled any imminent invasion. The second crisis—of national identity—took longer to resolve. In the postindependence period Kuwait's rulers tried to nurture and mold the embryonic sense of patriotism that emerged at independence into a strong national identity through three sets of political institutions: the ruling institution of the al-Sabah family, the consultative institution of the National Assembly, and the sustaining institution of the bureaucracy. In large measure these institutions proved successful in consolidating the national identity and in doing so in such a way as to ensure loyalty to Kuwait's leaders. Nonetheless, the postindependence Kuwaiti government faced serious dissent. Although the regime generally chose co-optation over coercion, the opposition of the 1980s—from the Islamists to the prodemocracy movement before and after the Iraqi invasion of 1990—has caused the government to reassess its earlier strategies.

FORMAL STRUCTURES

Ruling Institutions: The Ruling Family

The most important ruling institution in Kuwait is the ruling family itself, led by the amir. In 1961 (as in 1990) the Iraqi threat strengthened

91

Qasr al-Saif, the presidential palace, before the Iraqi invasion (author's photo)

this institution by prompting Kuwaitis to rally around known leadership patterns. Shaikh Abdallah used the crisis to reiterate not only his personal claim to rule but that of the al-Sabahs more generally. As leader of an independent state, Abdallah changed his title to amir. In November 1962, immediately following the crisis, the amir drew up a constitution. This document declared Kuwait a hereditary amirate and stipulated not only that Kuwait's leaders come from the al-Sabah family but that they come specifically from male descendants of Mubarak the Great (a provision that has survived constitutional revisions). This clause codified what had become custom: the semiformal alternation of power since 1915 between the lines of Mubarak's two ruling sons, Jabir (r. 1915–1917) and Salim (r. 1917–1921).

The postindependence period has seen considerable evolution in the positions of both the ruling family and the ruler. The most important changes have been the expansion of the ruling family's role in politics and the increasing formalization of that role. Although Kuwait has been ruled by members of the al-Sabah family since the eighteenth century, the family has ruled as an institution only since the mid-twentieth century. The family's political role began to grow in the period between World Wars I and II when Shaikh Ahmad began selecting his brothers and cousins as advisers and then as heads of key departments such as municipality, education, and health. This practice of hiring relatives increased after independence and became formalized as the advisers became department heads and then cabinet members. The top posts—in the ministries of foreign affairs, information, defense, and interior—have since gone almost exclusively to al-Sabahs, first to the closest relatives of the amir, then to the relatives of his heir apparent, and finally to other family members. The ruling family has always held about one-quarter of the cabinet posts and always the most important posts.[1] Al-Sabah ministers start younger and stay longer: an average of more than nine years compared with a general average of five and one-half years. Second tier family members fill lesser posts in the higher civil service and military and in general constitute the recruitment pool for important state posts. It is a large pool, with over 1,200 members.[2]

The ruling family is less constrained than it was before the twentieth century. In many ways the family is literally above the law. Press criticism of both the amir and his family is forbidden. The constitution declares the amir immune and inviolable, a condition that has always extended to the family to some extent. The precise extent of this inviolability was an issue that the assembly tried to test before its 1986 dissolution as delegates demanded the opportunity to question high-ranking family members over corruption and mismanagement. Many attribute the assembly dissolution precisely to this attack on the family. Grievances among family members and between family members and outsiders that would otherwise reach a court of law are settled internally by family councils. Although above ordinary law, the family is not without restrictions. Internal disciplinary procedures limit the actions of shaikhs, and offending shaikhs have been exiled.

Although the family functions politically as a unified institution, it is nonetheless deeply divided. Gavrielides reported four different levels of Sabah membership.[3] The most important family division is between those Sabahs with some claim to the ruling line—that is, descendants of Mubarak's sons Jabir and Salim—and those without any. An early test case for this distinction was the political career of Abdallah Mubarak, the youngest son of Shaikh Mubarak and later head of the police force, who aspired to the leadership in the 1940s and 1950s when he served as deputy ruler. His challenge failed, ending in his exile from Kuwait in 1961, an exile from which he returned only in the late 1980s. No one else but a descendant of Salim or Jabir has put forward a credible claim. Although Abdallah's line no longer stands as a serious challenge, the historical threat still lingers, and as recently as 1989 the government banned the writing of Abdallah's wife, Su'ad Sabah. Even though the ban doubtless owed much to Su'ad's own activities as an intellectual (with a Ph.D. in economics), a generous patron of Arab human rights organizations, and especially, as a political poet, it was also a reaction by some Sabahs to the more prominent public appearances of a young adult son of Abdallah and Su'ad, raising again the question of the political role of that family's line. Within the ruling line, the major division is between the Jabir and the Salim branches. In addition to alternating the leadership, these lines have produced several ministers and top officials. Important descendants from Jabir include Sabah Ahmad, until 1991 the long-serving foreign affairs minister and deputy prime minister. Important descendants from Shaikh Salim include heir apparent Sa'ad Abdallah.

One interesting secondary branch of the family is descended from Jarrah and Muhammad, the murdered brothers of Shaikh Mubarak. This part of the family, exiled after Mubarak's accession, returned to Kuwait in the 1950s after coming to an understanding with Shaikh Abdallah Salim, who was interested in strengthening the political role of the ruling family and expanding his Sabah allies. Many members of this branch went on to important government posts, including Kuwait's ambassador to the United States, Sa'ud Nasir, a descendant of Muhammad.

The family is usually sufficiently disciplined to keep its divisions in check. Important decisions are made behind closed doors by the amir on consultation with an inner family circle. Dissent remains largely within the family, although it occasionally rises to the surface, as it did in 1981 when Shaikh Jabir Ali was dropped from the cabinet following his unsuccessful opposition to the assembly reopening. As there is no tradition of primogeniture, succession can bring divisions to the surface. However, succession has been regulated by the institutionalization of the successor in the roles of prime minister and crown prince prior to the succession and by the 1962 constitution, which stipulates the designation of an heir apparent within a year of the amir's accession. Contestation thus occurs far in advance of the ruler's actual death, preventing a succession crisis during the critical period of official mourning.

Postindependence successions have been smooth. Abdallah Salim, Kuwait's first postindependence leader, named his brother Sabah heir apparent in 1962, just after independence. This particular choice, the one exception to the alternation pattern between the Jabir and Salim lines, surprised those who had expected a candidate from the Jabir side. However, the leading contender from that line, Jabir Ahmad, the finance minister (and eventual successor), although popular, was still young and controversial owing to his support in the more progressive, pan-Arabist circles. Sabah was a compromise, a low-profile candidate who would offend the fewest. He was a less prominent figure, having long waited under the shadow of Fahad Salim and Abdallah Mubarak. Yet he was also a candidate with experience in government, primarily as commander of the new police force, later as director of health, and then as director of foreign affairs. When Abdallah Salim died in 1965, Sabah succeeded him.

This choice proved to be the only deviation from the Jabir-Salim alternation pattern.

With Sabah's accession Jabir became prime minister and, in May 1966, heir apparent, alternating the succession to the Jabir line. When Jabir succeeded Sabah on the latter's death in December 1977, he quickly named Sa'ad Abdallah, from the Salim line, crown prince and then prime minister, silencing speculation about the succession. Sa'ad's background was with the police, having had police training in England before heading the city police from 1945 on. In 1959 when Kuwait's police forces were consolidated, Sa'ad became deputy commander in chief, in 1961 chief of police, then from 1962 to 1978 interior minister, and from 1964 to 1978 defense minster as well. Sa'ad has been an active prime minister, playing a prominent role, for example, in the negotiations with the prodemocracy movement. Like his predecessors, Jabir has also relied heavily on his extended family for advice and staff support. He has been less enthusiastic in relying on the other important postwar consultative institution: the National Assembly.

Consultative Institutions: The National Assembly

Along with the ruling institutions, consultative institutions also emerged in the postindependence period. The most important was the National Assembly, which carried on a lively political debate with the government from 1963 until its closure between 1976 and 1981 and then its dissolution in 1986. This institution had its origins in earlier efforts at representation, especially the Majlis Movement of 1938. The long-term catalyst to the assembly's formation was the demand for political participation that lingered after the 1938 experiment. Even after the demise of the 1938 assembly the nationalist opposition kept alive the idea of political participation in some organized forum. In the 1950s an echo of participation survived in elected advisory government departments. However, as these departments lost power to the increasingly prominent shaikhs, demands for more formal representation grew. During the 1950s the opposition petitioned the government for a parliament. Ahmad al-Khatib, a physician and Arab nationalist leader, spearheaded these efforts through his National Culture Club, which along with other clubs formed the organizational network for opposition politics. Opposition leaders were particularly hopeful that Abdallah Salim, who had supported the 1938 assembly, would support this new effort.

The Iraqi territorial claim and the general crisis accompanying independence prompted Abdallah to reconsider some form of assembly. Just as the populace turned to the established leadership in a moment of political crisis, so too did the ruler turn to popular support. The Iraqi claim not only prompted an outpouring of patriotic spirit among Kuwaitis but concentrated that spirit in the amir as he faced down the threat. In part, the assembly was an effort by the amir to institutionalize that spirit and support. The 1962 constitution even held out the promise of future assembly limitation of the ruling family's power: The assembly was to approve the amir's choice for heir apparent and in the event of family deadlock to select the heir apparent from among three Sabahs named by the amir.

Other factors played a part in the decision to support the assembly. The rulers hoped to use the assembly to develop their own allies, in particular the newly settled beduin, who in time came to hold a critical progovernment position in the assembly. At various times the rulers encouraged the election of Shia, religious Sunni candidates, and nationalists, using the assembly to court the enemies of whatever opposition group they most feared. The rulers also hoped to use the assembly to pull Kuwaitis (to whom suffrage was restricted) apart from the many expatriate Arabs who had begun to arrive in Kuwait, bringing with them dissident political ideas. If the assembly has been an inclusive institution, it has not been all-inclusive. As elsewhere, suffrage was limited to citizens: In Kuwait that excludes the bulk of the population. Suffrage was further restricted by age, sex (men only), and citizenship status (only those in Kuwait's first category of citizens, descendants of Kuwaitis resident in 1920, could vote). Suffrage also excluded active members of the armed forces (inactive members could run for the assembly; in the 1981 elections some 100 army officers resigned their commissions to become candidates) and members of the ruling family (who could neither vote nor serve), accentuating the division of labor between ruling and consultative institutions.[4] The result was a small voter pool: In 1985 only 57,000 Kuwaitis, less than 5 percent of a total residential population of 1.5 million, could vote.

In December 1961 elections were held for the Constituent Assembly, which then drafted a constitution, and in 1963 the first National Assembly elections were held. The assembly held four sessions—in 1963, 1967, 1971, and 1975—before its suspension in 1976. The assembly reopened following elections in 1981; however, after elections held in 1985, the assembly met only twice before the amir again dissolved it in 1986.

The elections to the first assembly in 1963 produced a highly vocal opposition, the National Bloc, led by al-Khatib, which soon focused its criticism on the amir's cabinet. The National Bloc objected to the inclusion of merchant ministers, arguing that a conflict of interest existed between their private and public responsibilities. So effective was the opposition that it forced the ruler to return from India to dissolve the cabinet.

Following this assembly, the government began taking a closer interest in the opposition.

The 1967 elections, held amid credible charges of government interference and election irregularities (ranging from gerrymandering to ballot stuffing, miscounts, and mass naturalizations of progovernment beduins), prompted the resignation of seven representatives and popular calls for rescheduled elections. The next election, in 1971, did produce a more compliant assembly, one that included only four members of the nationalist opposition. Al-Khatib, the opposition leader, was not among them.

In the 1971 elections the opposition had focused on negotiations with the oil companies. In 1973 the assembly rejected a government agreement with KOC on Kuwaiti participation, demanding more radical steps toward nationalization—action that culminated in the company's complete nationalization in 1976. However, the assembly's position on oil also alerted the government to the dangers and possible power of the assembly opposition.

Elections for the fourth assembly were held in 1975. This assembly continued the tradition of opposition with far more enthusiasm than the amir was willing to tolerate. In August 1976 the amir dissolved the assembly and introduced new restrictions on the press and on public meetings. Several factors contributed to this decision. The first was the volatile nature of the opposition and the number of issues, foreign and domestic, on which the assembly opposed the government. The government was particularly concerned with ties that were developing between domestic opposition and opposition groups in the Arab world at large, fearing that this assembly opposition would harm its relations with other Arab states, among them Saudi Arabia, which had always disapproved of the legislative experiment. The government also argued that the assembly's volatility hindered its effectiveness: In its last months the body was paralyzed, delaying the budget and other issues in endless debate. The government also guessed correctly that the assembly had begun to lose popular support for the positions it had taken on corruption and government intervention in the economy, on planning and price controls, and on narrowly self-serving issues, such as its move to quintuple the pensions of assembly members. Although the suspension produced some opposition, it did not meet with as much as the assembly members might have hoped (although with the new press restrictions, it was hard to gauge the public reaction). Not until the end of the decade would they be able to rebuild the popular support that had brought them to office.

Following the suspension, the amir promised to restore the assembly and, to the surprise of many, he did. As in 1961 the pressing need for domestic support in the face of regional threats, this time emanating from the Iranian revolution, encouraged the ruler to reactivate this popular institution. In 1979 Shaikh Jabir opened talks with the former delegates, editors, and other political figures over proposed constitutional revisions, forming a committee to draft the revisions. Following the committee's work in August 1980, the amir announced the return of parliamentary life, and in December he announced that elections would be held in February 1981.

Although the elections themselves were relatively free and fair (the U.S. State Department, for example, reported them so, commenting only on the continuing prohibition of political parties and the limitations on suffrage), nevertheless, redistricting (creating twenty-five two-member districts instead of the previous ten), new electoral laws, and more subtle government support for favored candidates slanted the results.[5] In rewriting the rules and in monitoring the election campaigns, the government reacted to the nationalist opposition of the past. So eager was it to prevent a nationalist revival that it encouraged the Islamist, or politically religious, candidates—candidates it thought were hostile to the nationalists as well as politically malleable. These candidates did well in the campaign, with five Islamist delegates forming the core of the assembly opposition. Redistricting hurt both the progressive bloc, which took only three seats (among those who lost was al-Khatib, the erstwhile opposition leader), and the Shia, whose representation fell from ten seats to four. It helped not only the Islamists but also the progovernment beduins, who took twenty-three seats.

The fifth assembly (1981–1985), like its predecessors, produced a vocal opposition. A dispute over constitutional revisions emerged, representing a more general dispute over legislative-executive relations and power sharing. Other issues included the government position on the Iran-Iraq War, internal security, state corruption, press restrictions, and Islam and politics (the assembly introduced several bills restricting non-Islamic practices and calling for greater enforcement of Islamic law). The religious opposition proved so determined that by the end of the fifth assembly the government began reconsidering its earlier support of the Islamists.

The government did not repeat its perceived mistake in the elections for the sixth assembly in 1985. This time, in order to block the Islamists, the government encouraged both more beduin candidates (who took over half the seats) and, reversing itself, nationalists (the Islamists' natural opponents). It began allowing the nationalists more political space, participating, for example, in the public political rehabilitation of al-Khatib.

The nationalists did well in the elections. Al-Khatib won, along with three other nationalists. Two prominent Islamist deputies, Khalid Sultan and Isa Shahin, were defeated. Yet despite government efforts a core of Islamists remained, among them Abdallah al-Nafisi, a political scientist and erstwhile progressive Arab nationalist at one time banned for writing a book critical of the 1976 elections.[6] By the time he returned to Kuwait in 1985 he had adapted his progressive position to a leftist Islamist stance.

The result was two small opposition blocs: Islamist and nationalist. Rather than neutralizing each other, the two blocs showed an unanticipated ability to coordinate opposition. The new assembly succeeded in blocking several government bills, including some aimed at resolving the Suq al-Manakh stock market crash of 1982 that threatened to bankrupt thousands of Kuwaitis. More dangerously, the assembly began attacking ministers, including members of the ruling family. In 1985 its inquiries into corruption associated with the stock market prompted the resignation of Justice Minister Salman Du'aij in connection with allegations that he had used his position to arrange government compensation for the stock market losses of his young son, among other charges of financial irregularity. The opposition then began questioning Oil Minister Ali Khalifah over financial irregularities (some in connection with the 1981 purchase of Santa Fe International) and oil-field security, bringing him to the verge of resignation. Communications Minister Isa al-Mazidi, Finance Minister Jasim Khurafi, and Education Minister Hassan al-Ibrahim all came under attack, Hassan al-Ibrahim by the Islamists for his university reforms. Finally, as assembly members began actively calling for the resignation of the ministers of interior and oil, both from the ruling family, the government decided the assembly had gone too far. In July the amir suspended the assembly a second time.

Both domestic and foreign factors played a role in this decision. At home the assembly had criticized the government's handling of the stock market crash. It had taken on the issue of corruption and had been reluctant to approve state bailouts for those involved in the crash, earning it the enmity of those it charged with corruption and those who would benefit from the government's proposed reforms. The growing economic crisis facing Kuwait exacerbated the situation: Oil prices, which fell to $10 a barrel over the summer, the lowest price in years, left everyone on edge. The assembly had also begun to direct explicit attacks toward cabinet members, especially members of the ruling family. Finally, the dissolution decision followed a wave of political violence in 1985, including an attack on the amir himself. The amir pointed to the growing security concerns prompted by the Iran-Iraq War, the need for unity in the face of those concerns, and the inherently divisive nature of the assembly. He noted the danger of an assembly fanning secular divisions. As the government, feeling regionally threatened, drew closer to its Gulf allies, especially Saudi Arabia, it came under increasing pressure to support the Saudi position that parliaments were a security threat. Although the amir again left open the possibility of reinstituting the assembly, his commitment in 1986 was far vaguer than it had been in 1976.

Even closed, the assembly served as a powerful symbol for political opposition and as the focus for demands for political participation in the prodemocracy movement of 1989–1990 and again following the Iraqi invasion. The assembly always functioned with limited powers. It played no role in selecting the head of state or the cabinet, although on one occasion it did bring down a cabinet. However, it did function as a forum for debate and as a lively source of criticism of the government on important topics ranging from the annual budget and oil policy to women's rights and the role of religion in politics. In introducing bills and debates and questioning ministers, it placed issues on the agenda, forcing the amir to address them.

Sustaining Institutions: The Bureaucracy

As the ruling family was consolidating its hold and as the National Assembly was waxing and waning, a third institution was inexorably developing: the Kuwaiti bureaucracy. This bureaucracy, one of the largest per capita government machines in the world, barely existed before the oil era. Its predecessors included a small palace administration with clerks and tax collectors, a small religious administration that handled what would eventually become government judicial and welfare functions, and a few interwar institutions established by the merchants and absorbed by the state, such as the municipality and the Education Council. Because Kuwait was never formally a British colony and because its internal problems had never threatened regional security, it was never administered by the Colonial Office with colonial troops but rather at a distance by the India Office and, after the dissolution of that office, by the Foreign Office. One consequence was that a large colonial administration never developed.

It took oil revenues for a real bureaucracy to emerge. The bureaucratic demands of the oil industry were relatively small, as oil operations were handled by foreign-owned companies. However, a small government bureaucracy did emerge as liaison, to monitor the companies, to handle some oil-related operations, and eventually to take over the industry after nationalization. The real impetus for expanding the bureaucracy, however, came from the need to spend the vast revenues created by oil. After World War II Shaikh Abdallah began spending on development projects and social services. Quickly a new state machinery developed to handle these new functions. In the early 1950s the British tried to persuade Abdallah to hire British advisers to manage this bureaucracy. But Abdallah's reluctance, coupled with the resistance of key shaikhs, kept the British presence from overwhelming the new state. The bureaucracy was built, however inadvertently, not by the British but by the amir, to centralize his own power, and by the feuding shaikhs: Abdallah Mubarak, who developed the internal and external security system, and Fahad Salim, who oversaw development spending.

With independence the bureaucracy was reorganized. Following the 1962 constitution new ministries were formed from the old departments. Rapid growth continued as Kuwaitis were hired in large numbers as a way of distributing the oil revenues nationally and as expatriates were hired in still larger numbers to carry out the vast technical functions that the Kuwaitis, small in number and then less highly educated, could not yet assume. The new revenues following the price increases in the 1970s induced another spurt of growth. Unchecked, this bureaucracy continued to grow, surviving rulers and assemblies, carrying out the day-to-day state functions.

At the peak of the bureaucracy, beneath the amir, was the cabinet, dominated by shaikhs (who held one-quarter of the posts). In general, cabinet ministers have been young (in their thirties and forties), with the al-Sabah ministers the youngest of all. Most were highly educated: Of the seventy-five ministers who have served since 1962 nearly half had college degrees and several had advanced degrees (mostly in economics and business), mainly from U.S. colleges and universities. Most of them came to the position from government and, to a lesser extent, the business community (although only three ministers went directly from business to the cabinet). Many subsequently returned to business. The ministers were overwhelmingly Sunni; only three were Shia, and only one had tribal origins.[7]

The cabinet oversees the vast bureaucracy. The most important ministries and state institutions beneath the cabinet are those concerned with money. The institutions associated with the raising of revenues include not only the Oil Ministry and the Kuwait Petroleum Corporation but, of increasing importance, the Finance Ministry and the investment institutions. Because of Kuwait's great wealth, the largest state institutions are devoted to spending rather than raising money, especially the Ministry of Housing and the Ministry of Social Affairs. In some sense, the entire bureaucracy is devoted to distributing money, as state employment is guaranteed to all Kuwaitis.

The government has made a significant effort to Kuwaitize the bureaucracy. By 1989 the government staff of 144,286 included 64,203 Kuwaitis (or 44.5 percent of the total employees) according to a Civil Service Commission study.[8] Government efforts to increase Kuwaiti representation in management jobs, including limiting some posts to Kuwaitis and favoring Kuwaiti graduates, had succeeded to the point where Kuwaitis held 66 percent of all senior staff positions. As Kuwaitis constituted only 28 percent of the population, they were overrepresented in the bureaucracy.

The bureaucracy was large but not always effective, at least in terms of implementing the ruler's plans. To understand why, it is necessary to reexamine the relationship between the oil economy and the state. The oil economy is about as close as one comes in the real world to what economists and political scientists call a rentier economy. A rentier economy is an ideal type, a model that comprises a cluster of three attributes, all of which find their fullest real-world expression in oil-producing states. For a state to possess a rentier economy, the source of income, or rent, must be externally generated and involve little contact with the local economy, it must go directly to the state, and it must be very large.

In a rentier economy the revenues come from abroad, rather than from inside the economy—for example, from a foreign government or company. By this criteria the United States was never a rentier economy because its oil revenues came from within the country. Oil revenues in Kuwait, however, historically have come from foreign oil companies. The industry itself creates few local upstream and downstream linkages. It normally employs few local workers, indeed, few workers at all, as it is a very capital intensive industry. It is almost an economic enclave.

In a rentier economy revenues go directly to the state. A rentier economy is distinguished from most economies highly dependent on foreign trade because the income from foreign trade goes to the private owners of the commodity-producing properties and not directly to the state. This was the case in Kuwait before oil: The Shaikhs collected taxes on the pearling and trading boats owned by the merchants. Oil revenues, however, go directly to the state. In Kuwait (as in most of the Third World), the state, not private citizens or companies, owns the land or at least subsoil rights. The fact that oil revenues go directly to the state is important because it means that money is centralized in the state. Individuals can become rich only through their relationship to the state or the state elite.

Finally, in a rentier economy rents are large. Unless rents are the only important revenues in the economy, they will not set the tone of the economy. Yemen and Egypt both have some oil, and because of that those economies exhibit rentier elements, but they are not rentier economies. In contrast, Kuwait is highly dependent on oil; for much of the postwar period the direct sale of oil accounted for over 90 percent of the state revenues.

A rentier economy affects in three ways the kind of state that emerges. First, a state built on a rentier economy, a rentier state, has different functions. One of the most important administrative functions of most states, rich and poor alike, is to extract revenues, that is, to draw taxes from the population. Because rentier states do not rely on taxes on the local population for income, they do not have to carry out this extractive function. Instead of extracting revenues, they distribute revenues. In the Kuwaiti case pre-existing traditions—patterns of paternalism and group solidarity—already predisposed Kuwait to distribute revenues fairly widely. This distributive function developed in a particularly Kuwaiti way, but it nonetheless bears a family resemblance to the distributive functions carried out by all other oil-exporting states. This function has become institutionalized, and revenues are now distributed by the state through direct transfers, social services, and state jobs. One result of this different function is that the institutions of rentier states differ from most other states. On the one hand, Kuwait has no big taxing institutions, no IRS. On the other hand, it has huge distributive institutions such as the Ministries of Health, Social Affairs, and Education. It also has a large Oil Ministry to assure that its capacity to distribute will continue. Kuwait, however, despite its excellent distributive capacity, has virtually no redistributive capacity. It can give to the poor, but it cannot take from the rich. The lack of an extractive, hence redistributive, capacity means that the state has fewer policy tools, fewer fiscal options, and less flexibility should it need it.

A second consequence of a rentier economy is that it radically, if inadvertently, changes the relationship between state and society, primarily by creating new social classes. In Kuwait, as in other rentier states, oil weakened old classes, such as the merchants, because the state no longer depended on them for money and Kuwaitis no longer depended on them for employment. However, if oil destroys certain social groups, it also creates new ones: bureaucrats and middlemen-contractors, groups defined by their dependence on the state for their creation and sustenance. Initially a rentier economy increases political stability owing to its effect on social structure. Because the states do not tax, they do not have to worry about taxpayer-based groups pressuring them for accountability, demanding to know how their tax dollars are spent or demanding something in return for their contribution to the state. If there are groups with complaints, the large revenues allow these states to buy their compliance, to co-opt them. However, in more fundamental ways these states are potentially unstable. A rentier economy allows rulers to become detached from society. In a political sense, they become isolated. No longer relying on powerful economic groups for news, they soon cease to hear any real news at all, and they may be unable to hear opposition growing until it is too late. In some sense, this is what happened to the shah of Iran. When they are no longer dependent on the wealthy, rulers no longer have access to these autonomously powerful groups, who in turn no longer have as strong a shared interest in keeping these rulers in power.

The oil state has produced new groups of supporters, but are they reliable? To some degree they are. These groups have an interest in preserving the new state, and in time, out of this interest affection may also grow. For those individuals who have no strong interest, their connection to the state allows the state to both monitor and control them more easily than it could groups in the private sector. The state can thus rely on a degree of both affection and fear. However, that reliability is not complete. Once created by the state, these new classes can become privatized; they develop their own interests and agendas distinct from those of the rulers. They can turn on the ruler whom they may come to see as a dangerous force, one who can take away rights and privileges. More subtly they can use the state apparatus to sabotage the leaders' plans, using their bureaucratic positions to further their own private interests.

A third consequence of a rentier economy is that these rentier states are much more dependent on the outside world than are other states. Oil had a dislocating effect on Kuwait's external economic relations, bringing new dependencies: on foreign markets and, later, on foreign labor and commodities. This dependence was not completely new; Kuwait was never an economically autonomous entity, and oil only deepened a pattern already apparent early in the twentieth century. Even before oil, Kuwait's economy depended on the trading patterns of others: on the movements of the beduin and caravans from Baghdad and Aleppo, on the vagaries of Indian and African markets, and on the pearl-purchasing patterns of wealthy Europeans. That insecurity, however, is seriously heightened by oil. The new linkages created by oil left Kuwait deeply dependent on uncertain foreign sources for investment income, consumer goods, food, arms, and labor.

SHAIKH JABIR'S RULE: PROBLEMS AND PROSPECTS

Some social fault lines along which political opposition could form were suggested in Chapter 4: family, tribe, sex, sect, class, and nation. Opposition has in fact formed along all these lines. Family networks always constitute the practical basis for opposition organization. When the assembly was in session, sex and, especially, tribe were important lines of organization. Sectarian divisions—Sunni-Shia—continued to be important both within the assembly and after its closure. Class-based opposition proved less important, largely because oil weakened class identities by replacing the private sector with the state as the prime determinant of income. Nonetheless, trade unions such as the General Federation of Kuwaiti Workers dealt with labor issues and tried to protect

Kuwaiti workers from the encroachment of foreign labor. The oil industry, which saw both early Kuwaitization and labor organizing, was a very important source of labor opposition. Trade unions were also active in politics, working with professional associations and cultural clubs, earning them the government's approbation during times of political crisis. Foreign workers were not an organized threat to the regime prior to the Iraqi invasion, owing not only to the legal restrictions on their economic and political activity and to the government's deportation policies but also to their own cultural and economic divisions and to their desire to save money, keep out of trouble, and go home. Some—notably Iranian, Iraqi, and Lebanese Shia—did support Islamist opposition to the regime and engaged in political violence, but their activities were generally contained. These groups, however, formed the basis for potential political opposition, some of which was realized during the Iraqi occupation.

The three sets of institutions just discussed—the ruling institution of the al-Sabah family, the consultative institutions, and the bureaucratic institutions—all helped the amir maintain internal stability in the face of these divisions. The institutions were crucial in enabling him to respond to opposition and to maintain power in the face of several internal political crises, four of which are discussed in the following section: the Suq al-Manakh stock market crash, the politicization of women's issues, the rise in Islamist opposition, and the prodemocracy movement.

The Suq al-Manakh Crisis

One of the first crises that Shaikh Jabir faced was an economic crisis with a large political component: the Suq al-Manakh stock market crash.[9] The crash, the recession the crash prompted, and the government's handling of the crash all elicited popular dissent and exacerbated existing opposition. The Suq al-Manakh grew out of the financial optimism of the 1970s, when Kuwait's financial sector expanded along with oil revenues, prompting a new growth of banks, insurance companies, real estate firms, and investment houses. The government was slow to regulate this growth. The first laws regulating the markets date back to the early 1960s, but circumstances changed enormously in the following years. In the early 1970s the government began adding some new controls: a 25 percent liquidity requirement, suspension of forward market transactions, and a committee to study shareholding companies.

The first indication that something was wrong came in 1977 when the small speculation boom crashed and stock prices on the official market fell, leaving hundreds of investors facing bankruptcy. The government responded in two ways. First, it bailed out the investors, buying shares to shore up the market. Second, it introduced new regulations, among them

Suq al-Manakh (author's photo)

regulations excluding companies registered outside Kuwait from trading. Both these policies inadvertently had a disastrous effect. The bailout reassured investors that the government would back them up, encouraging still more speculation. The new regulations were so effective at curtailing speculation that they drove high-risk investors out of Kuwait's regular stock market and into the alternative market, the Suq al-Manakh.

The Suq al-Manakh was a new and technically illegal market that grew up in the shadow of the old stock market, a market so dominated by wealthy old Bani Utub families trading among themselves in large blocks of stock that it left little room for the eager new investors. Its investment opportunities could not keep pace with the demand the new revenues generated. This new market, the Suq al-Manakh, appealed to new investors, who could gain entry through a small initial investment, and it appealed to the old investors looking for new opportunities. In the end, it seemed to appeal to everyone in Kuwait. By the time it crashed, college students, old merchants, new merchants, cabinet ministers, illiterates, professors, and even members of the ruling family were all involved.

The market featured risky investments—paper companies banned in the official market, often for good cause, such as lack of decent records or even assets. The government did not officially allow the market, but neither did it close it, perhaps because it was popular, perhaps because it seemed harmless, and perhaps because ruling family members were involved. As oil revenues washed through the economy, augmented by easy bank credit, speculation increased and stock prices skyrocketed. In 1982 the market crashed. Several factors contributed: a changing mood prompted by the Iran-Iraq War, a small tightening of local credit by banks that had previously eagerly bankrolled speculation, the beginning of the decline in oil revenues. The immediate problem was the kind of transactions the market encouraged—in particular, the use of postdated checks, technically illegal in Kuwait but widely used in the market. Stocks were routinely bought on checks dated up to a few years later. Deals grew larger and larger and more outrageous until finally an investor got in way over his head and cashed a postdated check. It bounced, and the system collapsed. Debts quickly piled on debts until they reached a paper total of $97 billion.

There seemed to be no alternative but for the government to step in again. And after much discussion, that is what it did, essentially picking up most of the tab for the crash by agreeing to compensate banks to reschedule loans at low interest. For a time the hard-liners, led by Finance Minister Abdallatif al-Hamad, with some support in the press and an assembly critical of the government for favoring the largest investors, tried to limit the bailout, a position that led to Al-Hamad's eventual resignation. The government, afraid of the social and political pressures that uncontrolled bankruptcy might induce, insisted on a rescue plan and in 1982 introduced an emergency stabilization plan. It separated the small and large investors, eight of whom alone accounted for two-thirds of the claims (Jasim al-Mutawwa, whose bounced check set off the crash, was responsible for half the claims). In 1986 the Central Bank announced a plan for settling bad loans, setting up the Difficult Credit Facilities Resettlement Program to reschedule the debts of 1,300 participants. By 1987, 98 percent of the market debtors were involved in the program.[10] However, those outside the program included some of the largest debtors (a few with ties to the ruling family), many of whom were holding out for a more generous bailout. In 1989 proposals from a joint government–Chamber of Commerce committee formed the basis for subsequent government policy. They included, essentially, generous controlled bankruptcy proceedings to write off the debts of the smaller debtors (those owing less than 250,000 Kuwaiti dinars [KD], approximately $74,000), who would lose their savings but be guaranteed a reasonable standard of living, and to work with the larger debtors to increase their ability to repay. The proposals for the small debtors had a primarily psychological effect, as they comprised over half the total debtors but less than 3 percent of the total debt.[11] Write-offs were welcomed by the Kuwaitis with outstanding debts but not by the many Kuwaitis who had made good-faith efforts to repay their debts.

The stock market crash left several casualties. The government's reputation for fiscal management suffered. The ruling family's reputation suffered as three of its members—Khalifah Abdallah, Muhammad Khalifah, and Du'aij Jabir Ali—were not only caught by the collapse but implicated in efforts to affect the government bailout. In some sense the country as a whole suffered as the crash plunged Kuwait, at least its non-oil private sector, into a recession that lasted through the 1980s and that came on top of a small recession already induced by the fall in oil prices. Real estate prices fell—30 percent in 1985.[12] Banking suffered a severe recession as almost every financial institution in Kuwait was affected. Even civil liberties suffered as the government came to fear press and assembly coverage of its handling of this volatile issue. The crash certainly contributed to the government's decision to dissolve the assembly and issue new press restrictions.

Among the few who benefited, as a group, were the old merchant families. These families, heavily invested in the old market, were relatively less exposed on the new market (although in the end no family was left untouched). It was from their ranks that the hard-line opposition to widespread bailout of the investors emerged. These merchants were also the group to whom the government turned to staff the new advisory committees to work out a solution. The 1989 joint committee report included among its recommendations deregulation, privatization, and protection for local industries—all measures of benefit to local merchants.

Despite the government's intervention the crash bankrupted thousands of individual Kuwaitis, leaving a social as well as an economic impact as families were torn apart by the bad investments and exposure of one brother or son. In the end, although the crash strained relations among relatives, it may have strengthened the extended family. For a time it seemed that grandmothers were single-handedly holding together homes torn apart by bad loans and investments, forcing sons otherwise at odds at least to appear together on Friday visits. It was often the family as a unit that now decided the division of obligations. Debts incurred by one son in the name of (and on the credit of) the collective family might be repaid by another son, depending on a variety of criteria, including present and future potential (including political potential) to repay. The lack of resolution to the largest debts, however, left a bad feeling all around that would probably have resurfaced (and may yet) had not the Iraqi occupation redrawn Kuwait's entire economic landscape.

Women and Politics

Several women's issues have been on the political agenda in Kuwait. Women's issues are politicized not only because of their intrinsic importance but because of the way they intersect with other political issues and the role they play in defining the relationship between Islam and politics. Political Islam inevitably takes on issues, small and large, that affect women directly—from the veil and labor-force participation to larger questions about the role of women in society. Islamist efforts to achieve more visible signs of Islamic devotion in dress, though not limited to women (Islamist men, too, have a style of dress) have affected them more. Islamist efforts to make Islamic law *the* rather than *a* source of law affect women by introducing changes in family law and restricting women's efforts to support more protective divorce laws.

Women faced Islamist political thinking primarily from the opposition, not from the government. In Kuwait the Islamic establishment never gained control over female education, as it did in Saudi Arabia, nor are women in Kuwait obliged to veil, nor forbidden to drive; indeed, for security (and safety) reasons women must drive unveiled. Women's issues that have been important in Kuwait include suffrage, education, and labor-force participation.

Until the assembly dissolution in 1986 women's suffrage was a recurring, although not central, issue. In 1971 the Society for the Advancement of the Family, a women's advocacy group, petitioned the assembly to consider women's suffrage. A suffrage bill was introduced, but it was blocked by Islamists. In 1980 Shaikh Sa'ad, a proponent of women's suffrage, again submitted the issue to the assembly, which again voted it down. In 1982 when the assembly again blocked a women's suffrage bill, 10,000 women demonstrated in favor of it.[13] Women put forth a number of arguments. Some, like Lu'lu'ah al-Qattami, director of the Women's Cultural and Social Society, argued that suffrage would only be a natural extension of women's existing electoral participation in cooperative societies, governing boards of the many social societies, and in student politics at the university. In 1984 a group of women launched a legal challenge on the vote, arguing that denial of suffrage was sexual discrimination, constitutionally forbidden. Sixteen women tried to place their names on the election rolls but were refused by registration officials.[14] In the 1985 election many women worked behind the scenes giving campaign support to candidates in the progressive Democratic Bloc, which favored women's suffrage. After the election the bloc introduced a suffrage bill, but the assembly's Internal Affairs Committee forwarded it to the Islamic Affairs Ministry, which ruled that "the nature of the electoral process befits men, who are endowed with ability and expertise: It is not permissible that women recommend or nominate other women or men."[15] The issue was then tabled and finally became moot with the assembly's suspension in 1986. Women's search for allies has not been very successful. A 1985 poll indicated only 27 percent of Kuwaiti men favored women's suffrage.[16] The prodemocracy movement did not actively support women's suffrage, calling the issue divisive—a threat to the tenuous unity the progressive left had established with the religious right.[17]

Female education has been another important women's issue. The debate has focused on segregation of the sexes, especially at Kuwait University, and the role of the Islamist student opposition. Unlike many Gulf universities, some of Kuwait University's campuses have been sexually integrated since the 1970s (although a certain informal segregation exists within classrooms). In the Islamist revival of the 1980s university activists successfully segregated eating facilities; segregation of other facilities followed. In 1984 a Saudi religious authority sparked a controversy in Kuwait when he issued a ruling, widely discussed in Kuwait's mosques, on the request of a member of Kuwait University's Islamic Students Society that coeducation was anti-Islamic and corrupted women.[18] The reaction to the ruling was to square off progressives against Islamists. As with any issue, there was more here than meets the eye. In this case, some of the reaction was couched in nationalist terms, with writers criticizing the students for approaching Saudi, not Kuwaiti, religious authorities. Still other issues lay beneath the surface. Some men in Kuwait were concerned that Kuwait University was becoming a women's college. A majority of the students were female, for many reasons, one being the greater reluctance of families to allow women to study abroad. Women with strong records had been denied fellowships to study abroad after the opposition of husbands and parents.[19] The greater limitations on movement of Kuwaiti girls and women allowed more opportunity for study, promoting higher academic achievement. Not only were there more women at the university, but they got better grades and graduated in higher numbers. Indeed, the university was considering introducing quotas and lowering the admission standards for men in order to address this perceived problem.

As was suggested in Chapter 4, female participation in the labor force has also been a political issue, usually couched by the Islamist opposition in terms of family, modesty, and especially segregation of the sexes. Religiosity alone bears no relation to women's labor-force participation, according to a 1984 survey.[20] In fact, among younger, more educated women religiosity is associated with greater representation in historically male fields. Young, less educated, and more religious women are among those least opposed to women working (sharing this position with the older, better educated but less religious women). However, religious women are more opposed to women working with men.

Other issues complicate the topic of women and work. Low female participation rates conflict with the state goal of increasing the number of Kuwaitis in the labor force. On the one hand, the presence of Kuwaiti women in the work force has already reduced the reliance on foreign workers in two areas, professional and clerical, where women are concentrated.[21] On the other hand, increasing female labor-force participation increases the demand for foreign nannies. Education and labor issues are also linked. Increasing female education, especially higher education, creates more pressure for labor-force participation: Younger, highly educated women are more likely to work and to continue working (three-quarters did not believe women should stop working upon marriage).[22] Increases in both female education and labor-force participation are also associated with decreased fertility rates, thus putting these policies in conflict with the goal of increasing the Kuwaiti national population.

Some women, many highly educated, have been actively involved in Islamist politics. Al-Qattami's efforts to lead a group of women to the assembly to push for a vote on suffrage prompted a countermovement and a petition signed by 1,000 women stating that women's suffrage and Islam were incompatible.[23] Whether on suffrage, education, or work, women face a dilemma in putting forward demands. Even though the demands are generated by Kuwaiti women and are as indigenously Kuwaiti as any other, they resonate with positions put forward by Western women. Regardless of the fact that these positions are the product of similar social position and not of social contact, they nonetheless always run the risk of being tainted by any association with Western feminism, which is interpreted by men opposed to this kind of social change as another form of cultural imperialism. The unfortunate but deeply rooted Western misconceptions about Muslim women (a subcategory of misconceptions about Islam) likewise prompt Kuwaiti (and other Arab) feminists at times to distance themselves from anything that has the taint of Western feminism.

The Islamist Opposition

The Islamist opposition has been among the most important opposition movements facing Kuwait's rulers. It includes Sunni groups, such as the Muslim Brotherhood–oriented Social Reform Society and the Salafiyyin, as well as Shia—those who identify as Shia primarily on ideologically Islamist grounds and those who identify as Shia primarily as a form of communal solidarity or in reaction to discrimination against Shia. Ordinary Shia may or may not agree with Islamists on the appropriate relationship between religion and politics or on the best tactics for meeting the community's needs, but they still see politicization of the Shia community as its best defense against Sunni opposition.

Sunni and Shia alike have opposed the government both legally and illegally. In the assembly, Sunni and Shia Islamists acted as a loyal opposition, proposing bills, debating issues, and forming alliances. Because government redistricting had weakened other historical opposition, notably the Arab nationalists and the Shia, Sunni Islamists became the leading opposition in the 1981 assembly, joined on particular issues by the Shia. They called for a constitutional amendment to make Islamic law the exclusive source of legislation. They put through an amendment limiting naturalization to Muslims. They pushed an assembly ban on public Christmas celebrations. They banned diplomatic alcohol. They took positions on women's issues, including suffrage. In the short-lived 1985 assembly the Islamists succeeded in ousting the liberal education minister, Hassan al-Ibrahim, and joined others to question the oil minister and the finance minister. The Islamist opposition carried on a nonviolent political campaign outside the assembly as well, especially at the university. The early 1980s saw an increase in political pamphleteering and other nonviolent dissidence.

Some Islamists, Kuwaiti and non-Kuwaiti and primarily, but not exclusively, pro-Iranian Shia, also took their opposition outside the increasingly limited political space the regime allowed. Hardly had Jabir's term begun when the Iranian revolution began echoing through Kuwait. In 1978 when the Ayatolla Khomeini was forced to leave Iraq, Kuwait refused him residence. In 1979 as the revolution took off, Iranian Shia in Kuwait demonstrated in support of the revolution and of the taking of U.S. hostages in Iran. In September the Interior Ministry deported the family of Abbas Mahri, a Shia leader, charging him with seditious mosque speeches. In November the government also arrested Kuwaitis in connection with the attack on the Grand Mosque in Mecca. 1980 saw bombings at an Iran Air office, the Iranian embassy, the newspaper offices of *al-Ra'i al-Amm*, and the Social Reform Association headquarters, as well as an attack on the visiting Iranian foreign minister.

Violence soared in December 1983 when dissidents set off a series of bombs at several locations, killing six and wounding over eighty people. Truck bombs damaged the U.S. and French embassies. Other bombs went off at an oil installation, the airport, the offices of the U.S. Raytheon Corporation (which was installing a Hawk missile system), a building housing Raytheon employees, a power station, a passport office, and an oil refining complex. Large-scale arrests followed.

In 1984 a new state security court imprisoned seventeen men, mostly non-Kuwaitis, in connection with the bombings, sentencing five Iraqi Shia and one Lebanese to death (three of them in absentia), seven to life imprisonment, and seven to shorter sentences; five were acquitted. The seventeen imprisoned included members of the primarily Shia pro-Iranian Iraqi group, al-Da'wah al-Islamiyyah (The Islamic Call). The conviction of the seventeen prompted repeated efforts by their supporters for their release, efforts that included hijacking three Kuwaiti planes. In 1988 two of the seventeen were released after serving their terms; the remainder were released during the Iraqi occupation in 1990–1991.

In December 1984 hijackers took to Tehran a Kuwait Airways flight headed from Kuwait to Karachi, demanding the release of those imprisoned in connection with the 1983 bombings and killing two Americans in the process. Kuwait sent a delegation to Iran to negotiate but, as the members refused to accede to the hijackers' demands, no agreement was reached. Eventually the Iranians boarded the plane, ending the hijacking and releasing the passengers. The incident left a bad feeling in Kuwait, where many suspected Iran of bad faith in the affair—in part because the hijackers demanded the release of pro-Iranian prisoners, in part because of skepticism over the Iranian-claimed assault on the aircraft, in part because of Iran's refusal to extradite the hijackers to Kuwait.

In addition to Iranian support for the prisoners, Lebanese Shia groups also demanded their release. In 1985 hijackers of a TWA flight to Beirut demanded the prisoners' release. Hizballah, the Lebanese Shia Party of God, also repeatedly demanded their release, especially that of the three Lebanese Shia, as a condition for freeing U.S. hostages in Lebanon. Among the imprisoned were relatives of highranking Hizballah members—one, a brother-in-law of Imad Maghniyya, was reportedly an organizer of the hijackings; another, a cousin of Hussain Musawi, was head of the pro-Iranian Lebanese Shia group, Islamic Amal.[24] The United States also added its pressure for their release, secretly at first, hoping Kuwait would trade the seventeen for U.S. hostages in Lebanon.

Violent opposition reached its peak in 1985. In March an Iraqi diplomat was killed in Kuwait by men connected to al-Da'wah. Ahmad al-Jarallah, editor of *al-Siyassah*, also was wounded in an attack near his office. The most important political violence came in May with an attack on the amir himself, when an explosives-filled car drove into the amir's procession, killing two guards and one bystander and wounding the amir. Islamic Jihad, which had demanded the release of the prisoners connected with the 1983 bombings, claimed credit. The attack was followed in July by bombings at two shorefront cafes frequented by Kuwaitis, wounding ninety and killing eight, among them a high Interior Ministry official.

In 1986 the Interior Ministry announced several arrests in connection with the previous year's political violence. A state security court sentenced one Iraqi to death and another (in absentia) to life in prison for the attack on the amir. In December three Jordanians were convicted in the *al-Siyassah* attack and the cafe bombings. Political violence, however, continued with a June attack on Ahmadi's oil facilities.

In May 1987 another bomb at Ahmadi was blamed on dissident Shia. In July two Shia from prominent local families were killed, apparently while trying to rig a car bomb near the Air France offices. In October a bomb exploded at a Pan American office, days after Iranian missile attacks on an oil facility, which were in turn followed by an Iranian warning that the Gulf states should remain neutral. In November the American Life Insurance Company was hit in the eleventh bombing of the year.

In April 1988 hijackers took a Kuwait Airlines flight, whose passengers included three al-Sabahs, out of Thailand, demanding the release of the seventeen prisoners. The hijackers took the plane to Mashad, in Iran, site of an important Shia shrine and also the residence of many Shia expelled from Kuwait. There authorities allowed the plane to refuel and, according to passengers, allowed the hijackers to add arms and more hijackers. Next, the hijackers went to Cyprus, where they killed two Kuwaitis when Kuwait refused to release the seventeen prisoners. Finally, they went to Algeria, where mediators arranged for the release of the plane in exchange for the hijackers' release. The hijacking—in particular, the killing of the two Kuwaitis—hardened the national as well as the government resolve not to deal with such opposition. Violence had reached such a peak that the government felt it demanded a forceful response.

To the dissidents, political violence was a necessary form of opposition to a government that had closed all other forms of expression; that had declared a war of its own on the politically religious, especially the pro-Iranian Shia; and that was supporting the Iraqi opponents of the Iranian revolution. This was particularly true for the non-Kuwaiti Shia dissidents: the Iraqis, Iranians, and Lebanese. For the Kuwaitis, especially the Shia, the case was more complicated. Most Shia did not advocate the political violence asserted by the minority, but they certainly understood and agreed with the grievances from which such violence sprang.

For the government the political violence was terrorism, plain and simple. At first the government responded to the growing violence as criminal activity, but increasingly the limits the government placed on activities of potential dissidents came also to restrict the political space of all Kuwaitis. Shaikh Jabir came to power during a period when political and civil freedoms were already particularly curtailed. The previous government had just dissolved the assembly and introduced new press restrictions. Jabir initially continued this policy. When press suspensions prompted protests on both free speech and financial grounds (suspended papers did not sell), the government responded by increasing subsidies to newspapers.[25] It was less responsive to civil liberties concerns. In 1979 the government had the editors of Kuwait's leading dailies sign a press ethics charter that coupled guarantees of press independence with restrictions on content deemed vaguely harmful to the national interest. The government continued to suspend publications for press-law violations. In 1979 the government also adopted a public-assembly law that banned most public groups of over twenty without prior approval (which it all but stopped granting) and authorized the police to attend public meetings. Other measures included a ban on public night gatherings and the public carrying of arms. A 1980 general mobilization law promised still greater restrictions on public freedom in the event of a declared emergency.

By 1980 the government felt more confident, and the restoration of the assembly prompted some relaxation of state control. However, the 1981 assembly soon expressed its objection to the press and assembly restrictions and to the government's proposed constitutional revisions. In 1982 the assembly voted to drop a controversial article from the press law, introduced in 1976 following the assembly dissolution, that granted the government wide powers to suspend publications for long periods and to imprison and fine editors and publishers. In 1983 the government withdrew its attempt to amend the constitution following widespread opposition.

However, as political violence escalated, the assembly joined the government in supporting security-related restrictions. In August 1981 the assembly called for expansion and improvement of the security services. In November it approved a public-assembly law restricting public meetings. The Suq al-Manakh crisis also predisposed some members to tolerate more press restrictions. During assembly debate on the stock market in 1982 and 1983 delegates criticized press accounts of the crisis, with some delegates calling for new press restrictions.

The turning point, however, was the December 1983 bombings. In December the assembly held a session on security and reversed its previous opposition, backing the government with the Islamist bloc's enthusiastic support. The next critical event was the 1985 attack on the amir, which not only convinced the amir that more drastic security measures were needed but also galvanized public support that might not have been forthcoming ten years earlier. Following the 1985 attack the assembly passed a strong antisubversion bill, laying down heavy penalties for possession of explosives, knowledge of terrorists and terrorism, and political violence. In March 1986 the government submitted a bill to the assembly setting the death penalty for crimes against aviation safety.[26]

Jabir also responded by reassessing his relationship with the loyal and disloyal opposition at home. In 1986 the government introduced several serious restrictions on political life, including suspension of the assembly and constitution and creation of new laws limiting press and assembly. New decrees permitted newspaper suspensions for reasons of national interest or for receiving aid from abroad. The Information Ministry began censoring all periodicals. Some fifty expatriate journalists were fired, with several forced to leave the country. Crackdowns on trade union and student opposition followed.

Much of the government's effort to suppress dissent was aimed specifically at the Shia community, as much of the political violence was connected with pro-Iranian Shia (Kuwaiti as well as expatriate). Certainly Shia interpreted much state action as anti-Shia. In 1982 several Shia were arrested for politicizing religious ceremonies. The government also began censoring sermons in the mosques as well as over the airwaves. The government was also concerned about Shia links to Iran, including possible Iranian training of those engaged in violence in Kuwait. Although most of the ties between Kuwaiti and Iranian Shia were longstanding apolitical ties of family and business, all ties worried the government. In 1986 the government deported thousands of residents of Iranian origin and introduced a range of new restrictions on local Shia, including their exclusion from sensitive jobs, especially in security and the military, and closer surveillance of Shia neighborhoods. Increasingly, however, these actions backfired, radicalizing otherwise less political Kuwaiti Shia and further polarizing the communities. Among the Shia communal grievances were the lack of state support for Shia mosques and religious centers, government quotas and restrictions in employment and higher education, and private-sector discrimination by Sunni employers. Shia also expressed concern over restrictions on nonpolitical assembly and expression within their community. Anti-Shia incidents perpetrated by the Sunni increased Shia alienation—for example, a 1983 attack by a group of Sunni that halted construction of a Shia mosque.[27] As tension grew, more Kuwaiti Shia, including some from prominent families, appeared among the arrested.

Initially the end of the Iran-Iraq War in 1988 prompted the government to improve its relations with Iran and relax its response to dissent at home. However, in March 1989 the government introduced still another crackdown on Shia, arresting several Shia, including Kuwaiti nationals, for seditious activity and a conspiracy that the government alleged involved plans to assassinate state officials. In 1989 when the Saudis executed sixteen Kuwaiti Shia convicted of planting bombs on the pilgrimage to Mecca, Kuwait's Shia felt their own government had not pursued the interests of its citizens and their coreligionists with any enthusiasm. The events of the 1980s left Kuwait's Shia feeling increasingly excluded from the national political community.

The Prodemocracy Movement

The prodemocracy movement began in Kuwait in late 1989 and focused on restoration of the assembly and constitution, suspended since 1986. Throughout 1989 prodemocracy petitions, signed by prominent Kuwaitis, began appearing. The amir's initial response was cool. He agreed to meet with opposition delegates but not to accept their petitions. In November dissidents began holding prodemocracy meetings, evading the state ban on public gatherings by using the diwaniyyahs, notably those of former assembly members. When these popular meetings grew into weekly political events, the police responded by breaking up some of the meetings with what, by Kuwaiti standards, was unusual force, including the use of tear gas and police dogs. News of the movement, and the government's reaction, spread as videotapes of the speeches and even confrontations with the police quickly circulated. The movement spread from the diwaniyyahs to the university, with students circulating their own petitions for a return to parliamentary life and a free press.[28]

The movement began to take off in early December, expanding through a series of Monday-night meetings organized primarily by a group of former assembly members around the explicit goal of the restoration of parliament and the parallel reinstitution of all suspended clauses of the constitution. A December 18 meeting drew a crowd of 3,000.[29] The meetings were followed by more petitions, with the opposition claiming by mid-December that it had gathered 30,000 signatures, a significant percentage of Kuwait's small electorate, on an election petition.[30] The government expressed its displeasure with the meetings by restricting them, with the interior minister banning diwaniyyah discussions of certain political issues and declaring the meetings a violation of the 1979 law on assembly and warning the organizers to cease. This was new. In 1982 the U.S. State Department human rights report explicitly noted that the Interior Ministry permission normally required for public meetings was not required for diwaniyyahs, "which anyone can attend and there speak freely."[31] This response only escalated the dispute, with the opposition defying the ban. The meetings soon widened into demonstrations that resulted in an incident in January 1990 in Jahrah when the police closed a diwaniyyah rally, in the process roughing up some of the dissidents, injuring five and using tear gas on the crowd, whose number ranged from the official estimate of 1,000 to supporters' estimates of 10,000 to 15,000.[32] The interior minister again warned Kuwaitis against discussing national issues in the diwaniyyahs, noting in particular the Jahrah meeting, and repeated his intention to take action against those who did.[33] Nonetheless, there were signs that this heavy-handed approach was not working. The government began reconsidering its tactics.

By late January it was clear the government's position was beginning to shift as cracks appeared in official statements. The day after the Jahrah meeting the information minister announced that the assembly would not be restored, at least not in its old, failed form, but added that if the opposition had a new concept for reintroducing public participation to decisionmaking, the government would listen.[34] On January 11 Shaikh Sa'ad asserted that the government remained committed in principle to some form of popular participation in decisionmaking but that it had not found the appropriate formula for preventing the crises that had plagued legislative-executive relations in the past. Sa'ad also promised to reconsider press censorship, and subsequently newspaper editorials began tackling the issue of dialogue. On January 15 Ahmad al-Jarallah ran an editorial entitled "Openness Need Not Be Feared," calling for freedom of expression and reestablishing the democratic process.[35] He cited the cases of Jordan, which had recently taken steps toward political liberalization, and Egypt, where a free press and public freedoms had survived even the dismissal of the interior minister without compromising security—a lesson, he said, for the regimes of the world.

In an interview with the *Arab Times* on January 16 Sa'ad insisted that Kuwait was still democratic: "The state, headed by His Highness the Amir is not against popular participation, but it is important to arrive at a formula through which we can overcome the negative aspects of the past experience."[36] He cited the rigidities of official offices and contacts of a parliamentary system versus the flexibility of the current system. He also pointed to the regional instability; the danger of antagonizing class, ethnic, and sectarian conflicts; and the tensions associated with the recent economic crisis. Acknowledging the popular grafting of the assembly onto national traditions, Sa'ad tried to link himself with the same approach: "When popular participation took a legal shape in the sixties it emanated from the government's wish to emphasize the old tradition of Kuwaitis in sharing opinions, brotherhood, one family spirit and their strong-bonds of national unity." He reaffirmed that the 1986 closure was in some sense temporary and insisted that the assembly remained suspended, not abolished. He also addressed the issue of civil liberties head on: "The state here was not and is not a state of violence, or of political prisons or a state of secret police." However, he added, it was also the state's duty to protect the security of its citizens.

On January 20 the amir went on national television to announce his support, in principle, for participation and parliamentary life, calling for dialogue, avoidance of confrontation, and a widening of the consultative base as well as firmly establishing freedoms. He delegated to Sa'ad the task of opening negotiations with the opposition, whose response was mixed. Ahmad al-Sa'dun announced the temporary halting of the weekly meetings, and others followed. However, when a demonstration of 6,000 took place on January 22 in Farwaniyyah, the government responded with tear gas and violence, resulting in more injuries and arrests. The next day two Kuwaiti papers, *al-Anba* and *al-Siyassah*, called on the public to stop challenging the government now that it had taken steps toward public dialogue.[37] However, on February 13 hundreds of Kuwaitis met at the diwaniyyah of Ahmad al-Khatib, who spoke with unusual clarity: "We hope for peaceful change, but if people are frustrated violence cannot be ruled out."[38]

Meanwhile, Shaikh Jabir and especially Shaikh Sa'ad began a series of meetings with prominent public figures on the idea of dialogue. Sa'ad held a meeting with 28 former members of the assembly on February 7 on the preparatory principles of dialogue. Nonetheless, the government stressed the need to have in place guarantees that would prevent the mistakes that had led to the 1976 and 1986 dissolutions. In a February interview with *al-Qabas* Sa'ad expressed his support for the principle of dialogue; however, dialogue requires time, much time, he said.[39] Sa'ad insisted he would meet with former assembly members; in fact, he insisted he would meet with all the former members from the 1962 assembly on, as well as with a host of other citizens. He hedged on direct questions about the constitution, saying that appropriate formulas were still unclear, and likewise resisted questions on the creation of a national charter. The amir was stalling while working on a compromise. It was a clever one.

On April 23 the amir announced his compromise: the establishment of a National Council comprising fifty elected and twenty-five appointed members with fewer powers. It would not enact legislation; rather, its goal would be to propose "rules and regulations that would insure maintenance of stability and national unity in line with the spirit of Islamic law and the principle of the one Kuwaiti family."[40] It would not be a wholly open and elected forum, but neither would it be a wholly appointed, docile body. The amir scheduled elections for June 10.

This proposal divided the opposition. Although some prominent Kuwaitis agreed to serve on the council, the compromise was rejected by the movement's organizers, who proposed an election boycott. The government's response was swift and anything but conciliatory. In mid-May it began arresting prodemocracy organizers, breaking into the homes of former delegates who opposed the council and charging them with violating laws on public assembly. Although they were later released, the government had made it clear its tolerance was fading. In June the government held elections for the council and, despite the opposition boycott, felt it achieved a respectable turnout. The new council had barely begun to meet when the Iraqi invasion put an end to its operation. The prodemocracy movement that spawned it, however, continued—underground in Kuwait and in exile.

The prodemocracy movement arose for several reasons. Kuwait's political institutions played a key formative role in the movement. Once the demand for political participation emerged, Kuwaitis had a natural, if suspended, institution on which to focus their grievances. Former assembly members played a key role in the call for democracy. There had always been some opposition to the suspension of the assembly, although the subsequent strict press laws had masked much of it. After the 1986 dissolution a coalition of academics and former assembly members unsuccessfully petitioned the government for permission to organize a peaceful prodemocracy protest. Former members were also able to point out that the government's promise that affairs of state would be easier to handle without the assembly had not been realized. They pointed to the continuing problems with settling the Suq al-Manakh crisis, continuing problems with foreign labor, continuing sectarian tension, and continued corruption and incompetence in a government run without accountability.[41] The amir gave inadvertent encouragement to the opposition by his vague indications that he intended to restore the assembly in some form.

A second important factor was the diwaniyyah, an institution that the government had consciously encouraged after 1986 as an outlet for Kuwait's participatory impulses, an outlet that apparently worked only too well at organizing and articulating those impulses. Kuwaitis not only used the diwaniyyahs but stood on their right, embodied in the diwaniyyah, to be hospitable, accusing the government of being ill-mannered by breaking up the meetings. If Kuwait had relatively strong representative institutions, the opposition also drew support from the fact that Kuwait had relatively weak repressive institutions: no martial law, no real secret police, and no institutionalized repressive capacity.

Kuwait's economy played a role. The economic crisis of the mid-1980s had prompted the government to move toward introducing limitations and charges on social services and even to talk about introducing taxes—policy trial balloons that popped in the face of public opposition. These economic problems and the government's response helped repoliticize the population. However, the economic crisis was not severe enough to prompt a truly authoritarian austerity plan from the government, and by 1990 the economy had bounced back from the price lows of 1986 and had begun to recover from the Suq al-Manakh crash. The combination of new political concerns created by the slowdown followed by an economic recovery large enough to justify, to the opposition, the reopening of political space played a role in the emergence of the prodemocracy movement. Other factors included the secular shifts that had taken place in the oil and independence eras, among them the generally higher level of political awareness on the part of a well-educated population.

External factors played a role. Certainly the expansion of political participation in the Soviet Union and Eastern Europe, eagerly followed in the Kuwaiti press, played a part, giving Kuwaitis the feeling that a historical window of opportunity had briefly opened. Ahmad al-Jarallah, in an editorial entitled "The Lesson of Romania," starkly warned that other leaders, including the many in the Middle East who had oppressed their populations and suppressed personal freedom, should ready themselves for the same fate as Nicolae Ceausescu.[42] "The oppressive regimes," he concluded, "will certainly receive what they deserve of punishment. Souls of thousands of persons who died in jails are now certainly crying and searching for their revenge. It looks that the time of punishment is fast approaching." Kuwait was the first Gulf Cooperation Council (GCC) state to recognize the new regime in Romania. On January 20 al-Qabas ran an editorial, "This Is the Right Time," noting "On the international level, we see East approaching West and West approaching East, and everyone is seeking more popular participation in decisionmaking and shaping the future. Today's world is not a world of conflict and polarization, but one of participation and cooperation. It is a world of harmony among nations and also within nations themselves."[43]

The Intifadah was also a lesson in political defiance that the Kuwaitis absorbed. As Ahmad al-Khatib put it: "We are like the Intifadah. First we have broken the barrier of fear, then we will go on from there. The people of Kuwait deserve something better than rule by decree. We have a democratic tradition, thousands of educated men and women and a right to rule ourselves."[44] The end of the Iran-Iraq War also encouraged an outpouring of dissent long held in check in the interests of national security. Prodemocracy efforts in nearby states—notably Algeria, Jordan, and the Yemens (soon to become Yemen)—also played a role.

These nearby states, however, also offered the greatest threat to democracy in Kuwait, although this was not obvious at the time. One of the few agenda items that the new council was able to tackle before its suspension was the growing threat to Kuwait from its neighbor, Iraq. This dimension of Kuwait's environment is explored in the following chapter.

NOTES

1. Abdul-Reda Assiri and Kamal Al-Monoufi, "Kuwait's Political Elite: The Cabinet," *Middle East Journal* 42 (1988), p. 48.

2. Alan Rush, *Al-Sabah: History and Genealogy of Kuwait's Ruling Family, 1752–1987* (London: Ithaca Press, 1987), p. 1.

3. Nicolas Gavrielides, "Tribal Democracy: The Anatomy of Parliamentary Elections in Kuwait," in *Elections in the Middle East: Implications of Recent Trends,* edited by Linda Layne (Boulder: Westview Press, 1987), p. 158.

4. *Middle East Contemporary Survey (MECS),* 1980-1981, p. 474.

5. U.S. Department of State, *Country Reports on Human Rights Practices for 1982* (Washington, D.C.: U.S. Government Printing Office, 1983), p. 1192.

6. Abdallah al-Nafisi, *Al-Kuwait: al-ra'i al-akhar* (Kuwait: Another opinion) (London: TaHa Advertising, 1978).

7. Assiri and al-Monoufi, p. 48.

8. *Foreign Broadcast Information Service (FBIS),* November 21, 1989, p. 16.

9. See Jill Crystal, *Oil and Politics in the Gulf: Rulers and Merchants in Kuwait and Qatar* (Cambridge: Cambridge University Press, 1990), pp. 97–100.

10. *Middle East Economic Digest (MEED),* January 22, 1988, p. 28.

11. *MEED,* December 19, 1989, p. 6.

12. *MEED,* August 30, 1986, p. 29.

13. Noura Al-Falah, "Kuwait: God's Will and the Process of Socialization," in *Sisterhood Is Global,* edited by Robin Morgan (New York: Doubleday, 1981), p. 413.

14. J. E. Peterson, "The Political Status of Women in the Arab Gulf States," *Middle East Journal* 43 (1989), p. 44.

15. Quoted in Peterson, p. 44.

16. Peterson, p. 43.

17. Tony Walker, "Veil of Silence on Suffrage," *Financial Times,* March 13, 1990, p. 31.

18. *New York Times,* December 17, 1984, p. 8.

19. Nesta Ramazani, "Islamic Fundamentalism and the Women of Kuwait," *Middle East Insight,* January-February 1988, pp. 22–23.

20. Jamal A. Sanad and Mark A. Tessler, "The Economic Orientations of Kuwaiti Women: Their Nature, Determinants, and Consequences," *International Journal of Middle East Studies* 21 (1984), pp. 461–462.

21. Nasra Shah and Sulayman Al-Qudsi, "The Changing Characteristics of Migrant Workers in Kuwait," *International Journal of Middle East Studies* 21 (1989), p. 50.

22. Sanad and Tessler, p. 464.

23. Peterson, p. 43.

24. *Wall Street Journal,* April 13, 1988; *Christian Science Monitor,* April 21, 1988, p. 5.

25. *MECS,* 1977–1978, p. 429.

26. *Amnesty International Report, 1987* (London: Amnesty International Publications, 1987), p. 356.

27. *MECS,* 1983–1984, p. 404.

28. "Al-Kuwait: hal ya'ud haqq al-musharaka al-gha'ib?" (Kuwait: Will the absent right of participation return?) *Arab Organization for Human Rights Newsletter* 28-29, January-February 1990, p. 1.

29. *MEED,* December 19, 1989, p. 25.

30. *Middle East International (MEI),* January 19, 1990, p. 13.

31. U.S. Department of State, *Country Reports, 1982,* p. 1190.
32. *MEI,* January 19, 1990, p. 13; *MEED,* January 19, 1990, p. 24.
33. *FBIS,* January 10, 1990, p. 22.
34. *MEI,* January 19, 1990, p. 13.
35. *FBIS,* January 17, 1990, p. 16.
36. *FBIS,* January 24, 1990, pp. 17–18.
37. *FBIS,* January 23, 1990, p. 13.
38. Quoted in *Financial Times Survey,* March 13, 1990, p. 32.
39. *FBIS,* February 16, 1990, p. 18.
40. *New York Times,* May 20, 1990, p. 4.
41. *MEI,* January 19, 1990, p. 13.
42. *FBIS,* January 4, 1990, p. 14.
43. *FBIS,* January 24, 1990, p. 18.
44. *New York Times,* March 11, 1990, p. 6.

6

Foreign Policy

Kuwait's foreign policy has always been guided by its vulnerability. Kuwait is a small state with big neighbors. Diplomacy, not force, has historically been the usual key to its survival. Kuwait's 200-year history is dominated by efforts to balance locally influential powers. From Mubarak's alliance with Britain to Jabir's alliance with the United States, Kuwait's diplomacy has involved the repeated wooing of regional and external powers in an effort to achieve both security and a degree of autonomy.

THE HISTORICAL PATTERNS OF KUWAIT'S FOREIGN POLICY

By the late nineteenth century Kuwait had developed the package of strategies it would use in the twentieth. Mubarak's predecessors secured as close a relationship as they could with the dominant regional powers, the Ottomans and the Wahhabis, using them to head off threats from each other. Only when the Ottoman threat challenged his personal rule directly (in support of the allies of Mubarak's deposed brothers) did Mubarak side completely with Britain, signing the 1899 treaty that made Britain responsible for Kuwait's defense and foreign relations but left Kuwait with internal autonomy. This agreement, though it limited Kuwait's independence, allowed it to hold other international predators at bay, thus ultimately preserving Kuwait's independence.

From the 1899 treaty until independence in 1961, Kuwait's foreign policy was determined by Britain. In the 1950s Kuwait began moving toward independence as part of the postwar decolonization process. With the loss of India, the importance of Britain's hold over the Gulf as a security corridor to that colony declined. Kuwait was becoming more important as the source of 40 percent of Britain's oil and as a major investor in Britain's economy, but these links could be handled more effectively through diplomatic and trade relations, backed only when necessary by force. Britain's failure to achieve direct administrative control over Kuwait also prompted it to grant independence. In the 1950s Kuwait began participating in international organizations such as the Arab League, the International Labor Organization, and in 1960, OPEC. Kuwait's new status was formalized on June 19, 1961, when it received official independence from Britain. An exchange of letters between Abdallah Salim and the British resident replaced the 1899 treaty, and colonial links were superseded by diplomatic ties.

Kuwait's basic vulnerability, however, had not changed. The new agreement promised continued British protection. Iraq challenged that guarantee six days after independence when it announced that Kuwait was part of Iraq. Kuwait's army—consisting of 2,000–3,000 men, 8 planes, and 4 helicopters—was incapable of defending the state. On July 1 British troops arrived in Kuwait. On July 20 Kuwait joined the Arab League; in September the Arab League sent its forces, and Britain gradually withdrew. The Iraqi challenge reminded Kuwait that it would have no choice as an independent state but to cultivate powerful patrons outside the Gulf and careful relations with the most powerful local forces: Iraq, Iran, and Saudi Arabia.

KUWAIT AND THE SUPERPOWERS

Alone among the Arab Gulf monarchies, Kuwait had a good relationship with the Soviet Union. From Kuwait's point of view, relations with the Soviets grew out of strategic considerations in order to balance the Western presence and in deference to Iraq, with its strong Soviet ties. Domestic considerations also played a role, with the relationship mollifying the Arab nationalist opposition bloc in Kuwait, some of which was mildly pro-Soviet, owing to Soviet support for the Palestinian cause.

The Soviet Union, recognizing Iraq's 1961 claim to the state, initially blocked Kuwait's entry to the United Nations and established diplomatic relations only after Iraq did, following a regime change in Iraq in 1963. Kuwait reciprocated by encouraging Saudi Arabia and the shaikhdoms to improve relations with the Soviet Union. In 1976 and 1984 Kuwait concluded arms deals with the USSR, and in 1986 Kuwait signed an economic cooperation agreement. By the 1980s the embassy in Kuwait was the Soviets' largest in the Middle East, their listening post for the region.

During the Iran-Iraq War Kuwait strengthened relations with the USSR. When the Gulf Cooperation Council (GCC) was formed in 1981, the amir went to some trouble to win Soviet approval for the organization, a factor in the 1984 arms purchase. As the war progressed, Kuwait looked initially to the Soviet Union to counter growing U.S. involvement in the

Gulf, requesting that the USSR reflag its tankers, which were threatened by Iranian missile attacks, after an initial approach to the United States received no response. This move, however, ultimately opened the way for a new strategic alliance with the United States.

Kuwait's underlying relationship with the United States was closer than its ties with the Soviet Union were. The first contacts with the United States were through the private missions of the Dutch Reformed Church, which established Kuwait's first modern health services early in the twentieth century. The formation of the Kuwait Oil Company as half-owned by a U.S. firm guaranteed an enduring U.S. interest, and bilateral relations gradually grew. In the 1940s the United States requested consular representation in Kuwait, but Britain rejected the request, fearing the Shaikh would play off U.S. and British representatives and interests.[1] But as Britain's regional and international power faded, Kuwait turned increasingly to the United States. In 1971 the United States named its first ambassador to Kuwait. In 1972 the U.S. Defense Department drafted a major survey of Kuwait's national defense requirements, paving the way for future arms sales. At the same time Kuwait also built up a private economic relationship with the United States, investing heavily in U.S. property and industry.

Nonetheless, there was tension in the relationship. Aside from the larger fear that too close a tie to the United States would jeopardize Kuwait's assertion of neutrality and render it less able to balance local powers, U.S. support for Israel made an alliance with the United States unpopular domestically and regionally. Kuwait's formal relationship with the United States deteriorated somewhat after Egypt signed a treaty with Israel in 1979.

The Iran-Iraq War forced Kuwait to develop closer ties with the United States. Initially Kuwait continued to have reservations about the U.S. presence in the Gulf and was an outspoken critic of military cooperation with the United States. During the war secret U.S. pressures on Kuwait to trade the seventeen prisoners convicted in the 1983 bombings for U.S. hostages in Lebanon was another source of tension. However, as the war continued, Kuwait's security situation deteriorated, and reservations about U.S. involvement weakened. In 1984 Kuwaiti vessels became the target of Iranian attacks, producing casualties, raising insurance rates, and introducing a critical vulnerability in Kuwaiti trade. The 1986 Iranian occupation of Faw peninsula brought the Iranian threat to Kuwait's borders. With the war so near, Shaikh Jabir reconsidered his options.

The amir responded to the Iran-Iraq War as Mubarak might have, by seeking superpower support for his embattled tankers. Kuwait had tried other forums: the UN, the Islamic Conference, the nonaligned movement, and the GCC. These efforts proved inadequate, so in 1986, following a summer of increased Iranian attacks on Kuwaiti ships, Kuwait approached the USSR and the United States with a request to reflag its tankers. The United States procrastinated, and the Soviets agreed in February 1987 to protect Kuwaiti tankers. Within days of learning of the Soviet offer, the United States responded to the Kuwaiti request, agreeing to reflag eleven Kuwaiti tankers and place them under U.S. naval protection. The Kuwaitis then agreed to have the Soviet Union reflag only three tankers. For the United States, the reflagging decision was not only a counter to the Soviets but also a signal to the Gulf states of U.S. support in the wake of the revelations of secret U.S. arms deals with Iran in the Iran-Contra affair.

For Kuwait, reflagging was a policy motivated by desperation: Kuwait's failure to galvanize a Gulf effort sufficient to stop the war, coupled with its own dependence on Gulf trade. Unlike Iraq and Saudi Arabia, which had oil pipelines in addition to sea routes, Kuwait relied exclusively on the Gulf for its oil exports. Kuwait hoped not only to gain protection for its tankers but, by internationalizing the war, to bring U.S. and Soviet power to bear on Iran and thus end the war.

The reflagging decision prompted little visible internal debate, certainly not from the suspended assembly or censored press. In deference to possible opposition, the government portrayed the reflagging as a commercial, not a security, venture and refused the United States bases or formal access to facilities, although it did in fact offer logistical support to the U.S. escort forces.

The policy was successful in that it allowed the safe resumption of Kuwait's oil shipping (although initially it prompted an increase in Iranian attacks). The new U.S. presence, which was followed by a greater international involvement in the conflict, also played a key role in ending hostilities between Iran and Iraq. In July 1987 the UN Security Council passed Resolution 598 calling for an immediate cease-fire. In August 1988 international pressure, in conjunction with Iranian military setbacks, led Iran to accept the resolution, effectively ending the war. Although Kuwait's ties to the United States continued to be characterized by occasional tension, as in 1988 when congressional opposition based on support for Israel prompted the modification of an arms sale agreement with Kuwait (discussed below), the relationship remained strong.

So on August 1, 1990, Kuwait had good relations with both superpowers, but its ties to the United States were particularly strong. Although some tension had appeared over the 1988 arms deal, Kuwait felt confident it could rely on its U.S. ally.

KUWAIT AND THE REGION

The Israeli-Palestinian Conflict

Until the Iraqi invasion Kuwait had been very supportive, financially and diplomatically, of the Palestinian national movement. Although Kuwait never played a serious role in the military side of the conflict (in 1967 Kuwait sent a small unit to the Egyptian front; in 1973 it sent small units to the Egyptian and Syrian fronts), it gave the Palestine Liberation Organization (PLO) regular and substantial financial support. It also gave substantial financial aid to Egypt, Jordan, and Syria. Abdul-Reda Assiri estimated that of the nearly $30 billion Kuwait contributed to Arab causes between 1961 and 1989, a little over half went to the frontline states and the Palestinians.[2] In addition to its foreign aid, Kuwait collected a 5 percent tax on Palestinian salaries that went to the Palestine National Fund.[3] Kuwaiti leaders regularly spoke for the Palestinians in international bodies. In the 1973 war Kuwait was actively involved in the Arab oil boycott and production cuts (the OAPEC decision on price increases and production cuts was made at a conference in Kuwait). In 1979 Kuwait followed other Arab states in breaking relations with Egypt after its treaty with Israel.

Although the Palestinian cause had popular appeal, it never had the immediacy in Kuwait of either the Iran-Iraq War or other more pressing regional issues. When more urgent matters arose, Kuwait could shift its position on the Palestinians. In the 1980s Kuwait, concerned about the Iranian threat and looking to Egypt to support Iraq's war effort, became active in Egypt's rehabilitation. Following the Amman summit in November 1987, Kuwait and Egypt restored relations.

Kuwait's support for the Palestinians caused tension in its relations with the United States. In 1979 Kuwait's efforts to arrange a meeting between the U.S. ambassador to the UN, Andrew Young, and the PLO's UN observer, Zuhdi Tarzi, led to Young's resignation. In 1983 Kuwait refused to accept the U.S.-nominated ambassador, Brandon H. Grove, Jr., because he had served as consul general in Jerusalem. Kuwait's efforts to buy arms from the United States were handicapped by opposition stemming from Kuwait's support for the Palestinians. In 1988 the United States agreed to sell Kuwait $1.9 billion in arms only after modifying the deal in response to congressional opposition growing out of support for Israel. This opposition, centering on the sale of 40 F-18 Hornet fighter jets and 300 air-to-ground Maverick missiles, prompted the administration to add several restrictions to the deal, including extension of the F-18 delivery timetable, limitations on the use of the F-18s and on the antitank potential of the Maverick-Ds, and trade-in of older aircraft, thus limiting the size of

Kuwait's air force. Although Kuwait accepted these modifications, the process left a bitter aftertaste for a small country always anxious to maintain its independence.

Kuwait's support of the Palestinians grew in part from the presence in the country of a large expatriate Palestinian community, the largest single group after Kuwaitis. Published statistics do not disaggregate Palestinians and Jordanians in Kuwait (most of whom are probably Palestinians with Jordanian passports), but Shafeeq Ghabra put the number of Palestinians in 1985 at 350,000.[4] It certainly was large: Kuwait was the third largest diaspora home for Palestinians, after Jordan and Lebanon.

Palestinian-Kuwaiti relations predate the formation of the state of Israel. However, the close nature of those relations is largely the result of the rough coincidence in timing between the Palestinian exile and diaspora in 1948 and the parallel postwar development of the Kuwaiti oil industry and the concomitant need for labor. Palestinian-Kuwaiti relations go back at least to the 1920s when the mufti of Jerusalem visited Kuwait on a fundraising tour for al-Aqsa mosque.[5] In the 1930s collection drives for the Palestinian struggle raised money in Kuwait.[6] In 1936 the first Palestinian teachers arrived to teach in Kuwait's new school system. After the formation of the state of Israel and the resumption of Kuwait's oil operations in the immediate postwar years, the rate of Palestinian immigration increased. The intelligentsia were the first to arrive, several hundred of them between 1948 and the early 1950s, followed by the former peasantry. The Palestinians played a key role in building Kuwait's state administration: By 1965 they constituted nearly half of Kuwait's public sector employees.[7] Ghabra detailed the role Palestinians played in establishing Kuwait's education, health care, and other social services. Many entered the private sector as well, although their number was limited by Kuwait's commercial ownership laws.

The Palestinians in Kuwait were diverse, from different regional and class backgrounds, although as an aggregate they were high wage earners, ranking right after the Kuwaitis.[8] Laurie Brand divided them into three groups: peasants and unskilled or semiskilled workers who earned low incomes and who risked and feared replacement by non-Arab labor; skilled workers of middle income in the public and private sectors; and middle- and upper-class professionals.[9] Although the professionals were the most well known, poorer Palestinians were also numerous.

From Kuwait's point of view, the Palestinians were welcome primarily because of their availability and the skills they provided but also because of popular sympathy for their plight. Palestinians in Kuwait enjoyed a special political status: They were allowed an unusual degree of freedom in political and social organization. Unlike other Arab states, Kuwait did not sponsor its own Palestinian organizations in an effort to influence Palestinian politics, and consequently Kuwait played an important role in the formation of the Palestinian national movement. By the late 1950s Palestinian leaders made Kuwait an organizing center. In the 1960s Kuwait opened political and military training camps for Palestinians. The PLO opened its office in 1964; al-Fatah (the dominant group within the PLO, led by Yasir Arafat) was headquartered there until 1966. Political activity was expressed primarily through the PLO office and through a variety of popular, union, and mass organizations.[10] Activities ranged from social and cultural programs to union work, fund-raising, and demonstrations. All that was explicitly forbidden was a military presence. Implicitly forbidden was the use of Kuwait as a battleground for internal Palestinian divisions and involvement in domestic Kuwaiti political issues. The government did not hesitate to suppress demonstrations with force when these rules were breached.

For the Palestinians, the migration was motivated by several goals, which Ghabra has listed.[11] The first was the crucial need for employment. The second was to establish a Palestinian society in exile. The third was to develop and maintain exactingly high professional standards so as to make themselves invaluable to their employers, thus guaranteeing the economic resources not only for survival but also for helping their families and fellow refugees. The fourth goal was to tend to family responsibilities, to reunite divided families, and to reestablish family links. The last goal was to reestablish not only a personal but a political Palestinian identity.

In the years before the 1990 Iraqi invasion, the relationship between Kuwaitis and Palestinians was changing. The Palestinian role in the civil wars in Jordan and Lebanon prompted a Kuwaiti reassessment as fears about similar communal violence in Kuwait grew. In 1976 the government closed PLO schools in Kuwait, transferring the students into state schools.[12] In the 1980s the new attention to security was directed at Palestinians as well as at other nationals. However, Palestinians still continued to enjoy more political and economic freedom in Kuwait than in most of the Arab world.

The Intifadah had a mixed effect on Palestinians in Kuwait and on Kuwait's view of Palestinians. Initially the government was very supportive of the uprising, granting it wide media coverage. It deducted one day's pay from all state employees in support of the uprising. However, as the Intifadah began to affect Kuwaiti politics, serving as one more spur to the prodemocracy movement, the government reassessed its position. In February 1988 demonstrators marching in support of the Intifadah clashed with the police, prompting several arrests. These public political displays alarmed the government.

For the Palestinians the transformation was more subtle. Although years of residence and work had given many Palestinians a vague sense of entitlement to the benefits of Kuwait's wealth, the time in Kuwait had done little to erase the social, economic, and political disparities between Kuwaitis and nonnationals, Palestinians included. The other nationals, however, could look forward to going home (as indeed, most did after a few years); most Palestinians could not. They stayed, and they compared themselves to Kuwaitis. The Intifadah began to politicize this resentment.

So on the eve of the Iraqi invasion, Kuwait had a large Palestinian population in its midst. The government felt it had built a good relationship with this community through decades of financial and diplomatic support for the Palestinian cause and by offering high-paying jobs at conditions far better than Palestinians could find elsewhere in the Arab world. Perhaps the social and residential segregation of the communities, along with the generally loyal history of the community in Kuwait, prevented the rulers from realizing the extent of the Palestinian discontent. The government's comfort with the Palestinian population was evident in the political space it allowed the community. The rulers knew that the Palestinians had political grievances but saw them as directed against Israel, not Kuwait, and that they had economic grievances but felt high salaries had deflected them. The one alarm bell that did start quietly ringing before the invasion was the Intifadah: It had begun to galvanize the Palestinians in Kuwait in a way that surprised and disconcerted Kuwait's rulers.

Foreign Aid

As the discussion of the Palestinians indicates, an important and unusual component of Kuwait's foreign policy has been its foreign aid program. By international standards Kuwait has historically been a very generous donor. In per capita terms Kuwait has been one of the most generous states in the world, always standing among the top ten international donors. In the early 1980s, until the fall in oil prices in 1986, 3.8 percent of Kuwait's GNP went to development aid, an extraordinarily high figure.[13]

Much of this aid was distributed through the Kuwait Fund for Arab Economic Development (KFAED), Kuwait's major foreign aid agency, established in 1961 with principal of $140 million.[14] At first most KFAED aid went, as the name suggests, to Arab states. In 1974 KFAED began funding projects in Africa and Asia, in part to offset the harm done these states by the increase in oil prices. Between 1961 and 1989 KFAED gave $5.5 billion in aid in 351 loans to sixty-four states (another $70 million went in technical aid). Just half went to the Arab states, 18 percent to Africa, and 29 percent to Asia. The bulk of KFAED's aid went to unambiguous development projects, focusing on agriculture, infrastructure (water, electricity, transportation), and human resources (education, health care). Perhaps an equally large amount of aid (the figures are not published) was disbursed as direct, bilateral, government-to-government aid.

The aid program was motivated by several factors. The first and most important was security. Kuwait's real security concerns, prompted by its wealth and covetous neighbors, coupled with its limited military ability, forced it to develop other foreign policy instruments. Virtually every time a danger presented itself, Kuwait responded with foreign aid. This program also served Kuwait's basic foreign policy impulse of balancer: Aid could signal and reinforce a tilt toward or away from various states.

The program originated in the independence crisis of 1961 when Kuwait first promised Egypt development support in exchange for military and diplomatic support against Iraq. In 1963, in exchange for recognition, Kuwait made its first aid grant to Iraq of $80 million.[15] Conversely, after Iraq occupied a border post in 1973, a tentatively approved KFAED loan was dropped.[16] At the same time, a public statement by Kuwait's foreign minister that Kuwait would be unable to continue aid to the Arab states unless Iraq left Kuwait helped galvanize Arab support for Kuwait. Syria received no aid until 1969—first, because of Syrian support for Iraq's claim to Kuwait and then, after 1963, because of Syria's rivalry with Egypt, a country Kuwait supported. Kuwait cut off new aid to Egypt in 1978 when Egypt signed the Camp David Accords and then resumed aid in 1985 as Kuwait backed Egypt in its support for Iraq during the Iran-Iraq War. In 1983 the Fund cut aid to Liberia when it restored diplomatic ties with Israel. These political concerns also affected aid to non-Arab states. KFAED did not lend to those breaching the Arab League's boycott of Israel. When Zimbabwe abstained from a UN Security Council vote condemning Iranian attacks on Kuwaiti ships, KFAED suspended aid there.[17]

Although KFAED's lending was governed by security concerns, KFAED had more institutional autonomy and more insulation from Kuwait's domestic politics than did most state agencies. It had a separate budget and was directed from 1963 to 1981 by Abdallatif al-Hamad, a powerful and highly competent manager who could protect KFAED's interests. This autonomy allowed rulers to use KFAED to maintain lines of communication with states during periods of otherwise tense relations and thus engage in more subtle diplomacy. In 1970 Kuwait suspended direct aid to Jordan following the Jordanian-Palestinian civil war (resuming aid during the 1973 Arab-Israeli War), but the smaller KFAED operations in Jordan continued. A similar policy was adopted in Tunisia when Kuwait suspended state aid from 1965 to 1967 because of Habib Bourgiba's position on the Arab-Israeli conflict but allowed KFAED operations to continue. In 1978 Kuwait halted new aid to Egypt, previously the largest recipient, but allowed money in the pipelines to flow, including a large credit toward repair of the Suez Canal in 1979. The other side of this policy was that when direct state aid was working KFAED sometimes suffered. From 1967 to 1971 KFAED received no new state funds as money was eaten up in direct, short-term state aid to Egypt and Jordan following the 1967 Arab-Israeli War.[18] After 1973, however, the increase in oil prices allowed KFAED's budgets to grow.

A second and related motivation for the foreign aid policy was an awareness that aid could address some of the hostility that arose from the growing rich-poor divide, especially in the Arab world where shared nationalism heightened the non-Kuwaiti Arab sense of entitlement to a share of the oil revenues. The fact that KFAED's development projects were run in such a way as to actually facilitate development, that they were geared toward providing needed services to poor populations, that KFAED worked closely with the World Bank and other development organizations in setting up programs, that aid was linked to specific projects and evaluated by technical rather than political experts for economic soundness, and that the programs' efficacy was closely monitored and shared (with KFAED taking on no more than half the financing of any project)—these conditions suggest that Kuwait's nominal justification of helping the poor may also have actually been a factor. It also meant that most of the loans were repaid, the Sudan in 1983 being a rare case of default.

Other aid agencies included the General Board for the South and Arabian Gulf, established in 1953 under the Foreign Ministry, which gave aid, primarily in direct grants, to Bahrain, Oman, North and South Yemen, and the Sudan in the form of schools, hospitals, housing, and mosques. KFAED was also involved in the formation of multilateral aid agencies, including the Arab Fund for Economic and Social Development and the Inter-Arab Investment Guarantee Corporation. Although the bulk of Kuwait's foreign investment (public and private) went to the First World, some went to the Third World and supported Kuwait's foreign aid–foreign policy program.

So, on August 1, 1990, Kuwait felt that whatever tensions it had with its poorer neighbors—not only in the Gulf but in the larger Arab and Muslim communities and Third World—it had purchased at least a degree of political support through its aid program. Whatever other grievances these states might have, they certainly would not say Kuwait had not shared its wealth.

Kuwait's Relations with Saudi Arabia and the Shaikhdoms

Kuwait has always had an ambiguous relationship with Saudi Arabia. Even before state borders were drawn, Kuwait had to resist incursions from tribes in the area that would become Saudi Arabia. Under Mubarak, Kuwait's relations with its Arabian neighbor were good, but on Mubarak's death Ibn Saud claimed that some of Kuwait's tribes had turned their loyalty to him. As historically sovereignty over land followed sovereignty over people, Ibn Saud claimed much of the desert land once claimed by Kuwait. This claim was not resolved until after the Battle of Jahrah in 1920 when Kuwait nearly lost its independence. In 1922 when Britain set Kuwait's borders with Saudi Arabia at the Conference of Uqair, Kuwait lost substantial land—two-thirds of its claimed territory—to the new Saudi state. Ibn Saud continued to harass Kuwait militarily in the 1920s (forcing it to rely on British support) and economically in a blockade in the 1930s.

Postindependence relations between Kuwait and Saudi Arabia have been characterized by differences over approaches to Gulf security, differences that were, however, set aside whenever another power emerged as a serious threat. Kuwait's approach to Gulf security historically aimed at developing some variant of a federative alliance among the GCC states in which it would play the key role, an alliance that would balance Saudi Arabia and the other regional powers. After independence Kuwait hoped its neutrality (it was the only Gulf state with no territorial claims on its neighbors) and its history of successful diplomatic negotiation from a position of military weakness would give it credibility with the other shaikhdoms. Its semidemocratic institutions might also offer an alternative domestic political model. Unfortunately this model appealed only to the opposition, doing little to endear Kuwait or its federative ideas to the other Gulf leaders. In pursuit of federation, Kuwait used foreign aid to establish economic links with the poorer Gulf states. After Britain announced its withdrawal from the Gulf in 1968, Kuwait began working for a more formal federative arrangement. At first Saudi Arabia opposed this plan, hoping to keep the smaller states divided and dependent. Locally ambitious but militarily weak, Saudi Arabia would have preferred to dominate an arrangement among the shaikhdoms. Local rivalries among the small states also hampered Kuwait's efforts. Finally, the formation of the United Arab Emirates (UAE) in 1971 preempted a larger federation.

In the 1970s Kuwait worked for a variant of its earlier federative plan, a structured cooperation among the smaller states, focusing on economic integration—efforts that Saudi Arabia again resisted. The apparent settling of differences between Iran and Iraq in 1975 prompted Kuwait to promote economic cooperation among the smaller states to balance this emerging Iranian-Iraqi relationship. Both the temporary removal of Egypt from Arab politics with the Camp David Accords and the weakening of the shah strengthened Iraq's regional role, prompting a new closeness between Saudi Arabia and Kuwait. Then in 1978 revolution swept Iran, taking it momentarily out of the regional balance as an independent, powerful player. The revolutionary regime, however, posed an immediate ideological threat to its neighbors with its potential export of Islamist political activism. Saudi Arabia and the shaikhdoms pulled together, and toward Iraq, to counter Iran.

The Iran-Iraq War that broke out in September 1980 reinforced this new alliance structure. Saudi Arabia tried to bring the shaikhdoms into a formal security alliance, but they were reluctant—Kuwait most reluctant of all. Owing to assembly opposition, Kuwait alone among the shaikhdoms rejected Saudi Arabia's proposed internal security agreements to coordinate domestic political surveillance.

Kuwait, however, had not abandoned its hope for an important independent role in a regional security alliance, and this goal reappeared in the form of proposals for economic cooperation. The resulting compromise was the Gulf Cooperation Council, formed in 1981 by Saudi Arabia and the five shaikhdoms (Kuwait, Qatar, Bahrain, Oman, and the UAE), as an organization that included the defense and security arrangements the Saudis wanted but allowed Kuwait some autonomy in establishing economic and social relationships with the other shaikhdoms. Kuwait's economic and social cooperation plans were now incorporated in the GCC—indeed, initially the GCC stressed economic cooperation, downplaying its security functions. The main focus, however, was ultimately on war-related security cooperation and mutual defense arrangements and on internal security. Although Kuwait had reservations about such arrangements, its position so near the front and the continuing Iranian attacks finally brought it to agreement with the Saudis on external security matters. In 1982 the GCC states agreed to build a joint defense force. From 1983 on they engaged in joint annual exercises and exchanged visits between military staffs. Rivalries between the shaikhdoms and different security priorities—the other members were less hostile to Iran than were Saudi Arabia and Kuwait—along with the small size of the states, however, limited its effectiveness. As the war ended in 1988, it was becoming clear that the GCC was not an organization on which Kuwait could rely to counter a serious security threat.

With the war's end and the apparent absence of regional threats, Kuwait again distanced itself from Saudi Arabia. One area in which this shift manifested itself was oil policy, where the two states had historically been aligned, both being wealthy, large producers with small populations. Kuwait's growing downstream and upstream investments led it to focus more on long-term financial considerations and to advocate low prices, as higher oil prices would raise the price of the assets it was trying to acquire. Kuwait's wealth and small population meant it, unlike most other producers, could afford low prices. As the postinvasion period beginning in

August 1990 proved, Kuwait could in fact survive for a time without exporting any oil. Kuwait's position prompted a public disagreement with Saudi Arabia over quotas, as well as a disagreement between Kuwait and Iraq at the Vienna OPEC meeting in 1990 when Kuwait called for lower prices and rejected the quota offered.

Thus on August 1, 1990, Kuwait's relations with Saudi Arabia and the other Gulf shaikhdoms were not as close as they had been during the Iran-Iraq War. Kuwait, newly confident of its success in relying on U.S. support for the reflagging and less than confident of the efficacy of the GCC, had begun to distance itself from Saudi Arabia before it had reestablished good ties with Iran (although diplomatic relations had been restored) and before the Iran-Iraq War alliance between Iraq and Saudi Arabia had disintegrated—indeed, the formation in February 1989 of the Arab Cooperation Council by Iraq, Egypt, Jordan, and North Yemen prompted Saudi Arabia to sign a nonaggression agreement with Iraq. Kuwait, in trying to establish a new balance after the Iran-Iraq War found itself for a dangerous moment without Gulf allies.

Kuwaiti-Iranian Relations

Iran emerged in the 1980s as Kuwait's major regional threat owing to its ideological and material support for dissidents in Kuwait and actual attacks during the war. At first what Kuwait really wanted was a victory for neither power in the Iran-Iraq War, and although the government clearly tilted toward Iraq, other voices were heard. The assembly expressed its concern over a pro-Iraqi position that would necessitate more U.S. involvement, and it criticized the GCC as too anti-Iranian.

Kuwait initially maintained correct relations with the revolutionary regime. In July 1979 Sabah Ahmad visited the new Islamic Republic of Iran, the first Gulf foreign minister to do so. In 1980 Iran's foreign minister reciprocated with a visit to Kuwait. The government also set up formal economic and humanitarian links with the new regime. However, the distance between the two states was too great. The first worsening of relations had already begun in 1978 when Kuwait refused Khomeini residence, turning him back at the border after Iraq forced him to leave. By 1981 it was clear that the revolutionary regime in Tehran had hostile intentions toward Kuwait. Iranian efforts to export the revolution prompted ruling Kuwaitis to hope for an Iraqi victory. Iranian military attacks on Iraq also came frighteningly close to Kuwait. In October 1981 Iranian forces bombed oil installations in Kuwait, and relations quickly deteriorated. The battlefield struggle had also turned, and Iran was on the offensive. In December 1981 the assembly approved a $2 billion loan to Iraq, and Kuwait began backing Iraq as, it thought, the lesser of two evils.

Support for Iraq in turn worsened relations with Iran, and Iranian-supported violence within Kuwait grew. Kuwaiti authorities linked Iran to the many bombings in Kuwait, including the oil facilities and seaside cafes, to the assassination attempt on the amir, and to the hijacking of Kuwaiti aircraft. The 1986 Iranian occupation of Faw peninsula brought the war within earshot of Kuwait. The attacks on Gulf tankers threatened Kuwait's lifeline to imported food and other necessities and for exported oil.

In 1987 crowds attacked the Kuwaiti embassy in Tehran, protesting Kuwaiti support for Iraq. Kuwait withdrew its ambassador and closed its embassy, although it did not break relations. The incident was followed by the Kuwaiti expulsion of Iranian diplomats. In 1988 Iranian support for the hijacking of a Kuwait Airways flight, Iranian missile attacks on Kuwaiti territory and ships, and continuing Iranian accusations that Kuwait had allowed Iraq to use Bubiyan Island in its successful counterattack on Iranian forces in Faw all contributed to the continuing tense relationship between the states.

When the Iran-Iraq War ended in 1988, Kuwait's relations with Iran were just recovering from an all-time low owing to its alliance with the United States and its support of Iraq. Although Kuwait moved quickly to reestablish relations with Iran, sending a delegation to Tehran in September 1988 to discuss reopening the embassy and receiving Iran's foreign minister just days before the Iraqi invasion, Kuwait was not able to repair relations in time. Thus, on August 1, 1990, Kuwait's relations with Iran were close enough to frighten Iraq but still too distant to assure Iranian support.

Kuwaiti-Iraqi Relations

When Iraq annexed Kuwait in 1990, Saddam Hussain made two essentially contradictory claims: first, that *all* of Kuwait was historically, and therefore rightfully, part of Iraq; second, that only *part* of Kuwait was historically, and therefore rightfully, part of Iraq. The latter was a dispute about where the borders ought to be; the former about whether there ought to be borders at all. Underlying both assertions was the assumption that because something once was, it ought always to be—a troublesome logic, one that would as easily justify a Turkish claim to all of modern Iraq. In order to untangle the Kuwaiti-Iraqi relationship, it is necessary to glance ahead at what Iraq asserted that historical relationship to be in 1990.

The first claim, total sovereignty, is the easier of the two to analyze. If by rule we mean financial, administrative, or ideological control, Iraq did not have a strong case. Kuwait was never ruled by Iraq—Ottoman

Iraq or independent Iraq—either formally or (although here some ambi-
guities arise) nominally. Kuwait had an unbroken history as a self-
administered political entity since its establishment in the eighteenth
century, during which time it was ruled by locally chosen members of the
Kuwaiti al-Sabah family. The Ottomans had no control over Kuwait when
it was established; in the eighteenth century the area around Kuwait was
ruled by the Bani Khalid, an Arabian tribe.

In the late nineteenth century, Kuwait's relations with the Ottoman
Empire began to change. After Midhat Pasha's accession in 1869 as
Ottoman governor of the Iraqi province of Basra, Ottoman Iraq began to
take more interest in Kuwait. In 1871 the Ottomans sent a military
expedition into Arabia that Kuwait's Shaikh Abdallah supported, militarily
and logistically. For a brief time Abdallah also took the Ottoman title of
qaimmaqam (provincial governor), and it is with this title that the ambi-
guity of nominal rule arises. Iraq later invoked this as partial proof of Iraqi
rule; Kuwait asserted that the title was a mere formality. On this Kuwait
seems to be historically closer to the truth. Despite the title, the Ottoman
Empire continued to exercise no direct or indirect control: It did not collect
taxes, send administrators, police the area, interfere in the selection of
rulers or rules, or govern Kuwait in any of the ways in which it governed
its other provinces, even the most decentralized ones.

When Mubarak came to power, he reversed his predecessor's brief
pro-Ottoman position by formally siding with Britain in the 1899 treaty
and by relying on Britain for military support against Ottoman-supported
attacks. The new relationship differed from Britain's relationship with the
other shaikhdoms in that it came at Kuwait's initiative. One consequence
was a far-lower level of British involvement in Kuwait's domestic affairs.
In foreign policy, though, Britain settled in for a long stay. The 1899
agreement was followed by several more between Kuwait and Britain over
concessions and the handling of foreigners.

Ottoman opposition to the new arrangement with Britain emerged
quickly. Although the 1899 treaty was a secret, it soon became an open
secret; and when the Ottomans found out, they began a diplomatic
dialogue with Britain over Kuwait's status. This dialogue ended in another
document that is important to the debate: the draft Anglo-Ottoman Convention of 1913, initialed by British and Ottoman representatives, but
never ratified. In this convention Britain recognized Ottoman suzerainty
over Kuwait but declared Kuwait an autonomous district of the Ottoman
Empire and conditioned recognition of Ottoman interests on a promise of
Ottoman noninterference in Kuwait's internal affairs. Iraq later invoked
this convention as more proof of its historical sovereignty over Kuwait. In
rebuttal, Kuwait argued that the convention was never ratified, that no
Kuwaitis were consulted on or were party to the contents of the convention,

and that even this limited recognition of the Ottoman claim conceded Kuwait's historical internal autonomy and disallowed any interference in Kuwait's domestic affairs, a reservation that on the face of it would seem to preclude invasion and occupation. The convention did, however, for the first time set out a border between what would become Iraq and Kuwait.

The draft convention was soon superseded by events. World War I moved Britain into a closer alliance with Kuwait, and in 1914 Britain promised to make Kuwait a protectorate in exchange for wartime support. World War I also brought an end to the Ottoman Empire and led to the emergence of Iraq, whose borders now needed to be settled. Following the war, Iraq became a British mandate, and Britain tackled the question of its borders. In 1922 Britain called the Conference of Uqair in order to come to an understanding with Ibn Saud over the Saudi borders. This meeting set Saudi Arabia's borders with Kuwait and Saudi Arabia's borders with Iraq but not Kuwait's borders with Iraq. In 1923, however, Sir Percy Cox, high commissioner in Iraq, followed up the Uqair agreement with a memorandum to Major John More, the political agent in Kuwait, that set out the border between Kuwait and Iraq as that proposed in the unratified 1913 convention.

So far, nothing resembling an independent Iraq capable of making (or renouncing) its own claim on Kuwait even existed. In the 1930s, however, Iraq took its first steps toward independence. In 1932, in preparation for application to the League of Nations and termination of the British mandate, the Iraqi prime minister addressed the border issue in a letter to the British high commissioner, presenting a description of Iraq's border with Kuwait based on the 1923 memorandum and, consequently, the 1913 convention.

At this point, Iraq had not actually claimed Kuwait; indeed, the 1932 letter seemed to acknowledge Kuwait's independence. In 1938 the first Iraqi claim to Kuwait appeared. In a speech before the Iraqi parliament the Iraqi foreign minister declared Kuwait an inseparable part of Iraq and Iraq's natural outlet to the sea. The Iraqi press followed with articles with such titles as "Why is Kuwait not annexed to Iraq?"—prompting the amir to ban Iraqi newspapers.[19] As in 1990 two factors motivated this Iraqi move: money and security. First, oil had just been discovered in Kuwait (the first oil concession was granted in 1934; oil was discovered in 1938). Second, Kuwait offered an alternative to the port of Basra, then Iraq's only port, which recent disputes with Iran over the Shatt al-Arab waterway rendered problematic. Iraq began looking at the possibility of building a port along Kuwait's coast.[20]

As in 1990 Iraq claimed all of Kuwait and also just part of it, basing its claim on the 1913 convention. Britain rejected the first claim, noting that as Turkey had renounced claims to Kuwait and all the erstwhile

Ottoman provinces in the 1923 Treaty of Lausanne, there was no claim for Iraq or anyone else to inherit. Iraq then raised the partial claim, approaching both Britain and the amir for border adjustments; and when that failed, Iraq finally approached the opposition, working with those Kuwaitis involved in the Majlis Movement who also owned land in Iraq. But the rebellion fizzled, and the only legacy of Iraq's support was a handful of rebels who fled to Iraq (most soon returned home). In the following years Britain tried to arrange the formal demarcation of the border but to no avail, the Iraqis holding out for a border adjustment that would give them Bubiyan and Warbah, two islands off the entrance to Umm Qasr (Iraq's alternative to the Shatt al-Arab) clearly on the Kuwait side of the 1913 line. There the matter stood until Britain left.

On June 19, 1961, Britain and Kuwait announced the termination of the 1899 agreement, and Britain promised assistance to Kuwait if needed. On June 25 Iraq's leader, Abdalkarim Qasim, announced Iraq's claim to Kuwait. Iraqi military action was forestalled by the return of British and then Arab League forces. This did not dissuade Iraq from its claim, however. In November 1961 the Soviet Union vetoed Kuwait's application to the UN at Iraq's request.

It was not until a new Iraqi regime came to power in 1963 that relations improved. The new government formally recognized Kuwait's independence and in October signed an agreement recognizing the borders as those set out in the prime minister's 1932 letter. If it could be argued, as Iraq later did, that Iraq had not freely signed the 1932 letter, being still under effective British control, no such argument could be made in 1963. Iraq had been clearly independent since its revolution in 1958, and its leader in 1963 freely and publicly acknowledged both Kuwait's independence and its borders. Iraq went on to accept Kuwait as a member of the UN and the Arab League and to engage in a range of diplomatic agreements, including the exchange of ambassadors, consistent with such recognition.

But the dispute was not over. Despite the 1963 agreement, Iraq continued to contest Kuwait's borders in a variety of ways. In 1969 Iraq pressured Kuwait into permitting it to station troops inside Kuwaiti territory, near Umm Qasr. In 1973 Iraq captured Kuwait's al-Samitah border post, killing two soldiers and prompting Kuwait to close the border, halt aid, and recall its ambassador. Iraq then offered recognition of the borders in exchange for long-term leases on Warbah and Bubiyan. The consolidation of regional opposition to Iraq forced it to retreat (although not to withdraw its claim) as Saudi Arabia, Jordan, and Iran offered Kuwait military support.[21] In 1976 Iraq again seized some Kuwaiti territory; and although Iraq and Kuwait soon reached an agreement on the withdrawal of Iraqi forces, Iraq did not relinquish its claim to the islands.

Relations between Iraq and Kuwait appeared to improve during the Iran-Iraq War, but it was only the greater fear of Iran that compelled Kuwait to support Iraq. The most important form of support was direct aid: upward of $13 billion in loans between 1980 and 1988.[22] When Syria closed the Iraqi pipelines in its territories in 1982, Kuwait and Saudi Arabia also agreed to give the revenues from the 300,000–350,000 barrels per day of Divided Zone oil to Iraq. Kuwait allowed military and commercial trade for Iraq to pass through its ports and over its borders. In deference to this support and busy with its other border, Iraq did not pursue its claims on Kuwait, except to continue pressing for long-term leases on Bubiyan and Warbah.

Thus, as the war ended, Kuwait thought it was still on generally good terms with its Iraqi neighbor, owing to the support it had given Iraq during the war. There remained, however, the troubling issue of the borders. A 1989 visit to Iraq by Shaikh Sa'ad to discuss the matter produced no results, although it did lead to an agreement to supply Kuwait with Iraqi water and Iraq with Kuwaiti electricity.

THE INVASION

The crisis began in July 1990. On July 16 Saddam Hussain sent a list of complaints to the Arab League, accusing Kuwait not only of overproduction but of siphoning from Iraq's side of the Rumailah oil field—a long, ovoid field that straddles the undemarcated Iraqi-Kuwait border—and, oddly, of putting military forces inside Iraq. On July 17 in a Revolution Day speech, Saddam Hussain directed a particularly sharp attack at Kuwait, linking its oil policy to imperialist efforts to hold back Iraq and threatening to use force against oil producers exceeding their quotas. On July 24 Saddam Hussain sent two armored divisions to Kuwait's border. However, he assured Egypt's Husni Mubarak and Saudi Arabia's King Fahd that he would not attack Kuwait while talks were in progress, and they passed this reassurance on to the amir. To make sure that talks continued, the Saudis sponsored a meeting between Iraq and Kuwait in Jiddah; but on August 1, after the first round of discussions, the Iraqi representative walked out. Iraq now had 100,000 troops on the border.

On August 2 Iraqi troops invaded Kuwait and occupied the country and a week later declared it part of Iraq. Kuwait no longer existed.

What happened? Why did a foreign policy that had worked so well in the past—a foreign policy geared toward appeasement, balance, and good relations with all—fail and fail so thoroughly?

The primary reasons lie not with Kuwait but with Iraq. In justifying the invasion, Saddam Hussain continually returned to financial issues. Iraq did have real economic problems, originating in the financial exhaus-

Downtown Kuwait before the invasion (author's photo)

tion it experienced in its eight years of war with Iran. Iraq's financial disagreement with Kuwait focused on two issues: Kuwait's reluctance to write off its war debts and replace them with postwar economic aid and Kuwait's oil policy. Kuwait's financial support ended with the war (although the revenues from the sale of Divided Zone crude continued for a short time). On oil policy Iraq asserted, correctly, that Kuwait had been overproducing in defiance of its OPEC quotas, contributing to the lower oil price that hurt Iraq. Iraq claimed the collapse of oil prices due to overproduction had cost it $14 billion in lost revenues—a figure remarkably close to its debt to Kuwait. The low oil prices reduced revenues for other producers, giving Iraq considerable support for its goal, if not necessarily its means, of bringing Kuwait back in line. Iraq went further, however, asserting that Kuwait was hurting Iraq on purpose. Kuwait, Iraq argued, had already declared economic war on Iraq. Iraq also claimed that Kuwait was stealing oil from the Iraqi side of the Rumailah oil field. During the war Iraq had halted production from the field, mining its side to prevent it from falling to Iran. Kuwait went on producing on its side. After the war Iraq resumed operations and demanded $2.4 billion it claimed Kuwait had pumped out of Iraq's side. Kuwait asserted it had taken oil only from its own side.

These financial issues were real, but they were also exactly the sort of split-the-difference disagreements for which diplomatic negotiations had generally worked in the past. Kuwait certainly could have offered more—how reasonable one thinks the Kuwaitis were (but they offered him *$500 million*; they *only* offered him $500 million) depends on where one stands on a number of issues. It is less clear whether Kuwait could have made a large enough offer to make a difference to Iraq. The smoothness of the operation indicates that Saddam Hussain had already made the decision to invade; still, he may not have been committed to a full occupation. What is clear is that Kuwait and Iraq were talking past each other. While the Iraqis were talking about Kuwait's extending more support, Kuwaitis were disappointed that reconstruction in Iraq had proceeded without any substantial business being assigned to Kuwaiti firms. But still, down to the invasion, they were talking. Negotiations had hardly been exhausted; in fact, they had hardly begun. Kuwait was willing to discuss the loans and economic issues, but it would not make territorial concessions.

Iraq also raised the issue of the borders. This was not, in itself, an important factor in precipitating the invasion. The issue of borders was not even raised until a week later, after Iraq's failure to cobble together a collaborationist government in Kuwait forced it to resort to direct administration. On August 2 Iraq claimed to respect Kuwait's sovereignty and to invade in defense of a rebellion. Once the border issue was raised, it was raised in a particularly muddy way, with Iraq asserting, as in 1938, both a claim to all of Kuwait and a claim to specific parts of Kuwait. The first claim, as previously noted, had no real historical merit (although Saddam Hussain could count on a widespread ignorance of the historical details to work in his behalf); as for the second, even though there is no historical evidence to support an Iraqi claim to Kuwait town and bay or the islands of Bubiyan and Warbah, it is less clear where in the desert sand the appropriate line should be drawn. Iraq disputed the line across the Rumailah oil field, citing both historical reasons and economic need. It also put forward a claim, based more on strategic need than historical title, to Bubiyan and Warbah. The historical claims were not strong enough to be a factor prompting the invasion, but the felt economic and strategic needs behind them were.

Other factors prompting the invasion included a fear of the political and economic claims returning soldiers from the Iran-Iraq War might put, indeed were already putting, on the state. These problems encouraged Saddam Hussain to look for distracting foreign adventures. The need to give an Iraqi population something, some victory for the years of war, was also a factor. The end of the Iran-Iraq War in 1988 left Iraq with a well-armed military but no money; Kuwait had the money but no military. It looked like an easy victory. Saddam Hussain certainly did not anticipate trouble from Kuwait. The preinvasion period was one of political turmoil there; perhaps he believed the opposition would even join him—he initially tried to set up a quisling government based on opposition members. Saddam Hussain certainly did not anticipate opposition from the Arab states. Nor did he anticipate Soviet opposition to his moves; indeed, he may have expected Soviet support. He apparently did not anticipate the U.S. reaction. He may have believed that the lessening of tension between the superpowers meant that neither would intervene in a local dispute. Whether this misunderstanding was due to U.S. statements is unclear: The U.S. ambassador and Saddam Hussain remember their first, and last, conversation differently. Finally, Iraq had virtually no mechanisms for communicating either public opinion or dissenting views as correctives to the leadership's own. Saddam Hussain could learn of his miscalculations only after the fact.

There were principles attached to the conflict. They may not have been important in motivating the main parties, but they were part of the conflict, and they account to some extent for the support the two sides received. The key principle involved not the specific claim to Kuwait but a more general argument about the artificiality of state borders in the region and the historical unfairness of the process of setting those borders. Iraq appealed to pan-Arabism and drew its support from those parties, notably the Palestinians, who had suffered the most from the introduction of the state system to the region. Iraq also capitalized on an anti-Americanism that, although diverse in origin (the most important source being U.S. support of Israel) was widespread in the region. To sweeten the pot, Iraq also invoked the sense of entitlement and resentment the poor Arab states felt toward their rich neighbors, deftly sidestepping the fact that Iraq itself fell clearly on the rich and not the poor side of that divide. Finally, Iraq linked its claim to the broader Arab issue of Palestine. Kuwait and its supporters appealed to state sovereignty, a key tenet of the international state system. It appealed to the norms that linked respect for state sovereignty to nonintervention (including noninvasion) in other states' affairs and to the diplomatic (as opposed to military) practices connected historically with those norms. It drew support from those states that had the most to gain from preservation of the international state system and state sovereignty.

The key causes for the invasion thus lay outside Kuwait: in Saddam Hussain's domestic economic and political problems and, beyond that, in the broad historical processes of state formation in the region. These were things over which Kuwait had no control.

Kuwait's foreign policy was not the primary reason for the invasion, but it was also important. The end of the Iran-Iraq War found Kuwait in alliance with the United States but at odds with virtually all its neighbors and with much of the foreign community within its own borders. During the war Kuwait had retreated on some of its key foreign policy principles, replacing nonalignment, neutrality, and opposition to outside intervention with a clear U.S. alliance. In doing so Kuwait had lost flexibility and with it the support its historical balancing act provided, all at a key juncture. Both the end of hostilities and Kuwait's new alliance with the United States also brought complacency. Peace initially brought tremendous relief to Kuwait. It no longer worried about the war spilling over onto its territory, nor did it worry about the security of its oil exports and its imports. The closeness of its new ties with the United States and the success of the reflagging operation gave it a false sense of security.

Part of the problem lay in the process of formulating foreign policy in Kuwait. Foreign policy was always an executive matter, the amir being the final arbiter, although he relied heavily on his long-serving (1964–1991) foreign minister and deputy prime minister, Sabah Ahmad, whom only the tradition of rotation between the Jabir and Salim lines had kept from becoming crown prince. His political longevity made Sabah the greatest single influence on Kuwait's foreign policy. From time to time other important players emerged—Prime Minister Sa'ad (frequently at odds with the foreign minister), the defense minister, and the oil minister. The National Assembly had once played a small role, but it had been silenced since 1986. If errors were made in Kuwait's foreign policy—and after the invasion the population came to believe errors were made—they were made by the amir, the foreign minister, and a few key advisers. Opposition leaders point to this closed and nondemocratic policymaking process as a major factor in failing to avoid the calamities of 1990–1991.

Another problem lay with Kuwait's military, which was caught completely unprepared. Kuwait's external security force had always been small, with Kuwait depending instead on diplomatic arrangements. Its military was intended only to cause an aggressor to hesitate long enough for Kuwait to mobilize diplomatic support, but it failed even to do that. Kuwait had expanded this force during the 1980s, doubling defense expenditures in the first three years of the Iran-Iraq War. In 1978 the government, alone among the Gulf shaikhdoms, introduced conscription and compulsory high school military training. All Kuwaiti men (with minor hardship exceptions) ages eighteen to thirty, al-Sabahs included, were obliged to serve. In 1980, when the Iran-Iraq War started, the government introduced a general mobilization law authorizing the call-up of Kuwaiti men from age eighteen to fifty and the registration of certain nonnationals with the Interior Ministry if security required it. In February 1981 the government doubled regular military salaries in an effort to increase volunteers and reenlistments. Still, on the eve of the invasion the army had only about 20,000 men, many of whom were non-Kuwaiti and, according to one account, over 60 percent of whom were on summer leave![23] As the Iraqis massed on the border, the Kuwaiti military was taken off alert and tanks pulled from the border so as not to antagonize Iraq. As the Iraqi forces advanced, the defense minister ordered the army not to fire. Iraq captured all the country's key positions within twenty-four hours.

Kuwait, in defeat, had no choice but to turn to the United States for support, which was forthcoming. President Bush lost no time in sending Defense Secretary Richard Cheney to Saudi Arabia where he convinced King Fahd to agree to the deployment of U.S. troops in the area. Operation Desert Shield had begun. An Arab contingent followed, with Egyptian, Syrian, Moroccan, and GCC troops. Britain and other European states sent forces as well. The UN Security Council approved a series of resolutions condemning the invasion, imposing economic sanctions on Iraq, and—at the end of November—authorizing the use of force against Iraq. In January 1991 Operation Desert Storm began.

On February 26 coalition troops marched into Kuwait. In April UN Security Resolution 687 concluded the war. It called for respect of the borders on the basis of the 1963 agreement and reaffirmed previous resolutions calling on Iraq to rescind all steps taken against Kuwait since August 2. Sovereignty was restored.

THE NEW FOREIGN POLICY ENVIRONMENT

In Kuwait the foreign-policy making process did not undergo any serious revision as a result of the invasion. The dismissal of Sabah Ahmad in a cabinet shuffle in 1991 was a dramatic change, as was to a lesser degree the demotion of Defense Minister Nawaf Ahmad to minister of social affairs and labor and the removal of Finance Minister Ali Khalifah, but their successors did not suggest any radical new approach to foreign policy. The amir, and his family, remained at the helm.

Kuwait and the United States

Kuwait's primary interest in its relationship with the United States following the war lay in obtaining continuing protection against any Iraqi threat. Kuwait's leaders believed a large and visible U.S. military presence would best serve that interest. The crown prince called publicly for the continuing presence of U.S. troops. To that end, Kuwait's rulers were as visibly pro-American as Third World leaders can be. As Kuwaitis pointed out, the U.S. embassy in Kuwait had to be the only one in the world with *pro*-American graffiti on it.

The United States had the same interests in the Gulf after the war as it had before: guaranteed supply of oil at affordable prices, regional security, and access to the markets of the oil-producing states. The war added a vested interest in Kuwait's own security, for it would surely be an embarrassment to lose Kuwait, having gone to such lengths to regain it. In September 1991 the United States and Kuwait signed a ten-year defense agreement under which the United States agreed to pre-position military equipment in Kuwait and conduct joint military exercises with Kuwaiti forces. This agreement assured a long and visible U.S. presence in Kuwait.

The U.S. military presence remained large and had a direct and continuing impact on Kuwait. The end of the war found the United States deeply involved in internal Kuwaiti politics. The U.S. Army's 352d Civil Affairs Command, a reserve unit of lawyers and bureaucrats, immediately began working to restore order. The Army Corps of Engineers supervised repairs to Kuwait's infrastructure—electricity, water, roads—and restoration of its police, firefighting, and postal services. This presence inevitably influenced the dynamics of Kuwaiti internal politics. In the months following liberation Kuwait's rulers vacillated over the central domestic issue of political liberalization (detailed in Chapter 7). The U.S. presence intruded on this debate. Yet despite some rhetoric to the contrary, the United States did not in the end support democratization in any practical way. Secretary of State James Baker did visit the amir in April and discussed movement toward democracy, going so far as to say that "the ability of the United States to continue to support Kuwait politically and from a security standpoint . . . would be enhanced if they evidenced full respect and commitment to the preservation of human rights."[24] What pressure was exerted was not sufficient to prevent the government from halting an opposition press conference called during Baker's visit to protest the slow pace of liberalization.

The president's own statements were still more equivocal. When asked in June whether he was disappointed with Kuwait's failure to institute democratic reforms, George Bush replied, "The war wasn't fought about democracy in Kuwait. The war was fought about aggression against Kuwait."[25] Although the United States supported democracy in principle (a place apparently somewhat west of Kuwait), it would not interfere in Kuwait's domestic affairs.

The lack of U.S. support for the prodemocracy movement flowed from several factors: the necessary emphasis on short-term reconstruction; a limited knowledge of the Kuwaiti political system (including a recurring inability to distinguish Kuwait from its less liberal Saudi neighbor) that allowed policymakers to mistake the amir for the status quo and ignore the historical role of the opposition; and even the notion that the United States should not meddle in Kuwaiti politics, normally appropriate but irrelevant in this case of already deep involvement. A fear of the sort of political opposition a democratic system would produce (Islamist or Arab

nationalist), that is, an emphasis on stability, coupled with a weak understanding of the factors that enhance stability (a tendency to equate short-
term authoritarian continuity with stability, overlooking the longer-term
stability offered by democratic regimes capable of genuine commitments),
played a role. Finally, the fact that Kuwait was not an enduring issue in
the United States, off the agenda once the troops were home and the
yellow ribbons off the trees, contributed to the lack of support for
democracy in Kuwait. Intentionally or not, the United States in supporting
the amir and the ruling family supported the least democratic forces.

The close relationship with the United States will continue to have
consequences for Kuwait's foreign policy. A visible U.S. presence will be
a constant focus for regional opposition, serving, as it did in the war, as a
lightning rod for ambient regional anti-Americanism. It will attract opposition from the Arab states that opposed the war, from Iran, and, in
degrees, even from Kuwait's wartime allies. Kuwait's new relationship
with the United States, though protecting Kuwait's sovereignty, constrains
its policy choices and makes it harder both regionally and internationally
for it to play its historical balancing act.

Soviet relations with the Gulf monarchies improved in some ways
as a result of the Iran-Iraq War, as the Soviets opposed the Iraqi invasion
and supported the American-led invasion forces. This improvement, however, came at a time when the USSR was experiencing a much broader
economic, military, and political disengagement from the region, as well
as from the rest of the Third World. Domestic turmoil left the USSR
unable to engage in any major new regional initiatives. This change was
well underway before the Iraqi invasion. After the war, domestic problems
continued to limit the involvement of the Soviet Union and its successor
states in postwar Gulf affairs.

Relations with the Region

The Arab-Israeli Conflict. Although the war demonstrated the enduring popular appeal of the Palestinian cause, it did little to affect the
underlying realities of the Arab-Israeli conflict itself. In an effort to broaden
his international support, Saddam Hussain brought Israel into the war by
launching missiles at Tel Aviv and raising the issue of linkage, offering to
consider withdrawing from Kuwait (although never offering to actually
withdraw) if Israel withdrew from the West Bank and Gaza. This support,
however, ultimately had little effect on the war's end. The war did not
leave the Palestinians and Israelis any closer to agreement; indeed, it
hardened positions.

If the war did not change the basic dynamics of the conflict or the
positions of the key players, it did affect both Kuwait's relationship to its

resident Palestinians and to the Palestinian national movement. The first change in Kuwait was the reduction of the Palestinian community from its prewar level of an estimated 350,000 to 50,000 within a few months. The second was a change in the status of this community, from the most-privileged to the least-privileged expatriates. Although some PLO leaders condemned the invasion, more supported it, while remaining silent on human rights violations inside occupied Kuwait. This silence, given the historical financial support Kuwait had provided the PLO and the role Kuwait had played in the movement's early history, led to a sense of betrayal among Kuwaitis. Although the Kuwaiti leaders in exile reiterated Kuwait's support for the Palestinian people and reaffirmed "that the position adopted by some Palestinian leaders will in no way affect our unswerving solidarity with the Palestinian people," in practice, policy could not be the same.[26] Pictures of Yasir Arafat hugging Saddam Hussain would not soon be forgotten. After the war this anger focused on the Palestinians remaining in Kuwait (discussed in Chapter 7). The collaborator trials, in which Palestinians were prominently featured, and the government's decision not only to limit overall levels of foreign labor but to give preference to the nationals who had supported Kuwait during the war meant that Kuwait would not soon again become a political or economic haven for the Palestinian community.

In terms of foreign policy, the war moved the issue of a solution to the Arab-Israeli conflict off Kuwait's agenda. Kuwait was in no mood to deal with the continuing Palestinian leadership, and it was happy simply to tolerate an international show of attention to the issue. Kuwait now lacked the financial ability to use foreign aid in the service of its policy toward this conflict as it had in the past. The substantial aid to the Palestinians, halted during the occupation, did not resume.

Eventually Kuwait will have to make peace with the Palestinians. In April, Shaikh Sa'ad said that Kuwait would no longer provide financial aid to Arafat and his supporters in the PLO but that Kuwait would aid other Palestinian groups.[27] Probably, Kuwait will also mend its relations with Jordan's King Hussain, if for no other reason than fear of the alternatives. Support for the Palestinians has reached a nadir in postwar Kuwait, but the broader pan-Arab identity, although shaken, remains. Kuwait will eventually resume some sort of support for the Palestinian movement, but it will not do so with any enthusiasm in the short term.

Foreign Aid. Kuwait's wealth prompted much of the support for Saddam Hussain among the nationals of the poorer Arab states. Although one response might be a more generous foreign aid program, Kuwait has drawn the opposite conclusion: Foreign aid does not buy loyalty and indeed can prompt contempt and bitterness. After all, the Kuwaitis reasoned, hadn't they been generous with their aid and wages? And what did it win them? Besides, money is in shorter supply. The Arab world's grievance over the unequal distribution of wealth is so fundamental that, ironically, Kuwait may conclude there is no serious way of addressing it. That said, once oil revenues resume, government-to-government aid will continue to play a role, simply because it is such an attractive short-term way of renting support. What is less likely to resume is development aid at prewar levels as a cornerstone of Kuwait's foreign policy.

Foreign aid for the coalition partners is another matter. Kuwait paid cash for the war, contributing $13.5 billion toward U.S. military costs, with additional support for the other coalition partners. It was happy to pay for the peace as well. Kuwait tried to privatize part of its foreign policy, offering the United States the bulk of its alluring reconstruction contracts, with lesser amounts going to other supporters. Although the boom did not prove as large as U.S. firms had hoped, what business there was, went to them. The U.S. Army Corps of Engineers signed a $45 million contract in January 1991 with the Kuwait Emergency Reconstruction Program. In March the contract was doubled. U.S. firms such as Bechtel and Raytheon signed contracts for the first phase of reconstruction even before the war ended. By June U.S. firms had sold $1.5 billion worth of goods to Kuwait, double the prewar annual average.[28] Kuwait also continued its arms purchases from the United States: In April when the Defense Department awarded McDonnell Douglas a $153 million contract for work on forty F-18 fighter jets for Kuwait as part of the 1988 arms deal, Kuwait's defense minister announced that Kuwait was planning to rebuild its army with weapons as advanced as possible, the United States being the logical source.

Relations with Iran. Iran proved to be a winner in the war. Being able to credibly claim neutrality (even a willingness to mediate between Iraq and the United States) and longstanding opposition to both the Iraqi and the U.S. leadership, it used the war to continue its international political rehabilitation and to reiterate the importance of an Islamist approach to political problems.

Iran's main goal after the war was to limit the U.S. presence in the Gulf. Although Kuwait had little interest in such a limitation, it was interested in maintaining good relations with Iran. For a time during the occupation Iran helped thousands of Kuwaiti families escape by providing identity cards.[29] Following the Iraqi invasion Kuwait virtually apologized to Iran for supporting Iraq during the Iran-Iraq War. It also dramatically increased trade relations with Iran. Although Kuwait could not agree with Iran on the U.S. presence, after the war Kuwait did support a more active Iranian role in Gulf security.

After the war, Iran set out to restore peaceful relations with its GCC neighbors and to play a more active role in postwar Gulf security arrangements. In order to limit the U.S. presence it worked to obtain a more formal security arrangement with the GCC states. Iran made rapid progress in improving relations with Saudi Arabia, reestablishing diplomatic relations (broken since 1988) in March 1991. Improved relations with Saudi Arabia brought pressure on the other GCC states, Kuwait included, to improve relations with Iran.

Relations with Saudi Arabia and the GCC. Kuwait felt only somewhat less beholden to the Saudis than it did to the United States. The war ended with a close alliance between Kuwait and Saudi Arabia, which had consequences for Kuwait's domestic politics. Saudi Arabia had a real interest in limiting a prodemocracy movement in Kuwait that might resonate at home. It was particularly concerned about the last assembly's opposition to ratification of the GCC's security pact. The Saudis, afraid of constitutionalist contagion, pushed for limits on participation and were one factor prompting the amir to move slowly in setting an election date.

There were, however, differences between Saudi Arabia and Kuwait. Although the Saudis wanted a U.S. presence as long as Iraq remained a threat, they wanted an Arab cover for this presence. The invasion demonstrated the inadequacy of existing Gulf security arrangements, especially the ability of the GCC to defend itself militarily. After the war Saudi Arabia hoped to build a more permanent Arab defense arrangement out of the wartime coalition. In March 1991 the GCC states signed the Damascus Declaration with Syria and Egypt, which provided for an Egyptian- and Syrian-based Arab peacekeeping force in exchange for increased financial aid from the Gulf states to Egypt and Syria. This new formula, GCC + 2, was to create a regional security arrangement that would avoid the internal political problems associated with a visible U.S. presence.

This effort faced the same problems such efforts had faced before the war: disagreements among member states that hampered coordination efforts and limited military capacity. The plan began to unravel within two months over disagreements about money (both aid and the allocation of reconstruction contracts for labor and services), the role of (and respect for) Arab forces and technology, and the roles of Iran and the United States in any future security arrangements. In May Egypt (which was also concerned with its workers in Kuwait, including seventy Egyptians to be tried as collaborators, and the property of those who had left) expressed unhappiness with the postwar security scheme and announced the withdrawal of its 36,000 soldiers. Following the Egyptian announcement, Kuwait worked with Saudi Arabia to try to reverse the damage. Although they may cobble together an Arab regional security arrangement, the underlying tensions and disagreements remain.

Relations with Iraq. Kuwait's relations with any new Iraqi government would depend on the nature and composition of the regime. The only situation worse than Iraq with Saddam Hussain would be the same regime without him—the same threat, with the veneer of international legitimacy that Saddam Hussain's absence would purchase.

As long as Saddam Hussain remains in power, Kuwait will see Iraq as a threat. There is nothing to indicate his intentions toward Kuwait have changed; only his tactics have. Iraq accepted Resolution 687 only at gunpoint. Iraq has disavowed previous agreements, asserting that it did not sign them as a free agent. It could just as well invoke duress to reject Resolution 687. Although the war is over, the disputes over oil production and borders have not been settled. Kuwait has made it clear it is in no mood to make concessions to Iraq on borders, islands, oil policy, or aid. As far back as October 1990 the exiled oil minister, Rashid al-Amiri, in outlining his plan for Kuwait's postwar oil policy, said that in light of Kuwait's reconstruction expenses it would push for a higher OPEC quota and a moderate pricing policy.[30] Specifically he rejected the price of $25 per barrel backed by Iraq before the invasion. The war has added new issues of contention: reparations, the return of specific property taken during the occupation (for example, the contents of Kuwait's museums and hospitals), and the fate of Kuwaitis missing in Iraq.

The situation in Iraq will affect domestic Kuwaiti politics. As long as the postwar security situation remains tense and as long as the Iraqi threat is real, Kuwait's rulers will be able to invoke national security to quell dissent. If security is seen as *the* issue, then an enlarged military will come to play a more important role in domestic politics, shoring up the authoritarian impulse and weakening the impulse toward political liberalization. These issues are taken up in the final chapter.

NOTES

1. Abdul-Reda Assiri, *Kuwait's Foreign Policy: City-State in World Politics* (Boulder: Westview Press, 1990), p. 7.

2. Assiri, p. 40.

3. Laurie Brand, *Palestinians in the Arab World: Institution Building and the Search for State* (New York: Columbia University Press, 1988), p. 122.

4. Shafeeq Ghabra, *Palestinians in Kuwait: The Family and the Politics of Survival* (Boulder: Westview Press, 1987), p. 9.

5. Assiri, p. 50.

6. Rosemarie Said Zahlan, "The Gulf States and the Palestine Problem, 1936–48," *Arab Studies Quarterly* 3 (1981), pp. 1–21.

7. Ghabra, p. 41.

8. Nasra Shah and Sulayman Al-Qudsi, "The Changing Characteristics of Migrant Workers in Kuwait," *International Journal of Middle East Studies* 21 (1989), p. 46.

9. Brand, p. 117.

10. Brand, p. 123.

11. Ghabra, p. 34.

12. Brand, p. 124.

13. Abdul-Reda Assiri, "Kuwait's Dinar Diplomacy: The Role of Donor-Mediator," *Journal of South Asian and Middle Eastern Studies* 14 (1991), p. 26.

14. Assiri, "Kuwait's Dinar Diplomacy," p. 26.

15. Assiri, *Kuwait's Foreign Policy*, p. 41.

16. Walid Moubarak, "The Kuwait Fund in the Context of Arab and Third World Politics," *Middle East Journal* 41 (1987), p. 540.

17. Moubarak, pp. 548–549.

18. Moubarak, p. 540.

19. Jill Crystal, *Oil and Politics in the Gulf: Rulers and Merchants in Kuwait and Qatar* (Cambridge: Cambridge University Press, 1990), p. 53.

20. Daniel Silverfarb, *Britain's Informal Empire in the Middle East: A Case Study of Iraq, 1929–1941* (New York: Oxford University Press, 1986), p. 67.

21. Moubarak, p. 549.

22. Assiri, *Kuwait's Foreign Policy*, p. 70.

23. Shafeeq Ghabra, "The Iraqi Occupation of Kuwait: An Eyewitness Account," *Journal of Palestine Studies* 20 (1991), p. 113.

24. *New York Times*, April 23, 1991, p. 7.

25. *New York Times*, July 2, 1991, p. 3.

26. "The Final Communiqué of the Kuwaiti People's Conference," October 13–15, 1990, Jiddah, Saudi Arabia.

27. *New York Times*, April 18, 1991, p. 2.

28. *Wall Street Journal*, July 8, 1991, p. 4.

29. Ghabra, "The Iraqi Occupation," p. 125.

30. *MEED*, November 2, 1990, p. 15.

7

The Aftermath of the Invasion

The Iraqi invasion of Kuwait in August 1990 changed that country forever. Nonetheless, the invasion did not destroy Kuwait. The impact and the aftermath of the invasion were shaped by preexisting relationships in Kuwait, by the particular configuration of events at the moment of invasion, and by the realignment of forces during the occupation and in exile.

THE OCCUPATION

The Effect of the Invasion: Inside Kuwait

The most dramatic effect of the Iraqi invasion and occupation was the attempted systematic destruction of Kuwait. Iraqi soldiers gutted the downtown business district, ransacked the industrial areas, and looted the residential areas: streetlights, hospital supplies, computers, lab equipment, school blackboards, boats, windows, phone booths, power transformers, food—anything that could move, did. Kuwait's Entertainment City as well as its Islamic Museum were taken to Baghdad, as was most of the Kuwait Airways fleet.

Most of the looting was government-sanctioned, but some was freelance. Refugees described soldiers emptying not only stores but apartments and houses of electronics, jewelry, furniture—anything that could be readily transported. Hungry soldiers ate their way through the zoo. So many cars were taken from Kuwait—100,000 by early September according to the *Iraqi* oil minister—that long lines formed at gas stations.[1] Officially Iraq condemned the looting and on at least one occasion made a public display of executing an officer accused of it, hanging his body from a downtown construction crane. However, privatization of looting and the accompanying disorder seemed to be more the issue, as formal looting by Iraq continued. Oddly, the looting was initially so thorough that it left hope that Iraq really intended to withdraw, for surely if Kuwait were to remain an Iraqi province it would need hospitals and schools.

Infrastructure was severely damaged by both military means and government-sanctioned looting. Roads and ports were damaged, communications systems destroyed. Power outages hampered the effectiveness of the desalination plants. Kuwait's industrial area in Shu'aibah was destroyed, although this loss was not as great as it would have been had Kuwait invested heavily in local industry rather than favoring overseas investment. Although Iraq took gold and $1.2 billion in cash from the Central Bank and $1 billion from the commercial banks, economic sanctions kept Iraq from touching most of Kuwait's investments, which were safely overseas. Nonetheless, to finance the war and immediate reconstruction, Kuwait used $15 billion of its more than $100 billion overseas assets. The most important damage was sustained by the oil industry, and the overall harm done to Kuwait's economy was severe.

The invasion also catalyzed several demographic changes. Before the invasion Kuwait had a population of just over 2 million, of whom slightly more than half were expatriates. Because the invasion occurred in August, a popular vacation time, many Kuwaitis were outside the country; others soon fled. By October 100,000 Kuwaitis were in exile in Saudi Arabia; by January 400,000–600,000 of Kuwait's nationals were abroad.[2] For expatriates the situation was more complicated. Those who could flee, did. Refugee reports suggested that only those foreigners who could not finance an escape or those (such as many Palestinians) who had fewer options, stayed. In the process most lost something; many lost everything. Those who held money, often years of savings, in Kuwaiti banks went home penniless. Those who escaped with a few goods often lost them to Iraqi soldiers.

For a short time following the invasion the political situation was fluid. At first Iraq asserted it had entered Kuwait in support of a local rebellion. However, efforts to establish a quisling government failed when Iraq was unable to find reputable Kuwaitis willing to serve. The opposition was, if anything, more anti-Iraqi than the government. The prodemocracy movement included parliamentarians who had opposed Kuwait's wartime aid to Iraq. The National Council—the partially appointed, partially elected compromise body set up by the government in June—had been still more vocal in its opposition to Iraq. Nor was the underground opposition, dominated by Shia whose earlier wartime support of Iran placed them outside the Iraqi camp, any more amenable to Iraqi rule. When Iraq nonetheless named Kuwaitis to the new government, they refused to serve. Their supporters issued a communiqué opposing the invasion, calling for the restoration of the Kuwaiti government, and even affirming their commitment, albeit with reservations, to al-Sabah rule. Finally, Iraq rounded up a handful of naval officers taken prisoner in the first days to serve in the brief Kuwaiti cabinet.[3]

Ironically, had Kuwait's national identity been more fragile, had it in fact been the contrived historical creation Iraq asserted it was, Iraq would probably have succeeded in putting in place a nominally Kuwaiti government that would have granted it the financial and strategic concessions it sought. Then perhaps Iraq would have found annexation unnecessary. However, unable to set up even the semblance of a Kuwaiti government, Iraq had no choice but to put in place an occupation administration. It established a military government under Ali Hassan al-Majid, a cousin of Saddam Hussein. His background indicated the direction the occupation would take: From 1980 to 1986 he served as head of Iraq's State Security Department and after 1986 as the senior officer in Kurdistan (giving him occupational experience in occupation).

On August 9 Iraq formally annexed Kuwait. The northern part of the country, 7,000 square kilometers including the disputed Rumailah oil field and the coveted islands of Warbah and Bubiyan, was added to the province of Basra; a separate province was created out of the rest of Kuwait. The government issued new Iraqi currency and new license plates, and new pictures and statues of Saddam Hussein were put on display. For Iraq, Kuwait officially ceased to exist.

However, Iraq was slow to set up an occupation administration. Its more pressing military concerns, coupled with an opposition boycott of nonessential work and the ambient fear and nighttime curfews that kept many Kuwaitis from venturing out, brought public life to a halt. Garbage sat uncollected on the streets, and government offices and banks remained closed, despite notices that Kuwaitis failing to return to work would be hanged.[4]

The first strand of resistance moved into this administrative vacuum as Kuwaitis organized around the preexisting system of cooperatives to provide food, security, and essential services. These cooperatives were relatively old institutions in Kuwait, dating back to 1961. They were organized around neighborhoods and run by elected boards who knew their communities well. Each cooperative served a specific and usually cohesive residential area, supplying basic commodities—rice, oil, flour— at subsidized prices. The cooperatives also dealt with local social and community issues, handling constituency concerns on garbage collection and schooling and serving as a sounding board for community grievances. These cooperatives, along with the other strong local institution, the mosque network, provided the backbone of the resistance. As Islamists already dominated many of the cooperative boards, they worked well together. Finally, the old system of diwaniyyahs, regular weekly meetings in people's homes, was used to communicate information about the resistance.

Although some services reappeared—cooperatives distributed food, stores reopened for a few morning hours with rationed sales, even limited bus service returned within a few weeks—the overall situation was grim. By late August food was scarce. Medical care was nearly unavailable for Kuwaitis, and medicine was in short supply.

A second strand of opposition now emerged that was more organized, had more explicitly political goals, and was increasingly militant. This resistance harassed the occupation forces by removing road signs and distributing underground leaflets and posters. The Voice of Kuwait, which began broadcasting mere hours after the invasion out of a jerry-built workstation (later moving to Dammam), served as a symbol of opposition, airing everything from practical advice on air raids to patriotic songs, news, monthly addresses by the amir, and propaganda for Iraqi soldiers.[5] The more militant opposition was organized through the mosques, many of them Shia. At night the resistance attacked small groups of soldiers and occasionally military vehicles. Resistance members received arms initially from fleeing Kuwaiti army and police units and sometimes bought them from Iraqi soldiers. Later, exile groups in Saudi Arabia supported the resistance with weapons and money.

Iraq moved quickly to eliminate this opposition. It attacked the resistance directly, executing those belonging or suspected of belonging to the opposition, often in front of their families, and taking others to prisons in Iraq and Kuwait (Kuwait University was converted to a prison). Iraqis in Kuwaiti dress began attending mosque, and political imams disappeared, as did heads of cooperatives. Checkpoints were set up throughout Kuwait to detain Kuwaitis and expatriates. Some people were released; others were humiliated, tortured, imprisoned, or killed. When opposition flared, the Iraqi army sealed off neighborhoods, leveled buildings, and conducted house-to-house searches. Display of Kuwaiti flags or pictures of the amir prompted summary punishment, often capital. The number of Kuwaitis killed, estimated at a few hundred in the first few days, steadily rose. Finally, the Iraqis encouraged Kuwaitis to leave, although the policy was haphazardly implemented, and thousands began pouring across the border.

These policies had two goals: to destroy the organized resistance and to cow the population. Partly a deliberate reaction to circumstances in Kuwait, the Iraqi response (with the exception of encouraging flight) was also simply the product of institutional inertia, the application of Iraqi political institutions, in this case security institutions, to Kuwait. Iraq was in no position to fine-tune its coercive apparatus to fit Kuwait, nor did it need to.

The Effects of the Invasion: Outside Kuwait

As the occupation continued, a new Kuwaiti society began to emerge in exile. Kuwaitis already abroad joined those who soon fled to form an exile community based in Saudi Arabia, with outposts in London, New York, Washington, and the other Gulf states. An exile government was formed in Taif. Most of the ruling family had fled Kuwait quickly, even as the invasion occurred. Other government officials soon followed, until reportedly the entire cabinet of twenty-two ministers was out of the country, along with much of the staff. Several of these bureaucrats were given the task of drawing up a reconstruction plan. Others tried to carry on some of the welfare functions of the old state: arranging jobs for exiles, tuition payments for stranded students, medical care, travel expenses, housing.

The exile government was able to arrange access to most of Kuwait's largest source of revenues: overseas investments, estimated at over $100 billion. Although the government lost access to oil revenues of $40–$50 million a day, it retained some control of downstream operations and continued to market 450,000 barrels of oil per day. Kuwait had three months' production of oil in storage or transit; Gulf states supplied more, keeping Kuwait's overseas refineries and retail outlets working. The government even invested $6 million in updating seventeen gas stations in Hungary.[6] The government proceeded to arrange its financial affairs as best it could. The National Bank of Kuwait (NBK), which had the overseas facilities (and which had always maintained its own records in duplicate abroad), began coordinating the obligations of Kuwait's banks. The NBK set about bringing interest payments up to date, rolling over debts, negotiating with governments over frozen assets, and drawing up a postwar bank recovery plan.[7]

The exile government also carried out a foreign policy, negotiating with the United States and Arab allies for support. In Washington the Citizens for a Free Kuwait, a private group connected with the Kuwaiti embassy, even hired a public relations firm, Hill and Knowlton, to communicate Kuwait's plight. The reconstruction planners formulated an economic policy and began signing contracts. A small military force was formed in Saudi Arabia from Kuwait's exile air force, which stood at about 75 percent of its preinvasion size, and from a reconstituted army of 4,500 of the original 16,000 ground troops.[8] A few thousand additional volunteers given a hasty month of training by the United States beefed up the force (unlike most Gulf states, Kuwait had had a draft, so most volunteers already had basic training).

Slowly a government-in-exile began functioning. It exercised no territorial control, but it did have a fiscal capacity, a coercive capacity, a functioning bureaucracy, and even a loyal opposition. It collected and spent money. It exercised some bureaucratic and financial control over its population. It engaged in foreign policy. It even managed to put some troops on its border, albeit on the wrong side. And it began to plan for a postwar return.

As the government reconstituted itself in exile, so too did the opposition. After the invasion the ruler began to rely heavily on his family, tolerating shaikhly excesses and closing out other advisers and in the process alienating many Kuwaitis. Although some members of the family, notably the ambassador to the United States, Shaikh Sa'ud Nasir, carried on a very competent public relations campaign, the rest of the family was remarkably ill-attuned to public appearance. Shaikh Jabir's own reluctance to present himself in world forums did little for his standing at home. His reticent appearance before the United Nations in late August evoked a poor comparison with Haile Selassie's appearance before the League of Nations. Indeed, for a time one rumor was that the deal to be struck with Saddam Hussein was the face-saving abdication of Jabir in favor of heir apparent Shaikh Sa'ad, a move that might have enjoyed some popular support.

Following the invasion the amir began restricting state spending authority to ruling family members, taking top state officials off the list of approved signatories.[9] The family began to achieve a stranglehold in exile over the privy purse, threatening to return Kuwait to the early days of oil when the amir drew no clear distinction between his money and the state's. The ruler's hold on state funds in exile angered the opposition. Ahmad al-Khatib captured this complaint succinctly, claiming members of the ruling family were "handling Kuwaiti investments as though they were the private property of the family, not the people's money."[10] The merchants, galvanized into political action on the eve of the invasion, now remained politicized by the ruler's behavior in exile and by the fear that oil revenues would not be distributed to them as generously in a post-invasion Kuwait. To remain politically active they needed a forum, hence their support for the return of the assembly. Joining the call for an assembly were the Islamists, the former assembly members, and all the groups that had supported the preinvasion prodemocracy movement.

These different lines of dissent met in exile. The opposition, which also established itself outside Kuwait, lost little time in petitioning the exile government for recognition, offering to stand beside it through the crisis in exchange for a promise of greater participation in the new Kuwait. This understanding that liberalization would follow liberation was worked out in a three-day meeting in October 1990 between government and opposition leaders in Jiddah, a meeting that joined 1,200 Kuwaiti exiles spanning the political spectrum and including members of the state's five elected national assemblies as well as other opinion leaders, intellectuals, and merchants. At the meeting the opposition and the crown prince hammered out an understanding: The ruler would restore the constitution and a degree of public participation; in exchange, the opposition would stand loyally behind him in exile—although to achieve this, the opposition reportedly had to threaten to walk out and denounce the ruling family.[11]

In the communiqué issued after the meeting, the opposition gave a clear declaration of support to the amir: "We emphasize that the Kuwaiti people, one and all . . . stand solidly behind our legitimate leadership whose true embodiment is our Emir, Sheikh Jaber al-Ahmad al-Sabah and his Crown Prince, Sheikh Saad Al-Abdullah Al-Sabah. . . ."[12] The communiqué reiterated the unity of the Kuwaiti people, paying tribute to the Kuwaiti resistance but also calling on Kuwaitis in exile to "do their best each in his respective line of specialization and position." It concluded with the promise to rebuild Kuwait on the two foundations of Islam and participation: "the adherence of the Kuwaiti people to their national unity and the legitimate regime which it has chosen . . . which rests on the principle of taking counsel and the people's participation under the nation's constitution of 1962." Given the politically closed nature of the host country, this was a notable declaration. It was clear that both the opposition and the government understood they must hang together or they would surely hang separately.

LIBERATION AND RECONSTRUCTION

Economic Reconstruction

Shortly after the invasion a group of prominent Kuwaitis approached the amir with the outline of a reconstruction plan. In November a Kuwaiti Task Force of exiled bureaucrats began working on a formal recovery program, a three-phase plan to take Kuwait through several years of reconstruction.[13] It set up teams to design an emergency action plan so detailed that team members worried about which medicines to buy first and where to warehouse them, how many manhole covers Kuwait's ravaged roads would need and where to order them, and how many mobile phones the emergency teams would need and their appropriate broadcast frequencies. After identifying critical needs, the group began signing contracts. It ordered medicine and medical equipment, clothing, and food, pre-positioning critical goods in Gulf warehouses and contracting for basic services. The task force also established liaison with the World Bank and with several U.S. federal agencies (the State Department, the Army Corps of Engineers, the Commerce Department, the Federal

A destroyed portion of the Bubiyan Bridge (courtesy of U.S. Department of Defense)

Emergency Management Agency, the Civil Affairs Division of the Defense Department). And then it waited.

The liberation of Kuwait, when it came, was a momentous event. As the troops and camera crews drove into Kuwait, hope filled the air. Reconstruction, however, did not go according to plan. Although the government distributed free food and gas, there were still shortages and long lines. The population complained about the slow restoration of electricity and water; emergency workers chafed at the bureaucratic delays that held food convoys and even critical firefighting equipment at the borders.

The first problem was financial. The scale of destruction seemed awesome: Schools, hospitals, and offices were destroyed; electricity, water, and phones were out. Although the worst of the early estimates of damage proved inaccurate—there was, for example, less damage to roads and bridges than originally thought—the harm was nonetheless severe. Repairing it was expensive. In May officials estimated that Kuwait had lost $60 billion in foregone revenues and direct damage and that reconstruction expenses in 1991 would exceed state income by $10–$20 billion.[14]

The second problem was political. Fearing the potential independent power and political aspirations of the reconstruction administration, the amir in the end relied not on the trained planners but instead assigned his own people. Inexperienced, unprepared, and—their critics argued—

War-damaged and vandalized stores, buildings, and cars in Kuwait City (courtesy U.S. Army/Specialist Bill Mohl)

Cable repair work with electrical towers in background (courtesy U.S. Department of Defense/Lane)

corrupt, they haggled while Kuwait burned. Their refusal to work with the resistance and use its distribution networks was but one factor contributing to the feeling that those in charge were not focused on reconstructing Kuwait.

In this the administrators took their lead from the amir. His first priority seemed to be reestablishing his own creature comforts, much to the disgust of a Kuwaiti population without reliable electricity or water. As Kuwait lay in darkness, the amir ordered chandeliers, and his ministers imported generators to power their private homes. In late March the minister of water and electricity announced longer-than-anticipated delays in the restoration of power: Kuwait would spend Ramadan in darkness. Kuwaitis, accustomed to both a functioning infrastructure and a responsive government, complained loudly.

The one reconstruction matter that made its way to the top of the agenda was oil. In their final days in Kuwait the Iraqis set fire to 600 of Kuwait's 950 oil wells, leaving another 80 flowing out of control, but not ablaze. From 4 to 6 million barrels per day of oil were going up in smoke. Further damage was done to tanks, pipelines, terminals, pumping stations, and Kuwait's three refineries, which contained state-of-the-art processing facilities. Equipment, parts, and furniture were also stolen. The world's largest oil spill spread from Kuwait out into the Gulf.

The first priority was controlling the fires. While the war was still on, Kuwait signed contracts with the four leading international firefighting companies, but the scope of the destruction and the pollution problems associated with the fires prompted the government to bring in other firefighting experts. By April Kuwait had 80 percent of the world's oil-well firefighting capacity engaged; by fall the fires were out, although substantial environmental damage remained. Bureaucratic delays and lack of heavy equipment—as well as unexploded shells, ponds of burning oil, dark and hot air—all hampered relief efforts. In March the finance minister estimated the cost of rebuilding the oil industry at $10–$20 billion.[15] It could take years to return to prewar production levels. Bechtel, a firm with long experience in the region, received the contract to oversee the restoration of the oil facilities. By August Kuwait was exporting small quantities of oil.

Rebuilding Kuwaiti industry was less urgent because Kuwait had always emphasized overseas investment over domestic industrial capacity. Kuwait's recent experience had done nothing to suggest this was the wrong choice: The invasion demonstrated the political as well as economic importance of its overseas investments. The economic devastation raised the issue, however, of the relative economic roles of the government and private sectors in postwar Kuwait. The merchants favored increased privatization of public services including, to a degree, health care and

Kuwaiti workers repair a power line damaged by retreating Iraqi forces (courtesy U.S. Air Force/Sergeant Prentes Tramble)

Aerial view of oil-fire fighters at work: hoses blasting, fires blazing (courtesy U.S. Department of Defense/Lane)

education—a radical departure from a thirty-year policy of providing state employment to all nationals.

Social Reconstruction

Kuwait had a preinvasion population of about 2.2 million, of whom 700,000 were Kuwaitis. Some 150,000–350,000 Kuwaitis remained through the occupation.[16] In April the government, having restored the most basic of services, began allowing the rest to return, encouraging the reticent by ending subsidies to those abroad. However, the unanticipated delays in restoring many services as well as the environmental problems associated with the oil fires slowed the return of those who could afford to wait abroad. Doctors disagreed on the health risks posed by the fires that blackened the skies and killed the desert plant and animal life, but thousands of Kuwaitis were sufficiently concerned about them and about the lack of services to remain abroad or even, having endured the occupation, finally to leave. When the borders to Saudi Arabia reopened, many who had stayed inside Kuwait left.

Although the invasion strengthened Kuwaitis' sense of patriotism (occupation and military confrontation are great forgers of national identity), it also created one important psychological division: between those who had stayed and those who had left. The invasion initially had a unifying effect, prompting even the opposition to rally around the amir as a national symbol, but as the occupation grew longer, dissatisfaction with the old government began to appear. Those remaining in Kuwait, who took the brunt of the occupation, not surprisingly felt the most dissatisfaction with those leaders whose policies had contributed to the dilemma in which they found themselves. To allegations of al-Sabah corruption and general government mismanagement were added the charge of complete incompetence in defense and foreign policy. That the rulers were in relatively comfortable exile in Saudi Arabia and the West did not help their case; nor did the fact that they had abandoned the country with what seemed in retrospect indecent speed.

Although this division between those who stayed and those who left was quite real, it was less clear whether it would prove as politically important as it was psychologically important—whether, when forced to choose, people would ally themselves politically with those who stayed behind rather than with those from their own sect or family. Ultimately the division may be less politically important than it first seemed. Although the sense of entitlement from suffering under the Iraqis was powerful, it was amorphous. Owing to the diversity in their religious, economic, social, political, and legal status, the political allegiances of those who stayed behind were fragile.

The invasion also raised anew an old question about Kuwaiti nationality: the status of the bidun jinsiyyah, resident Gulfians unable to prove Kuwaiti residency but lacking other nationality papers. Often these were tribal families with Saudi or Iraqi roots, not considered Kuwaiti by most Kuwaitis. The catchall group also included the more opportunistic, who had discarded valid passports in the hope of becoming Kuwaiti in order to benefit from the state's wealth, as well as others with no other home who considered themselves genuinely Kuwaiti. Those whose papers were not in order could not slip through bureaucratic cracks created by the invasion: Kuwait's citizenship records were smuggled out of the country, complete with names, addresses, birthdates, and fingerprints. The behavior of the bidun during the invasion was mixed. Many served Kuwait loyally (before the invasion many worked for the army or police), working and dying in the resistance. Others, including many with Iraqi relatives (some of them in the Republican Guard), joined the occupation. The first death sentence (later commuted to life) in the postwar collaborator trials went to a bidun, a military technician who joined the Iraqi Popular Army. Others were simply caught in the middle. As the war ended, hundreds of bidun taken prisoner in Kuwait and held in Iraq languished on the border, denied admission by a government worried about their real allegiances and determined to reduce the number of nonnationals.

Kuwait emerged from the war intent on drastically reducing its reliance on foreign workers. The immediate issue was the composition of the labor force. The initial consensus was toward hiring more Koreans, Baluchis, Filipinos, and other politically controllable laborers rather than Arabs and to give preference to nationals of states that had supported Kuwait. The government hoped, however, for an eventual population of about 1.3 million, down from the prewar level of over 2 million, the reduction to come from the nonnational population.[17] Although expense was the primary reason, another was the feeling left by the invasion that foreigners were politically unreliable and that many had served as a fifth column, welcoming the Iraqi invaders.

About two-thirds of the nonnationals had left during the occupation, and they were not allowed to return. Political and economic conditions in postwar Kuwait prompted many of the remaining nonnationals to leave. In April 1991 the government began registering foreigners and preparing to issue new identity cards. In June it began busing foreigners, primarily Iraqis and Palestinians, to its Iraqi border.

To reduce its long-term dependence on foreign labor, Kuwait would have to change state employment practices that guaranteed all nationals easy work for the government. The outmigration after the invasion of Kuwaitis and non-Kuwaitis, the vast majority of whom had worked for the state, effectively dismantled the state bureaucracy. The war completed this process of administrative destruction with the massive loss of records and buildings, essentially a loss of much institutional memory, leaving the postwar government a nearly blank slate with which to work. Nonetheless, to Kuwaitize the work force would require more than reducing the size of the government; it would involve restructuring incentives to bring more Kuwaitis into jobs previously held by foreigners. To do so would require overcoming many obstacles.

The nonnationals still left inside Kuwait were not a serious obstacle to Kuwaitization. They were politically powerless. Ethnically, linguistically, economically, and politically diverse, nonnationals had never formed a political bloc. Most wanted merely to save money and return home quickly. Divided between those who opposed Iraq and those who did not, they posed no unified threat. Their energy was dissipated in individual efforts to cut a deal and stay.

Nor did cultural attitudes about work among Kuwaitis pose an overwhelming obstacle. Those attitudes were largely new, the product of market forces: With enough money most people in most places will choose, as Kuwaitis did, against manual labor. Market forces work the other way as well. With attractive pay Kuwaitis not subsidized by the state would choose to engage in manual labor, as they did before oil, and as they did during the occupation.

Kuwaitizing the work force would, however, require the reorganization of educational programs and the introduction of incentives to more explicitly balance educational products with social need, that is, substantial restructuring of Kuwait's education system to encourage movement into more technical fields. This action could prompt some resistance, as Kuwaiti students were historically free to choose their direction, but would ultimately produce more Kuwaitis for essential jobs, thus furthering the goal of Kuwaitization of the work force.

Another strategy, possible but less likely, would be to bring more Kuwaiti women into the work force. Women are an important potential labor pool. Although their work-force participation rate is quite low, they are highly educated, so training costs would be relatively low. Several forces have prompted women to play a more public role in postinvasion Kuwait. Women played a key role in the resistance, organizing demonstrations in the early days of the occupation. At Jiddah, Shaikh Sa'ad acknowledged that contribution, declaring that women would "play a greater role and make more noble contributions in liberated Kuwait."[18] However, women did not play a particularly important role in exile politics. The necessary centering of the exile government in Saudi Arabia did not give women a forum in which they could excel (and the fact that escaping Kuwaiti women helped prompt a driving demonstration by Saudi women did little to endear them to that government). Women were notably unrepresented at the meeting in Jiddah. Although women resumed the battle for suffrage that they had waged since the 1960s, the battle was not easy. The movement experienced setbacks before the invasion as its erstwhile Arab nationalist allies abandoned women's suffrage in deference to their Islamist coalition partners. If the government were to reopen parliament, Islamists would probably oppose increasing women's work-force participation. The amir promised to study the issue of allowing women to vote, but then the amir was still studying the issue of allowing anyone to vote.

Political Reconstruction

To understand political reconstruction in postwar Kuwait, it is necessary to briefly review the political transformations under way before the invasion. Oil, as I have argued, initially had a depoliticizing effect, removing previously active groups—in particular, the merchants—from politics. But as merchant dissatisfaction grew with the decline in state spending in the 1980s, merchants began to return to political life in alliance with other opposition groups. The prodemocracy movement brought together a unified array of opposition forces—including parliamentarians, intellectuals, Islamists, and merchants—all dissatisfied with the amir's reluctance to reopen the National Assembly. This pressure had already resulted in the formation of the National Council. The relationship between the ruler and the opposition was thus already under stress when the invasion occurred. The political crisis surrounding the invasion and the amir's behavior in exile solidified the opposition alliance, culminating in the October meeting in Jiddah.

Ironically, however, the opposition leaders in exile finally unified at the top just as they were losing their popular base to the resistance groups inside Kuwait. Kuwaitis who had spent months fighting the occupation had little need for opposition leaders who had spent the war in relatively comfortable exile. These divisions surfaced after the liberation as food rotted in warehouses while resistance leaders argued with returned administrators over the right to feed the population. Now that the invasion was over, the opposition seemed momentarily ready to collapse from its own divisions.

This was the moment of opportunity for the amir. Had he moved quickly, returned to Kuwait at the head of the armies of liberation, kissed the ground, and made some promises about rebuilding a better Kuwait, he might have been able to stand above the emerging factions and appeal to the natural desire of a population tired of war to retreat from politics to the private world of reunited families. The opposition, so briefly united, could well have redivided. The prodemocracy movement might have been scuttled and a relatively benign authoritarianism imposed.

Instead the amir hesitated, remaining in comfortable exile for weeks after liberation, to the astonishment of the Kuwaitis, and thus accomplished for the opposition what it could not itself accomplish. Unwittingly, his distanced behavior forged a united prodemocratic front that could truly challenge his rule. Instead of deflecting the opposition he was now forced to confront it. He could do so in two ways: by liberalizing or by imposing authoritarian rule.

Historically, Kuwait's record on political openness was mixed. For much of its independent history Kuwait had a functioning elected assembly. The government had a reasonably good record on human rights: Kuwait did not have a history of martial law, secret police, or disappearances. Its first jail dates back to the 1938 rebellion, its first state security courts only to the mid-1980s. Kuwait's revenues allowed the government to respect most economic rights and many social rights (health care, education) although restrictions on collective rights—notably of women, Shia, and expatriates—existed. But overall, the government record was not bad. Kuwaitis spoke freely both in private and in the semipublic diwaniyyahs. The press was not rigorously censored, although from time to time periodicals were suspended. Kuwait's constitution guaranteed free speech and prohibited torture and degrading treatment, arbitrary arrest, and the like—clauses that for the most part held considerable respect. The U.S. State Department's 1980 human rights report noted that "no available evidence indicates that the government of Kuwait engages in or encourages torture," although it conceded that overzealous police occasionally used "third degree" methods, especially on nonnationals.[19] Its charges against the state included such relatively benign accusations as "road blocks and spot checks of outdoor gatherings of expatriates." The government was not accused of engaging in disappearances, death squads, abductions, secret arrests, or martial law. In 1982 the State Department reported no political killings, torture, or even political prisoners in Kuwait and described Kuwait's prisons as "well-run along modern lines."[20] The sanctity of the home was respected, with warrants required and used. Travel restrictions were rare (they were applied to military-age men who had not served and people traveling as representatives of societies, trade unions, and associations), although they were imposed on a handful of dissidents and, during the stock market crisis, on investors the government feared would expatriate their money and themselves.[21]

Following the 1983 bombings the government became stricter. It informed local editors it intended to apply existing press laws more rigorously (a 1961 law restricted criticism of the ruling family, stories that might offend foreign states, and more loosely, stories that spread dissension and harmed the national interest). In 1983 the government convened a special state security court to hear cases of political violence. Still, according to the State Department's 1984 report, the seventeen convicted in the 1983 bombings were the only prisoners then jailed for political acts.

After 1983 Kuwait began paying particular attention to foreigners thought to be behind the wave of political violence, deporting ever-larger numbers. Amnesty International in its 1984 report (earlier reports do not even mention Kuwait) expressed concern that the government had reportedly detained large numbers of Kuwaiti, Iranian, and Iraqi Shia following the 1983 bombings and also that many Iraqis were deported to Iraq where they risked political imprisonment.[22] Amnesty expressed concern as well over reports of ill-treatment and incommunicado detentions. In 1984 Amnesty International wrote the prime minister expressing concern over the rights of the arrested and urging better treatment for prisoners. Kuwaiti officials responded, referring to the relevant sections of Kuwait's criminal code and stating: "We share with Amnesty the general concern for the rights of all accused to fair treatment and a fair trial. We feel however that concern for the rights of a few accused individuals should not overshadow a more serious threat to the rights of millions."[23] Amnesty expressed concern that political prisoners were tried secretly by the state security court with no appeal and reiterated its concern over the fate of deportees on returning home. It also expressed its concern over the death penalty.

By 1985 the situation had worsened. The large number of prisoners, especially expatriates, held after the attempt on the amir's life swelled the jails, leaving many in inadequate facilities. In 1985 the government deported 15,000 foreigners and in 1986, 27,000.[24] Security forces began searching homes and businesses without warrants, although when protests were lodged, warrants were ordered (the government publicly conceded it had ignored some legal safeguards in detaining expatriates but promised to stop such practices).[25] In its 1986 report Amnesty expressed concern over allegations of government-sanctioned torture of political detainees and reiterated its concerns about fairness of secret trials (especially state security court trials), lack of appeal procedures, and deportations. Amnesty was not reassured by a statement by the foreign minister in 1985 to the assembly denying electric-shock torture but admitting to and condoning other forms.[26] New restrictions were introduced again following the 1986 assembly dissolution. The government continued to maintain a dialogue with Amnesty, defending the death penalty, for example, and arguing the adequacy of its procedural safeguards. In 1987 a state security court tried sixty-five people secretly, most in connection with bomb attacks but some for distributing leaflets advocating political violence. Security forces also held nonsuspects under house arrest to induce the surrender of relatives accused of political violence.[27] In 1988 and 1989 state security court trials continued, mostly of defendants in absentia, for acts of political violence. In 1990 the government cracked down on the prodemocracy movement. The state security apparatus was growing.

This transformation prompted the emergence of a small but active human rights movement in Kuwait. These issues had been on the opposition's political agenda since independence. A short-lived Rights of Man Committee was established in 1978. That year Kuwait also sent a delegation to the second UNESCO Regional Human Rights Conference. In 1980 the government sponsored a regional conference on human rights in Islam. The government established a Council on Human Rights and various committees to respond to Amnesty International's inquiries. In the 1980s a group of private Kuwaitis led by Ghanim al-Najjar began a small Amnesty International group; although its work, like that of other Amnesty groups, centered on other states, it played a role in convincing the government to carry on a dialogue with international human rights groups such as Amnesty. An informal but important section of the Arab Organization for Human Rights was also established in Kuwait, with some very prominent Kuwaiti members. These human rights groups were part of the background environment supportive of the prodemocracy movement that emerged before the invasion. The human rights situation deteriorated rapidly under the Iraqi occupation, which established a security state in Kuwait even more vigilant than its own in Iraq. In the seven months of occupation Iraqis tortured, kidnapped, harassed, and murdered untold numbers of Kuwaitis and foreigners.[28]

After the liberation the new government celebrated the destruction of the Iraqi security regime—then began setting up its own. Within hours of the Iraqi withdrawal the amir declared martial law and appointed Shaikh Sa'ad military governor. On March 19 the government suspended publication of *February 26*, the first paper to begin publishing after the liberation. Before the electricity was back, the Interior Ministry had awarded a $1.3 million contract to the U.S. Computer Sciences Corporation to develop a new information technology infrastructure to handle internal security.[29]

The Palestinians were the first target of this new security system. Palestinians in Kuwait had reacted in mixed ways to the Iraqi presence. Shafeeq Ghabra, a naturalized Palestinian Kuwaiti in Kuwait during the invasion, wrote that most in fact opposed the invasion.[30] The Palestinians there were among the wealthiest in the region with the most to lose. Ghabra cited numerous instances of Palestinians helping Kuwaitis, working with the resistance, and sabotaging Iraqi efforts. When Fatah supporters in Kuwait distributed leaflets criticizing the occupation, the Fatah leader in Kuwait, Rafiq Ziblawi, was assassinated. After the initial occupation, Iraq sent 200–400 members of the Iraq-sponsored Arab Liberation Front and 400 members each from the Palestine Liberation Front and the Iraqi-controlled Palestine Liberation Army to watch the local Palestinian community.[31] Other Palestinians, however, supported Iraq, either out of the desperation of their circumstances or out of faith in Iraq's pan-Arabism. As the Iraqi occupation force treated Palestinians more favorably than it did other groups, their support grew. Several hundred mostly poor Palestinians joined the Iraqi popular army in Kuwait.

This support for Iraq, and the support of the larger Palestinian community outside Kuwait, was not soon forgotten by Kuwaitis. As the occupation lifted, they took their revenge. At first Kuwaiti vigilante groups, some linked to members of the ruling family, went after suspected collaborators. Amnesty International and other monitoring groups reported the murder of dozens of Palestinians and the arrest and torture of hundreds more. In March Sa'ad reportedly threatened some of his own family members over their paramilitary activity, and in May he publicly condemned the kidnappings. Public abuse of Palestinians began to decline.[32]

Its center, however, had merely shifted. The government now began a series of show trials of suspected collaborators. By June the courts had heard over 300 cases. The violations of due process, denials of representation, absence of evidence, allegations of torture, and occasionally, the nature of the charges (wearing a Saddam Hussain T-shirt) and severity of sentences (twenty-nine death sentences, fifteen years for the T-shirt) prompted an international outcry. In June the prime minister announced the commutation of the death sentences.

A security state once established, however, was not so easily dismantled. Initial optimism over government reform began to fade. Although the amir deferred to public grumbling over delays in restoring basic services and corruption in granting contracts by dissolving the prewar cabinet in March 1991, he did not respond to opposition demands to couple a new, reformed cabinet with an early election date. Although ninety-six opposition members spanning the political spectrum signed a declaration vowing not to participate in the new cabinet unless the amir committed himself to an election date, the amir announced no election date but rather a new cabinet that was, as far as the opposition was concerned, only more of the same. The most notable change was an increase in the number of cabinet members from Sa'ad's rather than Jabir's branch, a shift that normally occurs only after a succession. The most notable individual change was the absence of shaikh Sabah Ahmad, Kuwait's long-serving foreign minister. The departure of Finance Minister Ali Khalifah (previously oil minister) and the demotion of Defense Minister Nawaf Ahmad to minister of social affairs and labor were also notable, mild gestures to public dissatisfaction with the old foreign policy and defense establishment. There were, however, no reformers in the cabinet, no truly new faces. The opposition was particularly disheartened by the promotion to foreign minister of Shaikh Salim, the former interior minister responsible for the preinvasion crackdowns on the prodemocracy movement. Following the announcement of the new cabinet, opposition leaders, now organized into seven political groups, called a press conference to criticize the appointments and to repeat their call for an election date. The government responded by canceling the conference and turning the lights off on reporters trying to interview opposition leaders.

The opposition leaders were not the only ones who objected to the government's behavior. A group of senior military officers also requested the dismissal of the former defense and interior ministers—Nawaf in particular—for their action in the invasion, for fleeing the country, and for leaving the military without orders.[33] General Muhammad Badr, the most senior officer to remain in Kuwait through the invasion and an active resistance leader and outspoken supporter of parliament, now stated publicly that the resistance forces might be hard to control if political reforms were not forthcoming, reminding the government that many remained armed. This protest was an unusually public statement of displeasure from a member of a military establishment long subservient to central government. Aside from occasional incidents (such as the 1986 sentencing of an army major, Abd al-Rahman Fakhru, to ten years in prison for writing pamphlets calling for the government's overthrow) the military was historically remarkably silent.[34] The protest, therefore, was evidence of dissatisfaction within the military and perhaps also a signal of a growing role for the military in domestic politics, a trend not likely to ultimately bode well for political liberalization.

In June the amir announced an end to martial law. The press, however, remained censored and public meetings banned. Resisting pressures to set an early election date, the amir announced on June 2 that elections would be held in October 1992. The opposition objected to the distant date and to the amir's silence on the reinstitution of all sections of the constitution, calling instead for elections by the end of the year and the formation of a cabinet with opposition members. The opposition also objected to the amir's plan to convene a weakened version of the advisory National Council, a council the opposition had boycotted when first convened in the summer of 1990 before the invasion. On June 4 1,000 opposition members held a public protest in defiance of the ban on assembly. Nonetheless, in early July the government convened the council, to opposition protest. If the amir was moving in the direction of political liberalization, he was doing so with great circumspection.

FUTURE PROSPECTS

The amir faced two options: to concede to the prodemocracy movement or to try to destroy it. Historically, Kuwait's amirs have usually chosen to make concessions to the opposition even as they tried to undermine it. To do this, the amir could allow elections, yet also divide the opposition, perhaps—as in the past—by peeling the merchants off from the coalition, this time by promising them more revenues through the privatization of state services. A less attractive option would be to work with other opposition leaders, notably the Islamists. They might be harder to co-opt, however, as many enjoy some popular support, in part because of their role in the resistance. Or the amir could seek new allies among the beduin or other as yet unmobilized groups. Finally, the amir could try to balance the elite opposition by allying himself with the national population, as in the past. He could give priority to rebuilding the state bureaucracy that provided social services and employment and halt talk of privatization. Indeed, he did try to placate Kuwaitis by writing off bank debts and supplying free goods and services (food, phones). In March 1991 the government announced a cash grant of $1,750 to all Kuwaitis who had stayed through the occupation and back pay to August 2. The cancellation of debts and cash grants cost the state $6–7 billion.[35]

These are expensive strategies, probably prohibitively expensive, barring extremely high oil prices and a quicker-than-anticipated return to full production. Ironically the opposition's strength—its unity and widely inclusive nature—makes it harder for the amir to apply his old policy of conceding while dividing the opposition and thus may make him more likely to embrace the authoritarian stance to which he leaned in the first postinvasion months. If the government continues in this direction, its authoritarianism is likely to be far less benign than in the past.

The strengthening of the security state with martial law and collaborator trials has long-term dangers. It is not only a threat to those against whom it is presently directed. Eventually the security apparatus will turn on its own nationals. Indeed, one of the first victims of the postliberation violence was Hamad al-Ju'an, a Kuwaiti opposition member, shot and paralyzed at his home in Kuwait days after the liberation in an attack that prompted Abdalaziz al-Sultan, chairman of Kuwait's Gulf Bank and an opposition member, to publicly charge the government with forming hit squads. This authoritarian trend is the most dangerous trend, for the efficacy of the democratic impulse lies less in the strength of Kuwait's participatory institutions than in the weakness of its authoritarian institutions. If these are allowed to grow unchecked, the prodemocratic forces will never win regardless of the election promises they extract from the amir.

The jury, however, is not yet in. The amir may be willing to seek consent rather than coerce compliance if he sees the costs of coercion as high and if he sees some advantages from liberalization. By institutionalizing the opposition he can co-opt it, implicating its leaders in the difficult austerity measures Kuwait must adopt. Several factors work in favor of political liberalization. Kuwait has more experience than its neighbors with representative institutions: its National Assembly, the diwaniyyahs, and cooperative societies. Kuwait's social structure is conducive to political representation: Kuwait has few of the communal divisions that elsewhere inhibit representation. It does have a significant Shia minority, and indeed that is where repression has flourished; but Kuwait has no sharp class divisions, partly owing to oil but also because few of the pre-oil industries, notably pearling, survived into the oil age with their workers and working-class conflicts intact. Kuwait does have a relatively large middle class—elsewhere the historical carriers of parliamentary democracy—with the money and leisure for political activity, in part the consequence of the early state spending on human capital. Kuwait's political culture is also conducive to political liberalization, with its respect for civil rights and the value placed on the autonomy of citizens in their own homes. Indeed, the government's preinvasion crackdown on the diwaniyyahs was protested as rude: It violated the citizen's right to host guests. The prodemocracy movement resonates with long-standing popular sentiments. These factors encourage the impulse toward political liberalization and may balance the tendency toward authoritarian rule that emerged owing to immediate postwar conditions.

The immediate impact of the occupation and war was to sharpen both the democratic and authoritarian impulses in Kuwait. The coalition victory reestablished central power with an authoritarian cast at the same time that exile and occupation strengthened the prodemocracy movement's opposition to authoritarian rule. Both of these impulses, toward repression and toward representation, continue to play themselves out in postwar Kuwait. The long-term effect will either be the introduction of an authoritarian system unlike any Kuwait has seen before, as the opposition fears, or a real broadening of political power, as the opposition hopes.

NOTES

1. *Middle East Economic Digest (MEED)*, October 12, 1990, p. 9.

2. *Wall Street Journal*, January 31, 1991.

3. Shafeeq Ghabra, "The Iraqi Occupation of Kuwait: An Eyewitness Account," *Journal of Palestine Studies* 20 (1991), p. 115.

4. *MEED*, September 28, 1990, p. 26.

5. *New York Times*, January 30, 1991, p. 5.

6. *MEED*, November 2, 1990, p. 15; *New York Times*, January 10, 1991, p. 10.

7. *MEED*, November 30, 1990, p. 6.

8. *Washington Post*, December 18, 1990, p. 17.

9. *New York Times*, October 14, 1990, p. 1; *MEED*, October 19, 1990.

10. *New York Times*, October 14, 1990, p. 1.

11. *New York Times*, October 14, 1990, p. 1; October 7, 1990, p. 6.

12. "The Final Communiqué of the Kuwaiti People's Conference," October 13–15, 1990, Jiddah, Saudi Arabia.

13. Kuwaiti Task Force, "Kuwait Recovery Program," January 29, 1991; "Strategic Framework for Reconstruction of Kuwait: An Approach Paper," November 24, 1990.

14. *MEED*, May 3, 1991, p. 5.

15. *New York Times*, March 18, 1991, p. 1.

16. *Washington Post*, January 15, 1991, p. 12; also see estimates above. These are very rough ballpark figures.

17. *Washington Post*, January 14, 1990.

18. "The Final Communiqué."

19. U.S. Department of State, *Country Reports on Human Rights Practices for 1980* (Washington, D.C.: U.S. Government Printing Office, 1981), p. 1024.

20. U.S. Department of State, *Country Reports, 1982*, p. 1188.

21. U.S. Department of State, *Country Reports, 1985*, p. 1293.

22. *Amnesty International Report, 1984* (London: Amnesty International Publications), pp. 345–346.

23. *Amnesty International Report, 1985*, p. 322.

24. U.S. Department of State, *Country Reports, 1986*, p. 1206.

25. U.S. Department of State, *Country Reports, 1985*, p. 1290.

26. *Amnesty International Report, 1986*, p. 341.

27. *Amnesty International Report, 1988*, p. 243.

28. See Amnesty International, "Iraq-Occupied Kuwait: Human Rights Violations Since August 2, 1990," December 1990; Middle East Watch, "Kuwait: Deteriorating Human Rights Conditions Since the Early Occupation," November 16, 1990; Arab Organization for Human Rights, "Taqrir 'an halat huquq al-insan fi al-Kuwait munth al-ghazw al-'Iraqi" (Report on the human rights situation in Kuwait since the Iraqi invasion), October 16, 1990; U.S. Congress, House Committee on Foreign Affairs, *Hearings on Kuwait and Human Rights Violations in Occupied Kuwait,* January 8, 1991; and various newspaper accounts, e.g., "Refugees' Picture of Kuwait: A Plundered, Fearful Nation," *New York Times,* August 27, 1990, p. 1.

29. *MEED,* March 22, 1991, p. 14.

30. *Middle East International,* April 5, 1991, p. 21.

31. Ghabra, p. 115; *Middle East International,* April 5, 1991, p. 21.

32. *MEED,* April 12, 1991, p. 14.

33. *New York Times,* May 24, 1991, p. 5.

34. *Middle East Contemporary Survey,* 1986–1987, p. 303; *Amnesty International Report, 1987,* p. 355.

35. *MEED,* May 17, 1991, p. 5.

Appendix: Chronology

c. 1756	A member of the al-Sabah family, Shaikh Sabah, is selected as amir
1896	Shaikh Mubarak comes to power (r. 1896–1916)
1899	Mubarak signs first treaty with Britain
1915	Shaikh Jabir comes to power (r. 1915–1917)
1917	Shaikh Salim comes to power (r. 1917–1921)
1920	Battle of Jahrah
1921	Shaikh Ahmad comes to power (r. 1921–1950); first opposition council formed
1922	Conference of Uqair sets Kuwait's borders with Saudi Arabia
1934	Kuwait's first oil concession agreement signed
1938	Majlis Movement; oil discovered
1946	Export of oil begins
1950	Shaikh Abdallah comes to power (r. 1950–1965)
1961	Kuwait becomes independent; Iraq announces a claim to Kuwait
1962	Kuwait's constitution promulgated
1963	First National Assembly elections held
1965	Shaikh Sabah comes to power (r. 1965–1977)
1967	National Assembly elections (government interference charged)
1971	National Assembly elections
1975	National Assembly elections
1976	National Assembly suspended
1977	Shaikh Jabir comes to power
1981	National Assembly suspension lifted, elections held; Gulf Cooperation Council established

1982	Suq al-Manakh Stock Market Crash
1983	Several sites in Kuwait, including U.S. and French embassies and Kuwaiti government buildings, bombed
1985	National Assembly elections; assassination attempt on amir
1986	National Assembly again suspended
1987	Reflagging of Kuwaiti ships
1989	Prodemocracy movement emerges
1990	Iraq invades Kuwait (August 2)
1991	Kuwait's independence restored (February 26)

Bibliographic Essay

CHAPTER 1: INTRODUCTION

Several books that survey the region also serve as useful introductions to Kuwait. These include Alvin Cottrell, ed., *The Persian Gulf States* (Baltimore: Johns Hopkins University Press, 1980), and Rosemarie Zahlan, *The Making of the Modern Gulf States* (London: Unwin Hyman, 1989). More journalistic but interesting introductory accounts of Kuwait include Ralph Hewins, *A Golden Dream: The Miracle of Kuwait* (London: W. H. Allen, 1963); Alan Villiers, *Sons of Sinbad* (New York: Charles Scribner's Sons, 1969); John Daniels, *Kuwait Journey* (Luton: White Crescent Press, 1971); Ralph Shaw, *Kuwait* (London: Macmillan, 1976); and David Sapsted, *Modern Kuwait* (London: Macmillan, 1980). The best general introductions to Kuwait are the books on history and politics noted in the following section. For a more extensive, albeit uneven, bibliography see Frank Clements, comp., *Kuwait* (Oxford: Clio Press, 1985).

CHAPTER 2: HISTORY

Kuwait's general history is surveyed by Ahmad Mustafa Abu-Hakima in *The Modern History of Kuwait* (London: Luzac, 1983) and in his *History of Eastern Arabia: The Rise and Development of Bahrain and Kuwait* (Beirut: Khayats, 1965). Those willing to dive into primary sources might consider Robin Bidwell, ed., *The Affairs of Kuwait: 1896–1905* (London: Frank Cass, 1971) and *The Affairs of Arabia: 1905–6* (London: Frank Cass, 1982). Interesting accounts by early travelers (and residents) include Edward Ives, *A Voyage from England to India, in the Year MDCCLIV* (London: Edward and Charles Dilly, 1773); J. S. Buckingham, *Travels in Assyria, Media, and Persia* (London: Henry Colburn, 1829); Lewis Pelly, "Remarks on the Tribes, Trade, and Resources Around the Shore Line of the Persian Gulf," *Bombay Geographical Society Transactions* 17 (1863); and Ameen Rihani, *Around the Coasts of Arabia* (London: Constable, 1930). The early Western residents were often missionaries. For their accounts, see Eleanor Calverly, *My Arabian Days and Nights* (New York: Thomas Y. Crowell, 1958), which offers a personal and professional account by one of the first Western physicians to live in Kuwait; Edwin Calverly, "A City of Pearls and Thirst," *Travel* 27 (1916); Paul Harrison, *The Arab at Home*

(New York: Thomas Y. Crowell, 1924); and Victor Sanmiguel, *Pastor in Kuwait: 1966–1978* (Leigh-on-Sea, Essex: Kevin Maynew, 1978). Memoirs by British officers in the area include Gerald deGaury, *Traces of Travel* (London: Quartet Books, 1983). The Dicksons (H.R.P. was for years Britain's representative to Kuwait) have written a number of books: H.R.P. Dickson's *Kuwait and Her Neighbours* (London: George Allen and Unwin, 1956); his wife Violet Dickson's *Forty Years in Kuwait* (London: George Allen and Unwin, 1971); his daughter Zahra Freeth's *Kuwait Was My Home* (London: George Allen and Unwin, 1956); and Zahra Freeth and Victor Winstone's *Kuwait: Prospect and Reality* (London: George Allen and Unwin, 1972).

CHAPTER 3: THE OIL ECONOMY

A few books cover Kuwait's economy generally. These include M. W. Khouja and P. G. Sadler, *The Economy of Kuwait: Development and Role in International Finance* (London: Macmillan, 1979); Y.S.F. Sabah, *The Oil Economy of Kuwait* (London: Kegan Paul, 1980); Ragaei El Mallakh and Jacob Atta, *The Absorptive Capacity of Kuwait* (Lexington, Mass.: Lexington Books, 1981); and Suad al-Sabah, *Kuwait: Anatomy of a Crisis Economy* (London: Eastlords, 1984). On Kuwait's economic history, see Archibald Chisholm, *The First Kuwaiti Oil Concession* (London: Frank Cass, 1975); The International Bank for Reconstruction and Development, *The Economic Development of Kuwait* (Baltimore: Johns Hopkins University Press, 1965); and Saba Shiber, *The Kuwait Urbanization* (Kuwait: Government Printing Press, 1964). Fida Darwiche covers the stock market crash in *The Gulf Stock Exchange Crash: The Rise and Fall of the Souq al-Manakh* (London: Croom Helm, 1986). On oil, see Mahmoud Kaboudan, "Oil Revenue and Kuwait's Economy: An Econometric Approach," *International Journal of Middle East Studies* 20 (1988). The concept of the rentier state and its specific applicability to Kuwait are discussed in Jacques Delacroix, "The Distributive State in the World System," *Studies in Comparative International Development* 15 (1980). A wealth of statistical information is available in the annual reports put out by Kuwait's Ministry of Planning Central Statistical Office in its *Annual Statistical Abstract*. Current economic events can be followed through the *Middle East Economic Digest*, *The Economist*, and *The Wall Street Journal*.

CHAPTER 4: KUWAITI SOCIETY

A good general introduction to Kuwait written by a historical-minded sociologist is Jacqueline Ismael's *Kuwait: Social Change in Historical Perspective* (Syracuse: Syracuse University Press, 1982). Interesting article-length treatments include Naseer Aruri, "Kuwait: Sociopolitical Developments," *American Enterprise Institute Foreign Policy and Defense Review* 2 (1980), and Hassan Hammoud, "The Impact of Technology on Social Welfare in Kuwait," *Social Service Review* 60 (1986). Tawfic Farah has carried out survey research in Kuwait on attitudes on a variety of issues. His work includes "Inculcating Supportive Attitudes in an Emerging State: The Case of Kuwait," *Journal of South Asian and Middle Eastern Studies* 2 (1979); his edited work, *Political Behavior in the Arab States* (Boulder:

Westview Press, 1983); Tawfic Farah and Faisal Al-Salem, "Political Efficacy, Political Trust, and the Action Orientations of University Students in Kuwait," *International Journal of Middle East Studies* 8 (1977); and Tawfic Farah, Faisal Al-Salem, and Maria Kolman Al-Salem, "Alienation and Expatriate Labor in Kuwait," *Journal of South Asian and Middle Eastern Studies* 4 (1980). There are a few quite interesting dissertations: Mohammad al-Haddad, "The Effect of Detribalization and Sedentarization on the Socio-Economic Structure of the Tribes of the Arabian Peninsula: Ajman Tribe as a Case Study" (University of Kansas, 1981), and Khaldun al-Naqeeb, "Changing Patterns of Social Stratification in the Middle East: Kuwait as a Case Study" (University of Texas at Austin, 1976).

A fair amount has been written on women in Kuwait: Jamal Sanad and Mark Tessler, "The Economic Orientations of Kuwaiti Women: Their Nature, Determinants, and Consequences," *International Journal of Middle East Studies* 20 (1984); Suad al-Sabah, *Development Planning in an Oil Economy and the Role of the Woman: The Case of Kuwait* (London: Eastlords, 1983); Ramla Nath, "Education and Employment Among Kuwaiti Women," in *Women in the Muslim World*, edited by Lois Beck and Nikki Keddie (Cambridge: Harvard University Press, 1978); Nesta Ramazani, "Islamic Fundamentalism and the Women of Kuwait," *Middle East Insight* (January-February 1988); and the discussion on Kuwait in J. E. Peterson, "The Political Status of Women in the Arab Gulf States," *Middle East Journal* 43 (1989).

Less has been written on tribes or sectarian differences in Kuwait. Tribes are discussed in Nicolas Gavrielides, "Tribal Democracy: The Anatomy of Parliamentary Elections in Kuwait," in *Elections in the Middle East: Implications of Recent Trends*, edited by Linda Layne (Boulder: Westview Press, 1987), and in al-Haddad's dissertation (reference in the first paragraph of this section). On the merchants, see Michael Field, *The Merchants: The Big Business Families of Saudi Arabia and the Gulf States* (Woodstock: Overlook Press, 1985).

Much has been written on expatriates in Kuwait. Expatriate labor is examined by Shamlan Alessa, *The Manpower Problem in Kuwait* (London: Kegan Paul, 1981), and Abdulrasool al-Moosa and Keith McLachlan, *Immigrant Labour in Kuwait* (London: Croom Helm, 1985). For more recent treatments, see Nasra Shah and Sulayman Al-Qudsi, "The Changing Characteristics of Migrant Workers in Kuwait," *International Journal of Middle East Studies* 21 (1989), and Sharon Stanton Russell, "Migration and Political Integration in the Arab World," in *The Politics of Arab Integration*, edited by Giacomo Luciani and Ghassan Salame (London: Croom Helm, 1988). Laurie Brand has an excellent study of Palestinians in Kuwait in *Palestinians in the Arab World: Institution Building and the Search for State* (New York: Columbia University Press, 1988). The most comprehensive book on that same topic is Shafeeq Ghabra, *Palestinians in Kuwait: The Family and the Politics of Survival* (Boulder: Westview Press, 1987).

CHAPTER 5: POLITICAL INSTITUTIONS AND PROCESSES

At the risk of appearing immodest I cannot help but note that the best analysis of Kuwaiti politics is my own *Oil and Politics in the Gulf: Rulers and*

Merchants in Kuwait and Qatar (Cambridge: Cambridge University Press, 1990). Other aspects of political life are dealt with in my "Coalitions in Oil Monarchies: Kuwait and Qatar," *Comparative Politics* 21 (1989), and "Abdallah al-Salim al-Sabah," and "Jabir al-Ahmad," in *Political Leaders of the Contemporary Middle East and North Africa*, edited by Bernard Reich (New York: Greenwood Press, 1990). Other interesting cuts at political life and political history include Naseer Aruri, "Politics in Kuwait," in *Man, State, and Society in the Contemporary Middle East*, edited by Jacob Landau (New York: Praeger, 1972); Hassan Ibrahim, *Kuwait: A Political Study* (Kuwait: Kuwait University, 1975); Ghassan Salameh, "Hangover Time in the Gulf," *Merip Reports* 139 (1986); and the sections on Kuwait in J. E. Peterson, *The Arab Gulf States: Steps Toward Political Participation* (New York: Praeger, 1988). Interesting dissertations on politics and public administration include Saif Abbas Abdulla, "Politics, Administration and Urban Planning in a Welfare State: Kuwait" (Indiana University, 1974), and Tarik Mohammad Alrayes, "Authority and Influence in the Government Civil Service in the State of Kuwait" (Claremont Graduate School, 1979). On Kuwait's political elite, see Ahmad Abdulla Saad Baz, "Political Elite and Political Development in Kuwait" (George Washington University, 1981), and Abdul-Reda Assiri and Kamal al-Monoufi, "Kuwait's Political Elite: The Cabinet," *Middle East Journal* 42 (1988). On the National Assembly, see Abdo Baaklini, "Legislatures in the Gulf Area: The Experience of Kuwait, 1961–1976," *International Journal of Middle East Studies* 14 (1982), and Ahmad Daher and Faisal al-Salem, "Kuwait's Parliamentary Elections," *Journal of Arab Affairs* 3 (1984). On the ruling family, a most useful book is Alan Rush, *Al-Sabah: History and Genealogy of Kuwait's Ruling Family, 1752–1987* (London: Ithaca Press, 1987). On the prodemocracy movement, see Mary Ann Tetreault, "Kuwait's Democratic Reform Movement," *Middle East Executive Report* (October 1990).

CHAPTER 6: FOREIGN POLICY

The best general introduction to Kuwait's foreign policy environment is Abdul-Reda Assiri's *Kuwait's Foreign Policy: City-State in World Politics* (Boulder: Westview Press, 1990). Some interesting observations on foreign policy in the subregion are offered in Hassan Al-Ebraheem's *Kuwait and the Gulf* (London: Croom Helm, 1984). On foreign aid, see Walid Moubarak, "The Kuwait Fund in the Context of Arab and Third World Politics," *The Middle East Journal* 41 (1987), and Abdul-Reda Assiri, "Kuwait's Dinar Diplomacy: The Role of Donor-Mediator," *Journal of South Asian and Middle Eastern Studies* 14 (1991). Relatively few sources touch on prewar Iraqi-Kuwaiti relations and fewer on the border issue. Daniel Silverfarb, *Britain's Informal Empire in the Middle East: A Case Study of Iraq, 1929–1941* (New York: Oxford University Press, 1986), devotes a chapter ("The Struggle for Kuwait") to the interwar claim. Ahmad Shikara, *Iraqi Politics, 1921–1941: The Interaction Between Domestic Politics and Foreign Policy* (London: LAAM, 1987), devotes half a chapter to the same topic. Majid Khadduri, *Republican Iraq: A Study in Iraqi Politics Since the Revolution of 1958* (London: Oxford University Press, 1969), devotes a subsection to the 1961 claim and the history behind it. The events of 1990 and 1991 can be followed in primary sources, the best (for political as well as economic events) being the *Middle East Economic Digest*, the *Wall Street Journal*, the *Economist*, and the chronology in the *Middle East Journal*, as well as the leading national papers (e.g., the *New York Times, Washington Post, Christian Science Monitor*).

CHAPTER 7: THE AFTERMATH OF THE INVASION

Very little has as yet been published on postwar Kuwait. On the occupation, see Shafeeq Ghabra, "The Iraqi Occupation of Kuwait: An Eyewitness Account," *Journal of Palestine Studies* 20 (1991), and "Voluntary Associations in Kuwait: The Foundation of a New System?" *Middle East Journal* 45 (1991), which includes a good historical background on associational life as well as a discussion of postwar prospects. The Kuwaiti Embassy and Citizens for a Free Kuwait in Washington have distributed informational packets with Kuwaiti views of events. Some Palestinian views of postwar events are found in the Jerusalem English-language weekly, *al-Fajr*. Some of the most interesting and up-to-date reporting on domestic events, in addition to the sources listed for Chapter 6, is found in the monographs and newsletters of several human rights monitoring agencies, notably Middle East Watch, Amnesty International, and the Arab Organization for Human Rights.

About the Book and Author

Kuwait, unlike most of its neighbors, has a well-established national identity and a long history as a nation, dating back to the eighteenth century. In this book, Dr. Jill Crystal focuses on two recurring themes in Kuwaiti history: one, the preservation of a sense of community in the face of radical economic, social, and political transformations; the second, internal rivalry over the conventions governing relations among members of the community.

Crystal skillfully weaves these themes into a broad profile of Kuwait, analyzing the nation's transformation from a pre-oil to an oil economy; its social structure and composition, including the country's tribal roots and key divisions involving class, gender, and immigrant labor; political tensions resulting from the nation's sudden wealth and the accompanying changes in social structure; and its relations with other countries in the Gulf and Middle East. In particular, she places Iraq's invasion of Kuwait in the context of Kuwait's historical foreign policy and examines the invasion's legacy, arguing that it reinforced Kuwaiti nationalism while renewing public demand for greater political participation.

Jill Crystal is assistant professor of political science at the University of Michigan. She is the author of *Oil and Politics in the Gulf: Rulers and Merchants in Kuwait and Qatar.*

186

Index